THE LAW AND STRUCTURE OF
THE INTERNATIONAL FINANCIAL
SYSTEM

The Law and Structure of the International Financial System

REGULATION IN THE UNITED STATES, EEC, AND JAPAN

John H. Friedland

QUORUM BOOKS
Westport, Connecticut • London

Library of Congress Cataloging-in-Publication Data

Friedland, John H.
    The law and structure of the international financial system :
regulation in the United States, EEC, and Japan / John H. Friedland.
        p.   cm.
    Includes index.
    ISBN 0–89930–837–6 (alk. paper)
    1. Financial services industry—Law and legislation—European
Economic Community countries.   2. Capital market—Law and
legislation—European Economic Community countries.   3. Financial
services industry—Law and legislation—United States.   4. Capital
market—Law and legislation—United States.   5. Financial services
industry—Law and legislation—Japan.   6. Capital market—Law and
legislation—Japan.   I. Title.
    K1066.F75   1994
    346′.082—dc20
    [342.682]   93–25950

British Library Cataloguing in Publication Data is available.

Library of Congress Catalog Card Number: 93–25950
ISBN: 0–89930–837–6

First published in 1994

Quorum Books, 88 Post Road West, Westport, CT 06881
An imprint of Greenwood Publishing Group, Inc.

Printed in the United States of America

The paper used in this book complies with the
Permanent Paper Standard issued by the National
Information Standards Organization (Z39.48–1984).

10 9 8 7 6 5 4 3 2 1

Contents

Acknowledgments

I would like to thank Jane D'Arista, Robert Litan, the Morin Center for Banking Law and the Brookings Institution. I would also like to acknowledge the assistance provided by the staff of the UK Securities and Investments Board, the staff of the Board of Governors and the staff of the SEC.

I would especially like to thank Lawrence N. Friedland for his valuable editorial assistance.

Abbreviations

AFBD	Association of Futures Brokers and Dealers
AG	mentioned as stock corporations in Germany
ATM	Automatic Teller Machine
ATRRs	Allocated Transfer Risk Reserves
BHC	Bank Holding Company
BHCA	The Bank Holding Company Act
BIF	Bank Insurance Fund
BIS	Bank for International Settlements
BSD	Banking Supervising Division
CAD	Capital Adequacy Directive
CAMEL	Bank Rating Standard: Capital, Assets, Management, Earnings, and Liquidity
CBR	Conduct of Business Rules
CCH	Commerce Clearing House, Inc.
CD	Certificate of Deposit
CFTC	Commodities Futures Trading Corporation
CME	Chicago Mercantile Exchange
CMLR	Common Market Law Review
COB	Commission des Operations des Bourses
Comm.	Community
CSD	Consolidated Supervision Directive
Dept.	Department
DM	Deutsche mark
Dow	Dow Jones Industrial Average

DTI	Department of Trade and Industry
ECB	European Central Bank
ECBS	see ESCB
ECJ	European Court of Justice
ECMF	European Central Monetary Fund
ECP	European Commercial Paper
ECU	European Currency Unit
EDS	Specialist in Education
EEC	European Economic Community
EMI	European Monetary Institute
EMS	European Monetary System
EMU	European Economic and Monetary Union
ERISA	Employee Retirement Income Security Act of 1974
ERM	Exchange Rate Mechanism
ESCB	European System of Central Banks
EST	Eastern Standard Time
Fannie Mae	Federal National Mortgage Association
FASB	Financial Accounting Standards Board
FBSEA	Foreign Bank Supervision Enhancement Act of 1991
FCC	Fond Common de Créance
FCM	Futures Commissions Merchants
FDIA	Federal Deposit Insurance Act
FDI Act	Federal Deposit Insurance Act
FDIC	Federal Deposit Insurance Corporation
FDICIA	Federal Deposit Insurance Corporation Improvement Act
FFIEC	Federal Financial Institutions and Examination Council
FHC	Financial Holding Company
FHLBB	Federal Home Loan Bank Board
FRA	Federal Reserve Act
FRB	Federal Reserve Board of Governors
FRN	Floating Rate Note
FSA	Financial Services Act
FSHC	Financial Services Holding Companies
FSLIC	Federal Savings and Loan Insurance Corporation
G–5	Group of Five Countries
G–7	Group of Seven Countries
G–10 Agreement	Committee on Banking and Supervisory Practices of the Group of Ten Countries, International Agreement on Capital Adequacy Convergence

GAAP	Generally Accepted Accounting Principles
GATT	General Agreement on Tariffs and Trade
GDP	Gross Domestic Product
Ginnie Mae	Government National Mortgage Association
GM	General Motors
GMAC	General Motors Acceptance Corporation
GSA	Glass-Steagall Act
IBA	International Banking Act
IBF	International Banking Facilities
IBM	International Business Corporation
ICI	Investment Company Institute
IMF	International Monetary Fund
IPO	Initial public offering
IOSCO	International Organization of Securities Commissions
ISD	Investment Services Directive
JUSEN	Japan's eight home loan finance companies
LBO	Leveraged Buyout
LDC	Less Developed Countries
LED	Large Exposure Directive
LIFFE	London International Financial Futures Exchange
LLR	Lender of Last Resort
LP	Listing Particulars
LTV	Loan to Value (ratios)
MMF	Money Market Mutual Fund
MOF	Ministry of Finance
MRP	Mutual Recognition of Particulars
NEC	a Japanese corporation
NIFs	Note Issuance Facilities
NOW	Negotiable Order of Withdrawal
NSCC	National Securities Clearing Corporation
NYSE	New York Stock Exchange
OCC	Office of the Comptroller of the Currency
OCC	Options Clearing Corporation
OECD	Organization for Economic Cooperation and Development
OFD	Own Fund Directive
OTS	Office of Thrift Supervision
R&D	Research and Development
RJR	RJR Nabisco

RUFs	Revolving Underwriting Facilities
S&L	Savings & Loan
SBD	Second Banking Directive
SEC	Securities and Exchange Commission
SIA	Securities Industry Association
SIB	Securities and Investments Board
SIMEX	Singapore International Monetary Exchange
SPV	Special Purpose Vehicle
SRD	Solvency Ratio Directive
SRO	Self-Regulatory Organization
SYN	together with
T-Bill	Treasury Bill
TSA	The Securities Authority
TSE	Tokyo Stock Exchange
UCC	Uniform Commercial Code
UCIT	Undertaking for Collective Investment Trusts
UK	United Kingdom
US	United States
VSTCF	Very Short Term Credit Facility
WACC	Weighted Average Cost of Capital

THE LAW AND STRUCTURE OF THE INTERNATIONAL FINANCIAL SYSTEM

Introduction

This book considers two kinds of financial markets: universal banking markets such as Germany and Japan where banks own equity shares, and where financing is dependent on long-term relations and cross-ownerships between borrowers and lenders, and arm's-length financial markets, where stock markets are largely independent of banks and where market prices, rather than long-term relations, determine financing (sometimes called "capital market"). The latter system prevails in the United States (US) and United Kingdom (UK). Although in Japan large securities firms do exist, and bank ownership of equities is limited pursuant to US influenced legislation, relational financing predominates over arm's-lengths financing.

In capital market countries, many shareholders may hold shares as part of an index, the securities markets are liquid, and consumer credit is plentiful. In universal banking market countries where there is bank ownership and control of industrial companies, where control is exerted because of bank domination of securities markets, there tends to be less financial innovation and less access to consumer credit.

Until the Insider Trading Directive of the European Economic Community (EEC) and the recent changes in Japan and Japanese attitudes toward capital markets, insider trading was commonplace in the day-to-day business in Japan and Germany. Securities laws, as Americans understand them, and the awesome authority of the Securities and Exchange Commission (SEC) are unknown in the European heritage. The United Kingdom, which has always entertained a system far closer to that of the United States in terms of its separation of securities and banking, enacted sweeping legislation only in the 1980s; stock markets were deregulated and banks allowed to enter into the securities market, primarily through subsidiaries. The reforms culminated in the Financial Services Act of 1986. A regulatory framework similar to that created in the United States during

the New Deal, and evidenced in such legislation as the Securities and Exchange Acts, is a recent phenomena in the EEC and in Japanese regulation and supervision of financial markets.

In July 1988, the Group of Ten (G–10) countries signed an agreement to abide by common rules for determining risk-based capital depending on the creditworthiness of the counterparty to transactions. This agreement, also known as the Basle Convergence Agreement (the G–10 Agreement), forms the basis of the EEC directives allowing for a single passport for banks throughout the EEC. Investment services firms engaged in securities activities compared to banks have traditionally held less, albeit more liquid, capital as a percentage of assets. Consequently, the EEC Capital Adequacy Directive (CAD) will require less risk-based capital for security activities of banks and securities firms. How EEC universal banks conducting investment services will be regulated in the United Kingdom is not yet clear. Lower capital adequacy standards for the securities trading activities of banks tend to undermine the basis of the 1988 G–10 Agreement.

The Financial Services Act of 1986 requires the securities activities of most banks and all other securities activities to be regulated by the Securities Investment Board (SIB) and self-regulatory organizations (SROs) depending upon the form of security business in which such firm is engaged. This scheme is understandably considered a regulatory maze by European banks.

The issues in this book are divided on a regional basis, with EEC issues being primarily addressed in Chapter 1, US issues in Chapters 2 and 3, and comparative Japanese and US financial structures in Chapter 4. While it might have been appropriate to divide the material by subject matter, such division would have altered the context of the issues. For example, capital adequacy exists within many fora, including the Basle Committee for Banking and Supervisory Practices, International Organization of Securities Commissions (IOSCO) forum, and the US domestic context. Since each of these fora could not be discussed separately, it is probably more effective to place the capital adequacy debate in the context of the EEC single market for financial services where it can be treated in light of the single passport for banking services, related issues harmonizing disclosure and other securities market issues. The US regime for legal regulation of securities markets (as opposed to self-regulatory organizations) began in the 1930s and cannot be done justice in the scope of this book. Since it has been so well explicated by commentators, anything that can be said in the space of these pages about this regime, and its development in the course of 60 years, would be superfluous. However, the pattern of US regulation has determined the focus of the EEC single market and of world regulation of financial markets in general.

Regulation of financial services will never be global. Rather, globalization is a trend along with regionalization (best characterized by free trade

associations such as the proposed North American Free Trade Association, which stands at the other end of the continuum from an individual country's establishment of rules attempting to create a distinct national framework in spite of the tendency toward world financial integration. While global harmonization and mutual recognition of financial regulation continue apace, it is necessary to understand that national and regional regulators have distinct criteria that clash with global harmonization and mutual recognition.

Chapter 1, which considers UK financial services in the context of the EEC single market for financial services, demonstrates the peculiar national regulatory initiatives of the United Kingdom and how such initiatives can and are integrated into the context of the EEC framework. The EEC is somewhere between a free trade area and a federal union. As students of US constitutional law will understand, it is difficult to consider federal law in complete isolation from state law. Similarly, an interpretive framework that considers both national law and EEC law must lay great emphasis on national law. If a similarly complex analysis of the interaction of other member states' laws with EEC financial law were attempted, this book would be too voluminous to carry. Ultimately, it is the methodology of analyzing international financial regimes that is considered here, rather than an exhaustive study of world financial regulation.

Chapters 2 and 3 review the current debate about reforming the US financial system in light of the financial innovation that has eroded the primacy of banks and the explosion of derivative markets, which have complicated securities regulation.

Specifically, Chapter 2 considers the line of judicial decisions that have eroded the Glass-Steagall wall separating banking and securities markets and examines the current banking crisis and new prudential rules in the Federal Deposit Insurance Corporation Improvement Act of 1991 (FDICIA) ensuring the capital adequacy of US banks. It also examines proposals going well beyond the G–10 Agreement such as proposals for reform of the banking structure, to include "narrow" banks, which limit access to deposit insurance and the payment systems to institutions with a restricted set of assets and liabilities, and broadening the definition of banks to include money market mutual funds and finance companies, so as to create a "level playing field."

Financial innovation is most advanced in the United States and has resulted in derivative markets that require intermarket regulation for manipulative practices, margins, capital and clearing systems. This is the subject of Chapter 3.

The incongruity between the US financial system, which entails liquid capital markets operating at arm's length and the separation of banking and securities, and the Japanese financial system, which involves relation-based financing, bank ownership of securities is the subject of Chapter 4.

The Japanese financial structure has become far more transparent since the Yen Dollar Accord of 1984. Nonetheless, the recent fluctuations in the Japanese stock market, which because of bank capital invested in the securities market have led to a reduction in bank capital of Japanese banks, have highlighted the tenuous financial structure of Japan. These recent developments indicate that the time is ripe for a change in Japan, while the poor performance of US companies in the international trade arena, which can be ascribed in large measure to the capital market structure in the United States, lead the student of financial markets to the conclusion that the US financial system is also in need of overhauling.

1

United Kingdom Financial Regulation in the Context of the European Community Single Market Program for Financial Services

As domestic markets give way to global markets, the European Economic Community (EEC) has been at the forefront of creating transnational regulation of financial institutions and enacting legislation, the objectives of which are the free movement of capital throughout the European Community.

The single market in financial services will allow communitywide branching of credit institutions and investment services as well as provide for mutual recognition of listing particulars and prospectuses,[1] all of which are part of the European single market program the most important of which became effective by the end of 1992.[2] This chapter will consider the way market risk in financial services is addressed in the context of EEC law and will explore the conflict between national (member state) legal regulation and EEC law, with emphasis on the law of the United Kingdom (UK).

Will EEC law, by attempting to create a "level playing field" of member states' laws through methods of harmonization and mutual recognition, start a "race to bottom" in which member states adopt liberal interpretations of EEC law and reduce any regulation more onerous? This chapter will attempt to demonstrate that despite the possibility of regulatory erosion, the probability remains that the UK regulatory regime is sufficiently sophisticated, futuristic and advanced to be subject to emulation by other member states.

The United Kingdom has developed sophisticated regulatory structures in such diverse areas as consolidated supervision of banking, securitization, regulation of exchanges and solvency of members of financial markets. The UK regulatory structure, which is second only to the United States (US) in its comprehensive regulation of securities, entrenched its premiere position by enacting the Financial Services Act (FSA) of 1986 in 1988. A major step was undertaken toward centralizing authority in the Securities and Investments Board (SIB) and

placing investment services' self-regulatory organizations under its auspices. A major obstacle to EEC financial integration is the separate
cultures of banking and investment banking in the United Kingdom
and the limited continental experience with securities markets. While
it is generally perceived that the "single passport" for credit institutions
provided for by the EEC Second Banking Directive (SBD) will establish universal banking (i.e., banks that perform deposit and securities
functions in the United Kingdom in the same corporate entity), this
may not be the case. Further, there may not be explosive growth in
securities markets on the Continent in spite of the worldwide tendency
toward pooled asset financing and away from tailored banking relationships, and continental banks may continue to perform mainly traditional banking functions.

Part I will examine the legal framework of the European communities. Part II will consider two different paradigms of the developed
country—the trade surplus country epitomized by Germany, which
employs the universal banking system (where banks perform most
financial intermediation, i.e., investment and securities related activities), and the capital market country such as the United Kingdom,
where financial intermediation is segmented into different sectors including investment banks, merchant banks and other finance-related
companies that entail complex securities markets subject to extensive
and particularized legal regulation. Part III will focus on the evolution
of international and EEC banking regulation and Part IV on investment
service regulation and its consequences. Investment services as separate
from banks exist only marginally outside the United Kingdom within
the EEC, although the discussion regarding securities exchanges is
relevant to all member states.

Part I: The Legal Structure of the European Community

The EEC has its origins in the Treaty of Rome which promulgated four
principles called The Four Freedoms: Freedom of Movement of Capital,
Labor, Goods and Services. In the context of financial services certain
provisions of the Treaty of Rome are particularly relevant: the provision
allowing for the right of establishment in other member states,[3] the freedom
to provide services throughout the EEC[4] and national (non-discriminatory)
treatment for member state institutions.[5]

The EEC, even after the Single European Act,[6] which although altering
voting procedures from unanimity to qualified majority vote[7] still allowed
member states to "opt out" in cases of extreme national exigencies relating
to non-economic matters and fiscal matters,[8] differs significantly from the
US federal system; however, the EEC involves measures of contractual
obligations and systematic law not found in other international treaty organizations such as the General Agreement on Tariffs and Trades (GATT).
Like the International Monetary Fund (IMF), the EEC Council of Europe

has a weighted voting policy and as in the IMF, more powerful nations play a disproportionately larger part in deciding issues.

The Single European Act formalized the role of the European Parliament in the decision-making process of the EEC. Under the new cooperation procedures that apply to harmonization of laws, amendments to the Treaty of Rome proposed by the parliament must be taken into account by the EEC Commission and the EEC Council. However, ratification of an amendment that is not supported by the Commission requires unanimous approval by the Council.[9]

The Single European Act also sets forth goals in other areas generally not included in the Treaty of Rome. In the monetary area the Single European Act committed the member states to further cooperation and, if necessary, to institutional changes, "in order to insure the convergence of economic and monetary policy" and the creation of a single European market for financial services.[10]

The Council (consisting of ministers from the member states responsible for the legislation considered) is the legislative body that determines by qualifying majority vote whether Commission recommendations will become law. Although the power of the European Court of Justice (ECJ) in interpreting the Treaty of Rome is not completely delineated, it is quite clear that the ECJ may mandate an approach for mutual recognition of products among member states.[11]

EEC law is accepted as prevailing over national law[12] and judgments and preliminary rulings of the ECJ based on community law are binding and enforceable and have "direct effect" in member states.[13]

Further complicating the EEC Federal System are the fora of the Group of Five (G–5), the Group of Seven (G–7), and the Group of Ten (G–10), which include non-EEC countries. Within the sphere of financial law, the forthcoming Investment Services Directive (ISD) together with the Capital Adequacy Directive (CAD) for investment services may undermine the Group of Ten Basle Convergence Standards for capital adequacy.[14]

In *EC Commission v. Germany*,[15] the ECJ, while striking down a German law requiring permanent establishment of insurance carriers in order to provide services, did find that in the case of insurance, host country controls were permissible in the public interest. This ruling can be extended to other areas including banking and, to a lesser extent, to investment services that require similar investor protection measures. In the area of investment services in the United Kingdom, such investor protection measures appear in the form of conduct of business rules.[16]

The judicial process in the EEC is unlikely to be the leitmotif of vast changes in law as is the case in the United States[17] and will only supplement in a broad objective, purposive way the progressive consensual process of creating a single market. In this regard, in spite of the supremacy of EEC law over municipal law, EEC law stands midway between the sort of judicial

process that occurs within a municipal legal system, and that which occurs under an international organization, such as the law of the International Monetary Fund, in which weighted voting and administrative decision are frequently eschewed in favor of consensus building.

EEC law at the highest level is by way of "directives," liberally worded documents enacted by the Council pursuant to a Commission recommendation, which are intended to be implemented in the national law of the member states by way of national legislation. The Commission has the exclusive right to propose directives, but their implementation is governed by the principle of subsidiarity which is precisely defined in the proposed Treaty on European Union[18] and is part of the common law of the EEC. Directives do not in themselves have direct effect in the member states, and variance in the wording of the implementation of directives in national legislation may create discrepancies among member state laws. However, directives are conceptually binding, and all national laws are subject to review by the ECJ.

Part II: Financial Systems in the United Kingdom and Germany

The principal difference in the financial arena between Germany and the United States and the United Kingdom is that Germany is a universal banking country—a country in which banks perform most investment services functions, while the UK financial system is a hybrid of the universal banking system and the US system, which rigidly separates banking from investment services under the Glass-Steagall Act.[19] Other continental countries have a system which tends toward universal banking and also have the high leverage which typifies the absence of non-bank–dominated securities markets within such countries.[20] As shall be discussed in Part III of this chapter, the United Kingdom has a separate regulatory structure to govern investment services, and the ISD is directed largely to UK concerns.

The gap between the economic systems of countries with high leverage, that is, high debt to equity ratio, such as Germany and Japan, and low-leverage countries, such as the United States and the United Kingdom, makes international agreement all the more difficult.[21] In Germany, two-thirds of all liabilities arise from borrowing from banks whereas in the United Kingdom the figure is one-quarter.[22] In Germany, three-fourths of bonds are bank issued bonds (debts initially taken on board by banks as borrowers) whereas the comparable figure for the United Kingdom is one-tenth.[23] The result in Germany and other universal banking countries (which are invariably those with high leverage) is that banks dominate the securities markets and are able to set the prime rate for lending to prime borrowers. That rate will in all likelihood be higher than that charged in

the London interbank market and the Eurobond market and will be particularly higher than the commercial paper rate.[24]

Furthermore, in universal banking countries banks may practice additional monitoring supervision because they frequently own large equity stakes[25] in the borrowers. Borrowers are recompensed to an extent by the fact that in these countries a lower dividend is usually required than in capital market countries such as the United Kingdom and the United States. The result is a higher price to earnings ratio for the shares in universal banking countries than in capital market countries. Under the Basle convergence setting capital risk weighting for international banks, banks are entitled to count toward capital 45% of the difference between book value and market value of the securities which they own[26] thereby further rewarding them for their lower income producing securities.

The complexities of negotiation regarding the CAD, with Germany attempting to create high capital adequacy standards and the United Kingdom attempting to maintain the more flexible[27] regulation approach that is currently used by the various self-regulatory organizations (SROs) highlights UK dominance and German inefficiency and inexperience in the financial sector in that UK markets function with less capital.[28] The fact that Germany is a net importer of financial services[29] is of course insignificant to the extent that financial services comprise only one component of trade, and Germany until unification was in substantial surplus.

The high leverage in universal banking countries and Japan[30] (which is not a universal banking country) is difficult to explain. It cannot be adequately accounted for by tax considerations[31] or the advantage of debt over equity. Apparently the ineffable investor-company relationships are the only possible answer. In general three factors characterize such systems: (1) the simultaneous holding of debt and equity claims; (2) the similar proportion of debt and equity; and (3) government policy.[32] German and Japanese banks have traditionally held significant equity holdings[33] and equity shares while bonds are closely held (about one-third Japanese and two-fifths German shares are held by non-financial enterprises)[34] thereby creating significant cross-holdings.[35]

German banks, as a class equity owner, rank fourth, behind non-financial corporations, individual households and insurance companies. As a group, the banks own only 9% of domestically listed shares of all German companies, but they also own more than 25% of at least 33 major industrial corporations.[36] In addition, German banks act as a depository for stocks owned by other classes of shareholders. At the end of 1988, DM 411.5 billion worth of shares, or approximately 40% of total market value of outstanding domestic shares, were deposited in German banks. When added to their own share ownership, nearly 50% of listed German corporate shares are directly or indirectly under the control of banks. This role as a share depository has been important to German corporate gov-

ernance because of the ability of banks to vote shares held in deposit on behalf of the depositors. Today this right is restricted insofar as the right of proxy must be renewed every 15 months.[37] In a study of board level linkages among German industrial and financial corporations, there were 453 primary and 1,175 secondary interlocks among directors sitting on supervisory boards of Germany's 325 largest corporations, with banks displaying the greatest number of linkages.[38] Thus, fundamentally high leverage countries have economic systems which do not partake of the same values as does the profit motivated portfolio investor of capital market countries.[39]

Frequently, national laws enhance the distinction in national economic systems within the EEC, for example in the arena of takeovers. The proposed Takeover Directive[40] will ostensibly regulate the terms and conditions of takeovers in the EEC. In the United Kingdom, takeovers are regulated by the Takeover Panel, which is a self-regulatory (i.e., nongovernmental) body, and hostile takeovers are, proportional to the economy, almost as prevalent as in the United States. In Germany, there have been no completely hostile takeovers.[41] However, the Flick Brothers acquisition of Feldmuehle Nobel in 1989 was the first step taken toward a hostile acquisition in Germany. Although this move was opposed by the target's board of directors, it was welcomed by the management. In spite of the Takeover Directive, French and German law confer particular rights on employees and their representatives. In France, employees, trade unions and workers' councils have the right to be consulted about a range of corporate activities.[42] In Germany, representatives of employees and trade unions have 50% of the seats on the supervisory boards of stock corporations (AGs) having more than 2,000 employees. In addition, workers' councils have rights relating to terms of employment and dismissal, and members of the supervisory board can be replaced only with a 75% vote of shareholders.[43] French companies are able to place serious restrictions on transfers of shares and voting rights of shareholders.[44]

Part III: Regulation of International Banking

THE INTERNATIONAL DEBT CRISIS AND THE BIRTH OF DERIVATIVE INSTRUMENTS

The regulation of international banking—as well as of other financial services—took on new dimensions in the 1980s. The current dialogue on banking regulation has been carried out at an international level. The urgency of international actions, like that of the monetary sphere proper, was precipitated by the proliferation of new financial instruments in the wake of overexposure of international banks, particularly US banks, to Less Developed Countries (LDCs). In 1982, the illiquidity of US loans to the LDCs created

a need for additional financing for banks,[45] thereby enhancing the Euro-bond market, as distinct from the syndicated loan market.

Commercial banks are perhaps the major source of international liquidity. The ratio of their capital to assets is a measure of their solvency. In order to bolster their supply of capital, banks issued floating rate notes in the Euromarket creating the threshold activity for the Eurobond market and ultimately enabling corporate borrowers to issue debt at far lower rates than in syndicated loans. While banks earned reasonable profit margins on bond underwriting, they were subject to competition from securities' houses. Furthermore, the process of disintermediation continued and led to the emergence of the European Commercial Paper (ECP) market, discussed below.[46] The LDC crisis also caused the development of off-balance sheet financing techniques, mostly as a self-induced response by banks to the insolvency of their loans and also in response to government regulation. These methods were successful in reducing the assets appearing on banks' balance sheets thus freeing up capital which could then be used for other purposes generating new fees.

The purpose of financial regulation is to provide a legal framework which will lessen the possibility of shock in the financial system; however, it may be that regulation can occur only after crisis. Prudential supervision is dedicated to the opposing concept. The 1982 shock has left in its wake a bewildering array of financial instruments which require complex and insightful regulation. The debt crisis created the rush toward off-balance sheet financing and caused the expansion of the Eurobond market. Banks required new sources of capital, which they obtained in large measure through use of the floating rate note (FRN) which consists of a perpetual sector and a dated sector. But the market was in large measure driven by banks needing to service floating rate business and lacking the requisite capital because of the debt crisis.[47] This market collapsed in 1986 amid fears that the Basle Committee would not allow perpetual notes to be considered part of capital under its capital adequacy solvency measure. (In fact, these notes were allowed to be considered part of tier-two capital.)[48] A second reason for the collapse was the expansion of the ECP market which imported the US commercial paper concept. There were several advantages to ECP; the turnaround time was two days as opposed to seven, and A-rated companies could often borrow at sub-Libid levels as opposed to higher sales commanded by medium term FRNs[49] (particularly if the ECP was enhanced by note issuance facilities (NIFs), or revolving underwriting facilities (RUFs), and ECP did not require direct underwriting, therefore making it less expensive than FRNs to issue.[50]

European Commercial Paper came into existence because the banking crisis had called into question the creditworthiness of banks and lenders. A-rated companies came to be considered better credit risks than banks, thereby giving corporate borrowers an advantage over their intermedi-

aries.[51] This disintermediation process poses grave dangers for the international banking system as it causes both a qualitative and a quantitative deterioration of banking loan portfolios.[52]

The geometric rise in international capital market volume has contributed significantly to interdependence in the international economic system. This is especially true with regard to the growth of derivative instruments including interest rate[53] and currency swaps[54] and financial futures.[55]

Dollar denomination of new financial instruments[56] enshrines the dollar as the world central currency. This fact, taken together with the US lead in financial innovation and deregulation, rules out any unilateral EEC initiative in financial market regulation, as US exchanges and the dollar denomination of financial instruments continue the pattern of US domination of financial markets and consequently, financial regulation; but the United States and the EEC in the late 1980s were about to embark on new terrain in international regulation.

THE EEC SINGLE MARKET IN BANKING: THE BASLE CONVERGENCE AND THE SECOND BANKING DIRECTIVE

By the mid–1980s, not only exposure to LDC risk but the off-balance sheet financing that had followed in its wake had aroused international concern. Thus, it became apparent to the Anglo-American regulators that something had to be done in the way of relevant regulation. The Anglo-American agreement led to the Basle Convergence Agreement of G–10 (G–10 Agreement)[57] which is far and away the most important agreement in the international monetary arena since Bretton Woods.[58] On December 30, 1989, the EEC concluded the SBD, the Solvency Ratio Directive (SRD) and the Own Fund Directive (OFD), which is largely based on the Basle Agreement.[59]

The underlying principle of the G–10 Agreement and these directives is a capital adequacy ratio for banks of 8% capital to assets by December 31, 1992, with assets being risk-weighted.[60] The G–10, the SBD and its corollary directives (the SRD and the OFD)[61] are broadly similar, although G–10 concerns only international banks while the SBD and its corollary directives concern all EEC banks. The only real difference in the risk weights attached to assets is regarding claims against domestic central government securities and against official sector institutions within the country or within Organization for Economic Cooperation and Development (OECD) countries. This discretion is afforded by G–10, while the SRD weights central government obligations at a 0% weight.[62]

In their determination of what constitutes a bank's capital (defined as "Own Funds" in the EEC directive), the G–10 and the EEC banking directives are fairly similar; however, some important distinctions do

emerge. Both the G–10 and the SRD require 8% of capital to assets ratio by the end of 1992. Both the SBD and G–10 allow different kinds of hybrid capital instruments, including non-cumulative preferred stock and subordinated term debt, to be included within capital[63] although only to a maximum of 50% of the core (tier-one) capital element. The OFD also allows general provisions and reevaluation reserves to be included to 100% of tier-one capital[64] and certain kinds of fixed term cumulative preferred and subordinated loan capital to a point of 50% tier-one capital.[65] What within the G–10 is described as hybrid debt capital instruments (i.e., perpetual debt instruments in the United States) would be treated similarly under Article 3 of the OFD, in which capital freely available to the credit institution is included as tier-one capital.

Under G–10 and the OFD, subordinated term debt of over five years' duration will be counted as tier-two capital. To debt of five years or less, a discount of 20% per year will be applied. Both the G–10 and the OFD require the deductions of certain categories of investment, including goodwill, from capital.[66] Under both G–10 and the SRD, loan loss reserves are limited to 1.25% of tier-two capital.[67]

Although loan loss reserves for specific loans are not to be included in general loan loss reserves, such inclusion has been effectively the result because the nature of loan loss provisioning in the EEC and Japan makes no clear distinction between general and specific loan loss reserves.[68] These anomalous approaches to loan loss reserves will yield different results for the United States and the United Kingdom, on the one hand, and universal banks in the EEC and Japan, on the other hand. Even more important, however, may be the requirement of specific provisioning for less than fully collateralized loans.[69]

The differences between the G–10 and the OFD are difficult to spot; however, here are a few examples. The OFD will allow only the inclusion of interim profits, that is, current year earnings, if such amount is net of any foreseeable charge or dividend.[70] The G–10 has a two-tier system of capital which in the first tier consists primarily of a bank's paid up capital and disclosed reserves while the second tier of capital includes general provisions, that is, general loan loss reserves and reevaluation reserves, which include hidden reserves and shares of transferable securities which may be marked up to their market value with a discount of 55% of the difference between historic cost book value and market value.[71]

There are no undisclosed reserves under EEC law but because banks own marketable securities, there is considerable unrealized market value of shares held at book value.[72] Two definitions of certain funds within Article 2 of the Own Funds directive require expansion: revaluation reserves[73] and value adjustments.[74] Revaluation reserves relates to concepts of consolidation and permits certain intergroup financial transactions allowing simpler treatment of assets within a consolidated group. Transfer-

able securities must be held either as financial fixed assets or as part of a portfolio trading book.[75] This is in fact the first formulation under EEC law of a "trading book option" important under the CAD, which is discussed below.[76] The higher value adjustment for capital adequacy purposes appears to state that under EEC regulation a member state may include the full market value of transferable securities as tier-one capital; in contrast, G–10 requires a 55% discount.

Another important distinction is in the treatment of subsidiaries. The OFD requires national regulators to deduct from capital all investments by banks in other banks (including equity and bonds), which exceed 10% of capital. G–10 requires banks to apply a 100% weight to such investments, thereby forcing banks to keep 8% of capital on hand against such risks,[77] a requirement less than one-tenth as strenuous as the OFD requirement that all investments by banks which exceed 10% in other non-consolidated banks (including equity and bonds) be deducted from capital;[78] but, the G–10 Agreement includes all non-consolidated subsidiaries, not just those over 10%.

Under the SRD, exposure to the private sector is listed at 100% weight. Most important, requirements to consolidate under the EEC are quite onerous. No definition of consolidation is given in the G–10 Agreement, highlighting the distinction between an international agreement and a legal regime. The SBD is subject to an earlier (1983) Consolidated Supervision Directive requiring consolidated supervision of credit institutions.[79] The supervision of credit institutions on a consolidated basis has been supplemented by a second directive on Consolidated Supervision of Credit Institutions Directive which involves consolidation of banking groups including financial holding companies.[80] However, it was the 1983 directive that began the process of consolidated supervision. The clearest statement regarding which institutions are to be consolidated appeared in the 1986 directive (the Eighth Directive on Company Law on the annual and consolidated accounts of banks and other financial institutions),[81] which provides rules of consolidation derived in large measure from the Seventh Directive on Company Law.[82]

The 1983 directive states that a credit institution having a 50% ownership participation in another credit institution or financial institution, "shall require either full or pro rata consolidation of the financial institutions concerned." The integration of this EEC directive into UK financial law illustrates the possibilities for misapplication of EEC law. The Banking Supervision Division of the Bank of England policy statement distinguishes between consolidated supervision and consolidation of financial returns.[83] This distribution is essential to understanding consolidated supervision as opposed to the consolidation supervision of capital ratios. In 1983, continental banking supervisors were implementing the same ratios for banking and securities activities, while the United Kingdom was implementing more

permissive ratios for securities firms.[84] The approach of the latest EEC Directives on Capital Adequacy of banking institutions as contained in the CAD and the trading book option which banks may use for their securities activities means that the consolidation of a securities subsidiary of a parent bank will involve the consolidation of its trading book with the bank's trading book at the same capital adequacy ratio, not at the higher investment book level. In 1986, the Bank of England issued a notice of consolidation supervision stating "that the supervisor of a securities company is the best judge of its capital adequacy."[85]

Under the SRD the solvency ratio of credit institutions which are parent undertakings shall be calculated on a consolidated basis by the method laid down in the two consolidated supervision directives.[86] The authorities responsible for authorizing and supervising a parent undertaking may also require the calculations of an unconsolidated ratio with respect to the parent undertaking. When the subsidiary of a parent is authorized in another state, the competent authorities of the member state in which the subsidiary is located shall require the calculation of a subconsolidated or unconsolidated ratio.[87] However, provided the Commission is informed, competent authorities may delegate the responsibility for supervising solvency to the competent authorities which have authorized and supervised the parent undertaking.

Where the SRD and the SBD utilize the traditional approach of consolidated supervision (they also create the subconsolidated or unconsolidated supervision), these directives are contrary to the doctrine embodied in the Basle Concordat of 1975[88] and the later Basle Concordat of 1981[89] under which the subsidiary is the responsibility of the state in which it is located.

Under the SBD, no credit institution may have qualifying holdings exceeding 15% of its "own funds" in an undertaking which is neither a credit institution nor a financial institution;[90] and the total amount of a credit institution's qualifying holdings, meaning direct or indirect holdings of more than 10%,[91] may not exceed 60%.[92] Credit institutions shall be given 10 years to comply with the qualifying holdings,[93] and compliance shall be on a consolidated basis.[94]

The Large Exposure Directive (LED) limits credit institutions on a consolidated basis to exposure to a client or a group of connected clients to 25% of own funds.[95] Credit institutions may not incur large exposures which in the aggregate exceed 800% of own funds (large exposures are defined as 10% of own funds).[96]

The background of the LED dates back to the 1984 failure of the firm of Johnson Mathey which created upheaval in the UK banking system, ultimately leading to the Banking Act of 1987.[97] At that time, the Bank of England employed a two-tiered regulatory system. In reaction to the First Banking Directive, the Banking Act of 1979 had provided statutory

regulation for deposit-taking credit institutions but continued to supervise other institutions ("recognized banks") like Johnson Mathey on a more informal basis. At the time of its failure, Johnson Mathey had surpassed the recommended 10% limitations on loans to non-banking affiliates.[98] The Banking Act of 1987 made the 10% guideline statutory, requiring post-notification and prenotification at 25%,[99] instituted a Banking Supervision Division which is required to report annually regarding compliance with the Act and eliminated the two-tiered system. Like the failure of Continental in the United States, the failure of Johnson Mathey revealed non-compliance with the recommended limits on affiliated loans. The Large Exposure Provision of the SBD limits to 15% exposure to an individual participation that is not a financial institution and total non-financial participations to 60%.[100] These two kinds of provisions—the SBD on participations and the LED on loans—are fundamentally developments toward statutory banking regulation to minimize systematic risk first introduced in the United States in the Banking Act of 1987.[101]

Within Europe differences exist regarding deposit insurance. Because the alternative to deposit insurance is very often a bail out by the lender of last resort (LLR), the emphasis on the LLR will vary depending on the degree of deposit insurance available. A European system of central banks[102] would require a uniform approach to deposit insurance and should provide a uniform policy for bailing out banks with difficulties. Liquidity under the Basle Concordat of 1975 and the revised Concordat of 1981[103] is generally considered to be the responsibility of the host member state, and the SBD did not depart from this approach; however, different EEC member states have different liquidity requirements.[104] Frequently, the regulator will have different rules governing the liquidity of domestic and foreign banks.

The risk weights of capital as well as the capital to assets ratio are all products of compromise, but they serve as a starting point for further international agreement, particularly with respect to off-balance sheet assets. Certain disparate treatment is apparent. Under both the SRD and G–10 a standby letter of credit will require a 50% risk-weighting.[105] One to four family residential mortgages bear a 50% weight under both the SRD and the G–10 Agreement.[106] As far as swaps contracts are concerned, a .5% weight is attached to interest rate swaps and 5% to currency swaps multiplied by the risk-weighted category of the counterparts as an add-on to replacement cost, although a higher weighting can be opted for which will not require a previous replacement cost component.[107] Novation will allow a netting of hedged positions whereas assignment or participation agreements will not. Under both G–10 and SBD, non-OECD government debts are rated at 100% risk, hardly likely to provide liquidity for developing countries.[108] Thus, the document has severe economic implications beyond G–10 and suggests the interlinking of trade, monetary and financial

law. Instruments which are traded on an exchange and marked to market are exempted under G–10.

Several aspects of banking regulation including deposit insurance, interest rate ceilings on deposits and reserve requirements are not included in the subject matter covered by the SBD and its corollary directives. It has been suggested that high profit margins for banks exist in such countries as the United Kingdom, Belgium, Denmark, France and Spain, while low margins exist in Germany, Italy, the Netherlands and Switzerland,[109] and that the difference is due in large measure to different reserve requirements.

A vexing problem is the wide range of reserve requirements, which run from a high of 25% in Italy, 18.5% in Spain and 12% in Germany to .5% in the United Kingdom and 0% in Belgium.[110] For banks to be competitive in a European market, it is necessary that reserve requirements be harmonized throughout the community so as not to disadvantage countries which require higher reserves. Reserve requirements, hitherto considered instruments of national monetary policy, may have to be replaced as a consequence of European Economic and Monetary Union (EMU). Otherwise, countries such as Italy and Spain, which have an excessive reserve requirement in order to provide cheap financing to ease fiscal deficits and to serve as an instrument of credit restraint, will be unable to maintain parity with stronger European currencies such as the DM.

Without harmonization of withholding taxes for residents and non-residents, investors would prefer to hold interest-bearing instruments and share certificates in banks in certain countries as opposed to others, thereby providing a certain advantage for non-withholding countries. In Belgium, for example, a withholding tax for both residents and non-residents of 25% is required for interest and dividends—whereas in the United Kingdom and Luxembourg, a similar 25% tax is required on interest, but there is no withholding on dividends.[111] Furthermore, there are variants in capital gains treatments. In general, the free flow of capital pursuant to the European Capital Liberalization Directive[112] acts as an impediment to tax collection since many member states use withholding taxes as a principal vehicle of tax collection. Without a common withholding tax, capital will flow to banks within the member states with the lowest withholding requirements thereby again favoring particular member states. A proposal for a uniform European system of withholding tax was defeated in 1989.[113]

The G–10 Agreement relegates many off-balance sheet items to 50% risk weights multiplied by the risk weight attached to the counterparty.[114] Certain risk participations will incur a weight with respect to the residual liability; however, other forms of residual liabilities will evoke different treatment in different EEC countries. One example is securitization.

Securitization, the process whereby loans or receivables are pooled and then sold for the purpose of moving assets off balance sheet to improve

the capital adequacy of the seller is not directly addressed by the G–10 Agreement or the SBD. Such receivables must have a reasonably ascertainable cash flow and include mortgages and credit card receivables. The market is vast in the United States[115] and is therefore an important factor in overall banking solvency. In the United Kingdom, the ability of banks to securitize assets (i.e., to achieve "sale" treatment) depends upon equity and voting rights held by the bank (original lender) in the Special Purpose Vehicle (SPV) created under the Companies Act of 1985.[116] Banks are allowed a one-time contribution to a SPV, and subordinated loans may be repayable only on termination of the SPV.[117] Certain situations allow more favorable treatment of mortgages.[118]

The United Kingdom requires consolidated reporting under the 1989 Companies Act (therefore requiring on-balance sheet treatment) of securitized assets where a parent has over 50% interest in the subsidiary or control thereof.[119] This use made of the EEC Eighth Company Law Directive[120] is illustrative of the manifold ways in which EEC financial law is incorporated into member state legal systems; UK law is particularly important in this regard as the United Kingdom is the European leader in financial services and financial innovation.[121]

In France, the equity investment in a Fond Common de Créance (FCC) by credit institutions operating through mutual investment funds may hold only up to 5% of the issue. The French legislation also contains certain investor protection measures which are lacking in the US and the UK legislation. The Commission des Operations des Bourses is responsible for overseeing establishment and the by-laws of the Fond Common de Créance.[122]

One aspect of risk which is not addressed by the SRD or G–10 Agreement is interest rate and currency risk. Traditionally, this area has been dealt with through consultation between banks and regulators. As the Committee on Banking Regulations and Supervisory Practices stated in the July 1988 G–10 Agreement: "The framework of this document is mainly directed at assessing capital in relation to credit risk (the risk of counterparty failure) but other types of risk most notably, interest rate risk, and investment risk on securities need to be taken into account by supervisors in assessing overall capital in relation to these risks."[123] In general, European countries have current rather than original exposure programs to monitor interest and currency exposure, but even though interest rate and currency futures in the United Kingdom are generally subject to the Association of Futures Brokers and Dealers (AFBD) of the London International Financial Futures Exchange, and to its exchange regulations, it is doubtful that regulators can fully grasp the extent of these positions given the nuances in the instruments used. However, off-exchange futures contracts and foreign exchange contracts are regulated by the Bank of England. Like the Federal Reserve Bank in the United States or other relevant regulators, the Bank

of England is responsible for regulating Treasury security futures for off-exchange, non-investment activities of banks.

The classic interest rate swap consists of an issuer with a high credit rating trading a fixed-rate obligation for the floating rate obligation of a borrower with a lower credit rating in exchange for a spread. It is possible that a period of stagflation could create a domino effect with the higher credit rating companies being forced to assume higher interest rates upon the default of the less creditworthy parties.[124] This is a particularly vivid example of the type of problem posed by financial innovation. The loss resulting from the *ultra vires* activities of Hammersmith & Fulham Boroughs in the United Kingdom pinpoints the problem of counterparty risks in interest rate swaps and the reason that netting is allowed only by novation under SBD and G–10 to determine capital to be held against credit risk. Unlike interest rate futures (T-Bill futures are traded on Chicago Board of Trade and Eurodollar futures on the Chicago Mercantile Exchange, and both on European Exchanges) interest swaps are usually off-exchange transactions in which banks function as intermediaries. The *Bank of England Quarterly* has questioned the depth of the secondary market in certain futures instruments.[125] The swap market, because of its insularity and possible illiquidity, may pose a greater threat to the banking safety net than do futures.

The growth of derivative instruments has hastened the process of international interdependence.[126] It has also made sharp regulatory directives more difficult.[127] Whether it has increased the global markets' volatility and reduced effectiveness of monetary policy or increased it, is a matter disputed by two different instrumentalities of the Bank for International Settlement.[128] Two real problems emerge when evaluating financial innovation. First, banking traditionally involved rule of thumb pricing, but the subtlety of today's instruments defies proper pricing.[129] NIFs, for instance, may seriously jeoparidze a bank's liquidity because the time at which such facilities will be drawn is unknown, although a "material adverse change" clause may provide some protection for banks. Second, no overall strategy exists for assessing interest rate risk on overall portfolio investment, according to the Bank for International Settlement report on banking innovation.[130]

The SBD requires implementation in the member state in which the credit institution is authorized. Complex amendments of national legislation are therefore necessitated. In the United Kingdom, the implementation of the SBD has been addressed in a consultative document issued by the Treasury and the Department of Trade Industry.[131] Specifically, a single authorization covering all the activities listed in the Annex B of the SBD for banks and their OFD (Article 18) subsidiaries is needed to make use of the passport to do business elsewhere in the EEC. This requires that different authorizations granted by various UK supervisory authorities

be replaced by a single authorization by the Bank of England; so that the Bank of England will exercise authority over non–deposit-taking activities carried out by the credit institutions elsewhere in the EEC. However, there will continue to be an interaction between the responsibilities of the Bank and those of other UK regulators.[132] It is also necessary to make this authorization the exclusive route for passportable institutions to carry on annex activities in other member states. A new definition of subsidiary undertaking and the current definition of parent undertaking must be introduced into legislation.[133] The current definition of subsidiary is much narrower than the term used in the directive. It may also prove necessary to redefine deposit taking institutions under Section 3 of the Banking Act of 1987. Primary legislation may be needed to make the 1987 Banking Act consistent with the European Communities Act of 1972 as regards the question of punishable offenses which relate to the powers of banking supervisors to obtain information and carry on investigations.[134]

The old reciprocity clause of the proposed SBD which required mirror image reciprocity for third country banking systems[135] has been replaced by an insistence on effective market access to third country markets[136] (which is mirrored in the ISD).[137] This is also the principle articulated in the financial services component of the current Uruguay Round.[138]

The impact of these provisions is limited in that existing third country subsidiaries within the EEC are grandfathered.[139] Furthermore, the Euromarkets have traditionally benefited from stringent regulation in the United States and Japan, such as the Interest Equalization Tax Act and Regulation Q,[140] both of which have since gone by the wayside, and Japanese restrictions on equity warrants.[141] In fact, the United States, through international banking facilities (IBF)[142] has created separate recordkeeping facilities within domestic US banking facilities which were not only free of Regulation Q restrictions, while they lasted, but were also free of reserve requirements. These IBFs were created in order to compete for the unregulated Euromarket business.

The reciprocity or effective market access provisions of the SBD are aimed at other restrictive practices in Japan. Japan has in fact undertaken serious reform and the lack of effective market access in Japan is often the result of the low rate of return on Japanese assets; and, a consequent reform of the Japanese financial system would result in a net loss to European banks.[143] The attempt to pigeonhole financial services within the principles of free trade, as enunciated by GATT and particularly the Uruguay Round which calls for the inclusion of services within GATT, fails to take into account the unique role of financial services delineated in this chapter.

EUROPEAN ECONOMIC AND MONETARY UNION
AND A EUROPEAN CENTRAL BANK

In 1979 the European Monetary System (EMS) was inaugurated pursuant to a resolution of the European Council at Brussels. The resolution estab-

lished an Exchange Rate Mechanism (ERM) allowing a fluctuation margin of 2.25% for the participating currencies, with certain EEC countries allowed to adopt a wider range of 6%. The resolution also adopted a European Currency Unit (ECU) as a means of settlement between member states monetary authorities, that is, central banks.[144]

Member states which opted to join the ERM of the EMS were obligated to intervene to support or sell their currencies if the currency deviated by more than 75% of the 2.25% fluctuation margin.[145] Italy operates within a wide band as did the United Kingdom during its participation.

The ERM of the EMS collapsed in September 1992. Its collapse was, in large measure, the result of high German interest rates caused by the expansion of the German monetary supply. This was a direct consequence of the rising demand created by German unification and the attendant German economic and monetary union. Initially, members of the ERM were attracted to the discipline imposed by the Bundesbank and its statutory independence, which other European central banks lacked. Its inauguration was particularly timely because of the fiscal stimulus employed by most member states to survive the economic downturn of the mid–1970s.[146] The demise of the ERM—which will be very difficult to resurrect because international money markets are unlikely to believe in the commitment of member states to monetary discipline—may have been precipitated by German monetary expansion as the result of unification and the reactive strict monetary policy; but the inability of the ERM to survive has created grave doubts about the possibility of European economic and monetary union any time in the next decade, although the Treaty of European Union requires monetary union to be accomplished as of 1999 at the latest.[147] Because relatively fixed exchange rates are a prerequisite to European monetary union and a European central bank, the entire European monetary program may not play an important part in the real time future.

In 1989 a committee chaired by Jacques Delors, president of the European Economic Community, issued a report on European economic and monetary union.[148] The Delors report set three stages for monetary union. The first two stages involve the setting of fixed exchange rates among the currencies of the member states of the European Community.[149] The third stage of monetary union under the Delors report calls for the establishment of a European system of central banks.[150] While the best-known function for a central bank is to determine monetary policy, another function of a European central bank would be to harmonize and administer banking and other financial regulation throughout the EEC.[151]

According to Otto Pohl, the former chairman of the Bundesbank, a European System of Central Banks (ESCB) must have "the monopoly of money creation."[152] Pohl's ESCB would operate very much like the Federal Reserve System of Central Banks and like Stage Two of the Delors plan. Pohl appears to see a single monetary policy for the EEC, which, like

Stage Two, would set rules for individual budgets and their financing. A natural corollary to Pohl's view is that additional liquidity should not be injected into the European financial system by independent non-ESCB supervision of securities markets:

The settlement of payments, open market operation with the banks, business on behalf of government institutions and the like should well be taken care of by the national central bank—according to the guidelines and instructions of the ECBS [ESCB]. In addition, the national central banks should, in my opinion, be responsible for bank and stock exchange supervision where (as, for example, in the Federal Republic of Germany)—this is not yet the case. This means the national central banks would play a role similar to that of the Federal Reserve Bank of the United States for the land central banks in the Federal Republic of Germany. However, they and/or the finance ministers would have to give up their right to formulate independent national monetary policies. Particularly for Germany, this would have far-reaching implications. The Central Bank Council, which today is the supreme decision-making body in the Monetary Policy field, would lose its most important function, a consequence which may not have become quite clear to every advocate of an ECBS [ESCB] in the Federal Republic of Germany.[153]

On February 7, 1992, the EEC memorialized negotiations undertaken within the intergovernmental conferences on European monetary and political union begun in December 1990 at the Rome Summit and ended in Maestricht in December 1991. This treaty, entitled "Treaty on European Union,"[154] enunciates an economic and monetary policy for the EEC.[155] Beginning on January 1, 1994, a second stage for achieving economic and monetary unions will begin with the establishment of the European Monetary Institute (EMI), precursor to a European Central Bank similar to the US Federal Reserve System. Each member state's national bank will operate in a system called the ESCB and in a manner similar to that of a member bank in the Federal Reserve System. The EMI is charged with the conversion of national monetary policies and with creating a system allowing for derogations from treaty responsibilities based on each nation's ability to fulfill the necessary preconditions for the adoption of a single currency.[156] The EMI is charged, by the end of 1997, to set a date for the beginning of the third stage of European monetary union which will in no event start after January 1, 1999.[157] One of the most important provisions for the establishment of a European Central Bank is that member states shall avoid excessive government deficits. Punitive measures are enumerated, including the requirement that member states concerned make a non–interest-bearing deposit to the community until the excessive deficit has been redressed. An excessive deficit[158] will be found where the ratio of all government debt to gross domestic product exceeds 60%. The EEC may also impose fines.[159]

Denmark and the United Kingdom have protocols to the treaty which

enable these member states to refrain from implementing the third stage of the treaty, that is, a single currency and a European Central Bank, to which they would derogate their monetary policy.[160] However, the practical ability of the United Kingdom to refrain from enacting the third stage of monetary union is limited in practice. The same motivations which caused the United Kingdom to join the ERM will be in effect at the time the European Central Bank (ECB) comes into existence. The maintenance of London as the principal financial market center of the EEC depends upon UK enactment of the ECB and attendant monetary policies implicit in fixed exchange rates or a single European currency.

The primary object of the ECB shall be to maintain price stability.[161] The ECB shall have the exclusive right to issue bank notes within the community.[162] In the protocol of the statutes, the ECB is guaranteed independence from national authority.[163] The governing Council consists of the members of the executive board and the governors of the national Central Banks,[164] and vote is by simple majority. Only where a decision regards bank capital will votes be weighted according to national bank shares.[165] The ECB is also charged with prudential supervision of the financial system of credit institutions and of the financial system in general.[166]

The delegation of powers to the ECB under the treaty in the areas of prudential supervision and exchange rate policy is not clear. No clear mandate is given in the area of prudential supervision. Article 105 of the treaty reads in pertinent part:

. . . the Council may, acting unanimously on a proposal from the Commission and after consulting the ECB and after receiving the assent of the European Parliament, confer upon the ECB specific tasks concerning policies relating to the prudential supervision of credit institutions and . . . other financial institutions with the exception of insurance undertakings.[167]

Under Article 104, the ECB is barred from lending directly to governments or buying securities from them. This ban on monetary financing makes it questionable whether the ECB is permitted to engage in open market operations. According to one estimate, if the ECB's domestic assets were to grow at 5% a year, and all of its purchases were of Italian government debt, purchases would be no more than 2% of the debt stock.[168] So, open market operations would not monetize national debts.

When countries join a monetary union, they forego the use of monetary and exchange rate policies to stabilize national economies. Without such tools, the only remaining tool is fiscal policy. Because the EEC budget is small, stabilization programs will have to be carried out at the national level without jeopardizing the fiscal stance of the EEC as a whole.[169] There are pros and cons to a monetary union vis-à-vis a federal system. Whenever

economic activity falls in a particular US state relative to other states, its citizens' federal tax payments fall and they receive more federal payments; this is not the case in a monetary union.[170] In addition to restrictions on excessive budget deficits discussed above,[171] the treaty contains a "no bail-out" clause.[172] The EEC budget could become more flexible in due course if certain programs were shifted from the national to the EEC budget, particularly unemployment insurance.[173] This would depend on the willingness of rich member countries to underwrite costs of adjustment in economically less developed member countries. But, as US experience has shown, off-balance sheet expenditures may be less politically sensitive.

Six countries would have failed the excessive debt and deficit criteria— Spain, Belgium, Ireland, Italy, Greece and the Netherlands. Here the idealism implicit in monetary union diverges from the reality and makes one question the sincerity and authenticity of the EEC.[174] No roadmap exists to define the trajectory that high debt countries are to follow to reduce their debt.

The EEC Commission has detailed what it considers to be the prime benefits of EMU.[175] In its view, the very purpose of an international regime is to set rules that apply to all participating countries and that can be maintained without hegemony. The Commission remarks that the flaw of the Bretton Woods System is that the leadership was given to one particular country (i.e., the United States) independent of the quality of its policy.[176]

Here is the impetus behind EMU. Although it is impossible to quantify the current role of the dollar, EMU and an ECB would undoubtedly limit the unilateral ability that the United States enjoys to monetize its deficit. The Maastricht Treaty even enunciates a procedure for the Council of Ministers[177] and the ECB to subscribe to an international monetary regime such as Bretton Woods.[178] This is the kernel of EMU. Consider the clout carried by the EEC in the GATT. If EMU had been in place in early 1992, it is not clear that the US Federal Reserve Bank could have lowered short-term interest rates without creating a dollar crisis.

The language of the statute that commits the ECB to price stability may be anathematic to the "lender of the last resort" function that a central bank must play. The role played by a central bank in a financial crisis is foreclosed under a strict interpretation of the statute.[179] Although national central banks must be involved in lender of last resort operations, an integrated financial market poses the possibility of EEC-wide contagion.[180] The tension between monetary policy and the lender of last resort function is all too clear.

The goal of price stability may have been appropriate to the 1980s, but conflicting goals of financial stability and economic growth may prove more important in the future. The ERM survived throughout the 1980s because of an EEC consensus on the primacy of price stability. A short-term eco-

nomic policy of price stability cannot serve as the foundation of EEC monetary and financial law.

A European Monetary Union will inevitably reduce the costs of transactions for EEC financial institutions operating within the EEC. Directly, there will be fewer charges for foreign currency risk, and, indirectly, financial institutions will be able to assess the value of banking and security issues in their own currency. Nonetheless, the absence of EMU will not substantially hinder progress in the arena of EEC integration in the financial sector.

The potential role of an ECB in the arena of prudential supervision is not readily apparent. Aside from its coordination of financial regulation, its attitude toward the bailing out of financially troubled institutions as a supplement to deposit insurance would be important in determining its functions. Even more important would be the role it would play in relation to the securities markets and the "securitized" markets (commercial paper and mortgage backed securities). The possibility of an ECB which would not respond to liquidity crunches in security markets is something to consider. Continental banking supervisors are not used to an independently functioning securities market requiring injections of liquidity through the easing short-term interest rates, as was found in the 1987 market break. The willingness to perform this function is a *sine qua non* of a successfully functioning ECB, which will provide support for all EEC securities markets, particularly those in the United Kingdom, which, as of this date, are the only ones that form a sector independent from the banking sector. The role of the central bank in providing credit to the securities markets is discussed in greater detail in Chapters 2 and 3 in relation to the United States.

Part IV: Investment Services: The Final Frontier

A. THE ROLE OF SECURITIES EXCHANGES

In the United Kingdom, The Securities Authority (TSA), a self-regulatory organization for the Stock Exchange, has promulgated the best execution rule to guard against self-frontrunning, a practice where a firm manipulates the market by trading ahead of its own order. International market manipulation which is best regulated at the exchange level suggests the increasing importance of international harmonization exchange regulation,[181] and UK exchanges have been the setting for US strategies of such manipulation by self-frontrunning.

The Investment Services Directive (ISD) includes the rights of establishment and the freedom to provide services as guaranteed under the Treaty of Rome.[182] Most important, member states may require that certain

transactions relating to services be carried out on a regulated market, provided the investor is habitually resident or established in that member state and the transaction involves an instrument dealt in on a regulated market.[183] Member states which do not permit credit institutions to become members of or have access to regulated markets unless they have specialized subsidiaries may continue until December 31, 1996, to apply the same requirements in a non-discriminatory way to credit institutions from other member states.[184] Spain, Greece and Portugal will have until December 31, 1999.

One of the most contentious debates surrounding the ISD concerned the publication of information with the timely screen-driven report of all information which makes it difficult for a market maker to operate efficiently. The compromise agreed on required publication at the start of each day's trading on the market of the weighted average price, the highest and the lowest price and the volume dealt with on the regulated market in question, and for continuous order driven and quote driven markets, publication at the end of each hour's trading of similar weighted average price and volume for a six-hour trading period and every 20 minutes of the weighted average price and the highest and lowest price on the regulated market in question for a two-hour period.[185] The directive does not state any clear date for implementation. The importance of requiring certain instruments to be regulated markets and traded daily reporting requirements, both of which are effective on December 31, 1996,[186] suggests that this will be the timing of implementation.

Additional EEC legislation relating to securities exchanges includes a directive making mandatory mutual recognition of listing particulars (LP),[187] which amends earlier directives the goal of which was the harmonization of listing particulars.[188] Another directive provides for the mutual recognition of prospectus requirements for unlisted securities except certain Eurosecurities, not generally the subject of an advertising campaign (the "MRP Directive").[189] The largely unregulated Eurobond market will remain unregulated.

Where the securities offered (including Eurobonds) are or are to be, listed in London, any advertisement or other information approved, or authorized for issue, by the Stock Exchange under Section 154 of the FSA will be exempt from advertising and public offer requirements as contained in the FSA, as will the listing particulars themselves and any other document required or permitted to be published by listing rules (found in the Stock Exchange's "Yellow Book").[190]

With the enactment of Part V of the FSA, the MRP directive becomes effective in the United Kingdom. The cumulative effect of the various LP and MRP directives is that:

1. Listing Particulars for exchanges of member states must comply with the minimum requirement of the LPD, must be drawn up and approved by the com-

petent authorities in member states and must be recognized as LPs in all member states.

2. Offers to the public however defined where official listing is not sought must, unless they fall within the exceptions in the MRP, comply with the minimum requirement of the MRP; and public offering prospectuses drawn up to the requirements of the LP Directive and approved must be recognized both as listing particulars and as public offering prospectuses in all member states.[191]

Notably, the MRP directive does not define "offer to the public" and thus this definition under UK law would be governed by Part V of the FSA. The absence of this definition is not in itself a major failing of the EEC legislation as it is intended to allow freedom of each member state to determine in its own terms what an "offer to the public" is or what minimum policing requirements are. The Department of Trade and Industry (DTI) in its consultative document essentially says that the prudential standards for issuance of securities which are not the subject of a public offering will be fulfilled by the requirement under Section 57 of the FSA that authorized persons approve the content of advertisements.[192]

Even listed securities that are public offers will have to comply with the MRP directive rather than the current Part IV of the FSA that governs all listed securities. According to the DTI this change will have little practical effect[193] although the text of Part IV and V of the FSA will have to be altered. The DTI says that there is a strong case for all securities not listed on an exchange to be subject to a prospectus requirement whether or not such offers are offers to the public.[194] The rationale given is that the admission of securities to dealing implies an expectation that a subsequent market will exist in the securities. It is odd that the DTI would suggest prospectuses for all securities whether or not offered to the public when the United Kingdom, with support from Luxembourg, was the primary opponent of extending the MRP to all offers of securities. In general, the FSA exempts certain private placements of securities from prospectus requirements for offers to the public by means of not requiring an advertisement (including an offering bulletin) to be considered an advertisement for the offering of securities within Part 1 of the FSA.[195]

UK law places no definitive restrictions limiting resale of privately placed securities as does US law, which requires a holding period of two years before resale to the public.[196] The MRP goes beyond the offer for sale type situations envisaged by the definition of secondary offer[197] and would cover a situation in which a share was offered to the public several years later[198] (Section 160 of the FSA might also cover such a situation). It is certainly to be queried as to whether the absence of any clear restriction on public resale under UK or EEC law represents a gap in investor protection. Furthermore, offers of short dated debentures are not deemed to be offers to the public.[199]

The DTI identifies three major approaches for determining what is an offer to the public:

1. the Guidance approach
2. the Objective Rules approach
3. the Hybrid approach

Under the Guidance approach, sharp lines are not drawn and thus there is a considerable degree of uncertainty.[200] The DTI has set forth a draft statute making obvious exemptions, including employee share schemes, and offers made to less than 50 persons, one of the first times the DTI uses a definitive objective standard.[201]

The MRP Directive list of exclusions is far larger than that provided for under US Securities Law.[202] Disclosure requirements under the MRP Directive[203] are considerably less specific than comparable disclosure requirements under Sections 5 and 11 of the US Securities and Exchange Act. There is mutual recognition under the MRP by all member states; however, member states may require the prospectus to include information specific to the market of the country in which the public offer is being made, concerning in particular the income tax system, the financial organizations retained to act as paying agent for the issuer in that country and the way in which notices to investors are published.[204] In the case of an offering for transferrable securities which are to be admitted to official listing on a Stock Exchange, the prospectus must comport with the LPD and at the same time be adapted to the circumstances of a public offer.[205] This information is more detailed than that required under the MRP Directive.[206] The MRP Directive must be contrasted with US prospectus requirements and liability for failure to disclose material information. Even to the extent that the United Kingdom has interpreted its domestic disclosure laws through a judicial line of decisions, these will be irrelevant to a non-UK firm doing business in the United Kingdom which will be held instead to the as yet uninterpreted disclosure requirements of the MRP (together with the domestic law of another member state that may, under a conflict of law approach, be interpreted by a UK court) with appeal to the ECJ. This level of investor protection is lower than that afforded by the US courts' 60 year's history of interpreting the disclosure requirements of the Securities and Exchange Acts.

The LPD and the MRP are feasible only because of the harmonization and mutual recognition of accounting principles used in the preparation of financial statements. Of the directives enacted on the harmonization of accounting principles, the most important are the Fourth Directive on Company Law[207] and the Seventh Directive on Company Law.[208] The Fourth Directive presents a compromise between the legalistic (statute-based) approach to accounting and financial reporting in continental Eu-

rope and the true and fair value approach prevailing in the English-speaking countries. It allows for a choice among many alternative treatments and gives member states options after implementation.[209] There are no requirements for cash flow statements or statements of changes in shareholders' equity. The income statement may be shown in four different forms, each of which is laid down in a separate article of the directive.[210] For measuring assets and liabilities, the Fourth Directive uses the term "valuation rules."[211]

The Seventh Directive of the Company Law requires consolidated financial statements for related companies. Fundamentally, the Seventh Directive requires consolidation where either the parent or the subsidiary is a limited liability company (i.e., a corporation), regardless of the location of its registered office. The legal concept of control, which is broadly defined, determines the obligation to consolidate. Article 13 specifies conditions allowing exclusion from the EEC consolidation obligation.[212] Article 14 of the Directive allows exclusion from consolidation if there are demonstratively dissimilar activities at the subsidiary level. Article 7 provides for mandatory exemption from consolidation of EEC parents' undertakings which are themselves 100%-owned subsidiaries of another EEC parent. Where the ultimate parent is an EEC undertaking, exemption from some consolidation is possible.[213] Where the parent is headquartered outside the EEC, exemption from EEC subconsolidations may be allowed.[214] Articles 16 to 23 address consolidation methods.[215] Article 34 deals with disclosure and involves considerable detail, including the disclosure of persons, registered offices of all related entities and a full description of consolidated net turnover broken down by categories of activity and geographical markets and tax considerations reflected in the financial statement.

The directive concerning annual financial and consolidated statements of financial institutions is an extension of the Fourth and Seventh Directives,[216] is tailored to financial institutions, adds other considerations, such as marking to market any instruments which are part of a trading portfolio, and begins to consider new financial instruments (particularly in forward transactions). The United Kingdom has implemented the Fourth and Seventh Company Directives through the Companies Acts of 1981, 1985 and 1989.[217] The one principal change is the requirement for geographic segment reporting.[218]

One effect of the Companies Act of 1989 is that it will permit settlement of securities and foreign currency transactions notwithstanding insolvency. Furthermore, the New Companies Act will also provide a process under which a defaulting counterparty will not be able to "cherry pick" among its various contracts and to disavow the one it does not want. Counterparty default will in general be given a higher priority than previously through additional safeguards. Cooperation between the bankruptcy trustee and the relevant regulatory and exchange official will be mandated.[219] These

new provisions will bring UK protection in line with that afforded in the United States.

Two paradigms of the future of securities regulation are evident. One is the "race to bottom" resulting from the level-playing, and the other is the necessity of conducting an orderly market, particularly in the area of exchange regulation. Although it is true that rigorous US securities regulation has caused the United States—like Japan—to lose business to the Euromarkets, the SEC has recognized the international market for sophisticated investors, as may be seen from the enactment of Regulation S,[220] which codifies the terms under which offerings in the Euromarket will be exempt from US jurisdiction, and Rule 144A,[221] which allows offerings to qualified investors as determined by a new worth test gauging ownership of liquid securities. These measures will enable the emergence of a sophisticated US market able to compete with the largely unregulated Euromarket. The London International Stock Exchange, because of its status as the most highly regulated exchange in Europe, is as likely to gain value as a result of increased European business in the wake of 1992 as it is to lose business to the less highly regulated exchanges of continental Europe. The idea that London will not continue to be a leading financial center competitive with Tokyo and New York[222] is, in my view, shortsighted, provided regulation of financial services, especially exchanges, payment systems and their attendant solvency issues, keep pace with that in US markets and regulations imposed by self-regulatory arrangements are not too onerous.[223]

The ISD requires member states to enable access to membership to exchanges located within their borders.[224] The mutual recognition of listing particulars mandates the minimum as well as maximum conditions to which issuers will be subject.[225]

B. THE CAPITAL ADEQUACY DIRECTIVE

The CAD is analogous to the various banking directives regulating capital. It is founded on the assumption that securities firms and securities activities of banks have short-term credit exposure and most of the instruments traded are marked to market. Generally, the directive regulates position risk and provides an overall safeguard for systemic risk. Position risk is the risk from the net position of the securities firm, and the capital requirement is 8% which is considered general risk. Also, an additional 2% to 4% risk weighting will be assigned against gross equity positions depending upon the diversification of the portfolio in order to capture specific risk under the latest draft of the CAD, the Common Position of the Council of Ministers dated July 27, 1992.[226] Interest rate risk is also divided into specific and general risk, depending upon the issuer.

These approaches enshrine what is entitled the building block approach,

under which different kinds of risk are added together. The earlier comprehensive approach looked at a securities position less arithmetically and in one stage rather than at two positions. The Committee on Banking and Supervisory Practices which has been chaired by the United States under the auspices of the Bank for International Settlements and the International Organization of Securities Commissions ("IOSCO") are the principal fora in which these issues are being discussed.

Under this draft, the provisions for minimum initial capital for most categories of investment firms have been increased to ECU 125,000 and ECU 730,000.[227] The ECU 730,000 level, which is equivalent to $900,000 to $1,000,000, is far higher than the SEC's minimum capital requirement for a full service firm.[228] The definition of a "qualifying" issuer of equity or debt has been broadened to allow regulators to consider securities which are neither listed nor rated as "qualifying items," taking into account the characteristics of certain markets.[229] Article 7 aims at providing a detailed regulatory framework for the supervision of market risks on a consolidated basis pursuant to the approach envisioned in the directive on consolidated supervisions of credit institutions (CSD).[230] The CAD preempts the CSD where the group does not contain credit institutions.[231] Groups not containing credit institutions may waive the principles of compulsory consolidation if certain strict conditions are met.[232] Specifically, entities of a group located in a single member state may offset their positions, even though they do not comply with capital requirements on a solo basis. Such offset is allowed if some entities of a group are established in another member state and comply with the CAD requirements on a solo basis.[233] The Council did maintain the Commission's amended proposal providing for the establishment of a regulatory committee; and the Council indicated its intention to come to a decision on the establishment of such a committee which would fulfill similar functions under the ISD and other securities markets directives.[234] Article 13 of the Common Position of the Council sets forth the Commission's undertaking to carry out further work and make suitable proposals for more appropriate capital requirements relating to commodities and commodities derivatives of units of collective investment of undertaking.[235] Under the new Article 14, a review clause is established to allow incorporation of developments in the work of the Basle group of banking supervisors and IOSCO, which is carrying out parallel work in the area of Capital Adequacy.[236] Under Annex 3 of the CAD, institutions may apply different weights for calculating capital requirements against foreign exchange risks in order to take account of the existence of groups of currencies characterized by high degrees of correlation, most notably in the ERM. Given the developments which are co-terminus with the report in the ERM, it is unlikely that such an amendment will have an immediate impact. Under the Common Position, the trading book is made mandatory for both credit institutions and investment services[237] and

the rules laid down in the SRD are also applicable to investment firms in respect of their non-trading book.[238] Alternative regulatory capital (i.e., that capital which is related to the trading book) is defined in a very similar fashion. Under the CAD, credit institutions and investment firms may use tier-three capital up to 150% of tier-one capital as defined in the Own Funds Directive. However, credit institution utilization of tier three beyond 150% of tier-one capital as defined in the Own Funds Directive requires authorization from the competent authorities. The same applies to investment firms beyond 200% of tier-one capital dedicated exclusively to trading risks, while the application of the 250% of tier-one ceiling involves compulsory deduction of illiquid assets.[239] The provisions for large exposures in the CAD are fairly similar to those in the LED[240] for credit institutions with some adaptations. Exposures to a single client or a group of connected clients arising solely from the trading book may exceed the limit contained in the LED subject to several conditions—(1) for a period of ten days an additional holding of Own Funds is required,[241] (2) after the tenth day additional capital, the amount of which is linked to the size of the excess, must be set aside,[242] and (3) overall limits on individual and aggregate exposures must be respected.[243]

The CAD offers major incentives for firms to move many assets from their bank book to their trading book, or, alternatively, to issue debt and equity securities (i.e., to securitize their assets) in order to achieve the lower risk ratings for position risk at the higher gearing allowed for trading books (tier-three capital). Consider a short-term loan to a non-governmental entity[244] or short-term commercial paper. Even a mortgage which bears only a 50% risk weighting may be preferable to hold as part of a securitized trading portfolio.[245] However, any fast move toward a growing market in underwriting of equities by continental universal banks that might tend to lower the price of the equity would be countervailed by the desire of these banks to maintain the value of their capital invested in equities and which is therefore includable in tier-two capital.[246] Tier-three capital, as distinguished from tier-two capital, includes the net profits or losses for the year to date[247] and subordinated loan capital having an original maturity of at least two years (versus at least five years maturity requirement with discounts thereafter for tier-two capital). Thus, the advantages of tier-three capital are its maturity period and the fact it can be up to 250% of tier-one capital for Own Funds of credit institutions.[248]

It is important to remember that the CAD calls for minimum capital rules; and, capital rules may be more prescriptive on a national level. The United Kingdom has a long history of detailed capital rules for securities firms. These rules, in their latest forms, are found in the Financial Supervision Rules of 1990 in the Securities and Investments Board rule book.[249]

The rules detail financial resource requirements for low-, medium-, and high-risk firms.

Since a firm conducting broker-dealer activities on an international scale tends to be a high-risk firm, we will concentrate on the application of capital rules for high-risk firms. There are stringent rules for deduction of illiquid assets and amounts due from connected companies.[250] There is a higher base rate requirement for firms in high-risk categories.[251] United Kingdom requirements may be more stringent in three categories: position risk for certain foreign equities, capital required for underwritings and large exposure, and reserves for non-qualifying debt which would encompass high-yield securities. The capital adequacy requirements for position risks for high-risk firms (meaning any large firm) are entitled the "more closely risk-based approaches to position risk."[252] Two different methods are likely to apply, depending upon the international diversification.[253] Only diversified portfolios of shares in the largest markets (United Kingdom, United States and Japan) can be treated in "Equity Method 3."[254] Ultimately, capital requirement for position risk is invariably lower for United States, United Kingdom and Japanese issues and will be higher for certain equities such as Hong Kong Equities, even though these are qualifying equities.

The SIB rule book has stringent discounts for non-qualifying debt instruments (which would include high-yield securities).[255] Capital requirements for underwritings may be higher in the United Kingdom than in the United States.[256]

The trading book option of the CAD applies only to certain activities of investment firms. The specific assignment of risk has been addressed by the building block approach (general and specific risk), and the netting requirements (of long and short positions) are similar to previous drafts of the directive;[257] however, a new system breaks down a long futures position, for example, to a combination of a loan maturing on the delivery date of a futures contract and the holding of an underlying security. (Options are treated similarly.)[258] A broadly diversified stock index future which hedges underlying equities will have a 0% specific risk weighting while the underlying equities will attract a 2% specific risk. Member states are responsible for insuring that additional capital is maintained to cover situations where indexes do not move in uniformity with underlying positions.

A new formulation is set forth for underwriting positions which are subscribed by third parties, reducing net positions for the first five working days of an underwriting, and unsettled transactions which do not cause exposure to a firm shall have no capital requirement.[259]

Large exposure to a particular client or group of connected clients is limited to 25%.[260] Competent authorities may authorize the limits to be

exceeded provided that: (1) the excess arises entirely on the trading book, and (2) the firm meets an additional capital requirement calculated by selecting those components which attract the highest specific risk requirement for up to ten days. For the ten-day period, the additional capital requirement is 200% of these components.[261] The limit is between 200% and 900%, but during the ten-day period, exposure must not exceed 500%. Any excesses for more than the ten-day period must not exceed 600%. Otherwise, additional capital is required; but the United Kingdom is fighting an uphill battle in attempting to allow securities firms to commit more than 25% of their capital because Continental regulators view this practice as inconsistent with the LED.[262]

A somewhat vague provision enables supervision on a consolidated basis and allows net positions to be offset, although each firm is obliged to meet its own capital requirements. The practical effect of this section is not quite clear; but, as rules and regulations about consolidated supervision follow the implementation of the directive, the section will become less ambiguous. Firms would not be subject to consolidated supervision if they deduct participation and other investments from their own funds.[263] The manner in which the trading option will work in practice is not quite clear. Certain assets may have been held for a long time but if they are traded it will be difficult to categorize such assets. In essence the Commission will probably spend several years in delineating the distinction between the two kinds of assets that derive from the two kinds of activities in which investment banks are engaged. The distinctions will be as complicated as those used to distinguish ordinary income from capital gains, and it is likely that this categorization will be used in promulgating the appropriate regulation. Currently UK banks that engage in trading under the lower capital adequacy do so through the use of a subsidiary and deduct the capital invested in that subsidiary from total capitalization of the bank.[264] While it is not known whether the same mechanism will be employed by banks in conjunction with the trading book, the failure to delineate a subsidiary for these activities will cause all EEC banks operating a trading book to be in all probability in violation of the G–10 Agreement. If such activities were not separated into subsidiaries, insolvency of the securities' activity of a bank may cause contagion in the international banking system. Because it is the Lender of Last Resort function of central banks that provides the banking safety net, it would be difficult to limit the safety net to non-securities activities. Furthermore, deposit insurance would have to be similarly limited. Even so, it is hard to envision a situation where failure of a bank's trading book operation would not lead to a bank run unless there were an effective Chinese Wall. Even if activities were segregated into a subsidiary and capital deducted, without Chinese Walls, banks could make loans to their securities affiliates and related issuers. Such practice is not possible in the United Kingdom where the Bank of England continues to

monitor such transactions informally. Yet France's system was similar to the United Kingdom's, and prior to the "petit Bang" of 1988, a Chinese Wall existed between banking and trading activities.[265] In all likelihood the United Kingdom concept of segregating the securities activities of banks is the result of the lower capital requirements for broker dealers in the United Kingdom. Such segregation is not prevalent in universal banking systems because securities firms, distinct from banks, have been of minimal importance or even non-existent in universal banking systems.[266]

Former SEC Chairman Richard Breeden remarked that measures may have to be taken to prevent US securities firms from conducting business in Europe because of the low capital requirements for equity position risk in the CAD. The possibility of such extraterritorial regulation is not evident. Today, American firms operate in the United Kingdom and their equity positions are subject to UK law, which is comparable to the CAD in many respects. As trading in securities becomes more international through concepts such as recognized exchanges and designated exchanges, it may be increasingly difficult to segregate out the territorial application of securities laws, particularly with regard to trading activities. Consequently, it is highly desirable that international agreement is reached on a framework for capital adequacy of securities firms.

C. CONSOLIDATED SUPERVISION

The CSD,[267] together with the LED,[268] provides a framework for EEC regulation of financial conglomerates. The LED, in general, limits exposure of any credit institution to any single borrower to 25% of risk-based capital. The CSD basically extends the concept of consolidated supervision to unregulated entities of financial conglomerates. The CSD expands the consolidated supervision approach of the EEC Banking directives to include the consolidation of credit institutions to all banking groups including those whose parent undertakings are not credit institutions. Consolidation is applied to almost all banking groups.[269] Matching provisions to those in the SRD exist for the subconsolidated ratio of the subsidiary in another member State[270] and for bilateral agreement to delegate responsibility for supervision of such a subsidiary.[271]

Where credit institutions authorized in two or more member states have their parent in the same financial holding company, supervision on a consolidated basis shall be exercised by the competent authorities of the member state in which the financial holding company is set up.[272] If no subsidiary is authorized in the member state where the financial holding company is set up, the competent authorities shall reach agreement on who shall exercise supervision. In the absence of such agreement, supervision shall be exercised by the authorities that authorized the credit institution with the greatest balance sheet.[273]

Where the liability of a parent undertaking is limited to a share of capital, there shall only be proportional consolidation.[274] Yet, consolidations may be complete depending upon control exercised.[275] Control is determined by "significant influence," single management or dominant management.

Member states are to negotiate agreements with third countries to promote consolidated supervision of credit institutions that have their parent undertaking in a third country and credit institutions in a third country which have their parent undertaking in the community.[276]

Under the 1992 CSD, supervision is of financial holding companies and their subsidiaries. Mixed activity holding companies are required to provide information to regulators and are subject to on the spot verification of information.[277]

The provisions in the CAD for consolidated supervision of investment firms that do not contain a credit institution include similar provisions to those in the SRD and the CSD. Member states may waive the applications of the requirements on an individual or a subconsolidated basis to an institution which as a parent undertaking is subject to supervision on a consolidated basis and to any subsidiary of such institution which is subject to their authorization and supervision.[278] The same right of waiver is granted where the parent undertaking is a financial holding company with its head office in the same member state. Competent authorities may delegate their responsibility for supervising the subsidiary's capital adequacy and large exposure to the authorities responsible for the parent undertaking.[279] Authorities may allow the offsetting of net positions in the trading book of one institution with positions in the trading book of another institution, foreign exchange positions in one institution to offset foreign exchange positions in another institution within the group,[280] and similar offsetting of these positions in third countries where capital adequacy rules are basically equivalent.[281] When a group does not include a credit institution, competent authorities may waive supervision on a consolidated basis, provided that each investment firm in such a group (1) uses the same definition of "Own Funds" as is required in the directive,[282] (2) meets the capital requirements imposed on a solo basis, and (3) sets up systems to monitor and control the sources of capital within the group.[283] However, should the waiver be given, authorities must be notified of the risks that could undermine financial positions and may take measures to limit transfers of capital from such firms to group entities.[284] Particular measures shall be taken to monitor risks of large exposures.

The CAD provides many exceptions to consolidated supervision and by allowing for the off-setting of net positions, consolidated supervision seems only to help the firm reduce its capital requirements. Nonetheless, the import of the consolidated supervision rule is that consolidated supervision may be waived only where a firm receiving the waiver of supervision complies with the rules of the directive. Therefore, it is quite likely that all

unregulated affiliates and subsidiaries of investment firms, together with unregulated affiliates of credit institutions, must comply with capital adequacy standards. This is in sharp contrast with the situation in the United States, where, although bank holding company structures are subject to rigid supervision, affiliates of securities firms may be completely unregulated.[285]

Last year, the Technical Committee of IOSCO published a paper which sets forth the principles which should govern the supervision of financial conglomerates.[286] In general, the need for supervision of financial conglomerates is mandated by the fact that many financial conglomerates include entities that are not subject to regulation. While some of these unregulated entities may be engaged in non-financial activities, others may be conducting financial activities or have close involvement with a group of companies engaged in financial activities. Leasing, consumer credit, bridge lending, foreign exchange and swaps are examples of financial activities which do not require authorization in many G–10 countries.[287]

While IOSCO enshrines the principle of solo supervision within group-based supervision, it clearly establishes the idea that the supervisor should regulate the group on a consolidated basis. In order to monitor the risk of contagion, the IOSCO report stresses that it is highly desirable for the securities regulator to have early warning of problems elsewhere in the group. In the United States, the failure of Drexel Burnham created legislation under the Market Reforms Bill of 1990 addressing the issue of the holding company of a financial conglomerate.[288]

The IOSCO report also addressed the question of prudential consolidation of banking groups and their securities affiliates. These concerns are particularly relevant to continental Europe, but not to the United States, the United Kingdom or Japan.[289] Although consolidation of capital adequacy standards between banking securities and insurance remain futuristic, as the joint Basle-IOSCO meeting in Geneva recognized, it is necessary for regulators to find some way of adapting the techniques they employ in undertaking prudential supervision of consolidated entities to take account of technical difficulties which result from differing capital adequacy requirements. The trading books option,[290] as enunciated in the CAD, is a highly efficacious means of creating parity between universal banks that conduct trading activities in the bank itself and banks which conduct securities activities in subsidiaries or independent securities firms; but by requiring lower capital for securities issues than for loans to the extent that these are hedged by futures indexes the trading book option inevitably promotes trading activities over investment activities. Whether this will be redressed or whether it will be desirable internationally is not at all clear from the IOSCO report; but it is likely that, without a strong policy at this moment from IOSCO, this trend will continue unabated.

A large number (200 plus) of bank insurance groups now exist within the EEC. There is an emerging consensus that something must be done to deal with the problem of double leverage. However, there is no agreement on the problem and the insurance sector itself is not even capable of capital consolidation where there is a life and a non-life company in the same group.[291] This lack of agreement poses a threat to financial transparency and the safety and soundness of financial institutions. Further exacerbating the problem is the fact that the risks of insurance are not understood by securities and banking regulators and vice versa.

The recent CSD for financial groups provide some rules for determining who should be the lead supervisor responsible for consolidated supervision of the group for the use of both banking groups and investment services. The lead supervisor will be the country in which the holding company is established, except where no banking or investment business is carried out on its territory. In that case, the supervision of the largest affiliate is designated. The Securities and Exchange Commission had a different opinion regarding the value of a group-based risk assessment standard and contrasted the experience of consolidating bank holding supervision with functional regulation of securities firms, which it believed to be superior.[292]

The IOSCO Technical Committee Report on financial conglomerates goes beyond the functional regulatory approach that is currently in use in Anglo-Saxon countries by considering whether it is feasible and practical for regulators to become aware of the corporate and managerial structure of financial conglomerates. A financial conglomerate operating internationally may have adopted a management matrix whereby accountability is organized on a functional basis spanning a number of different corporate entities rather than following a pyramid structure within each corporate entity. The IOSCO Report considers it crucial for regulators to be aware of the lines of accountability within the conglomerate that affect firms they regulate.

The IOSCO Report also goes beyond the current regulatory dimensions existing in the United States and the EEC in conjunction with relations with shareholders and management (IOSCO principles E and F).[293] Shareholders and managers of unregulated holding companies can exert significant influence on regulated entities and current legislation does not really address the ability of supervisors to refuse or withdraw licenses from regulated entities where the supervisor is dissatisfied with either the controllers or managers of unregulated holding companies. However, to the extent that the unregulated holding company exerts influence over regulated entities, the fitness of major shareholders of the manager of the regulated entity does become an issue, and this is clearly addressed in current legislation in the United States and the EEC.

The IOSCO Technical Committee on Technical Adequacy chaired by Richard Breeden, former Commissioner of the SEC, was able to agree on

common capital standards for debt instruments but not on equity issues. The area of disagreement concerns the position of the EEC that a net capital requirement obtained by the netting of long and short positions should reduce the capital requirement for securities firms. The SEC position was that had such capital rules obtained in 1987, market disruption would have been aggravated. Although this appears to be a simple case of disagreement as to the quantity of capital, it may be that regulatory differences regarding the unregulated entities which are affiliated with securities companies can account for a different approach. For example, if consolidations of futures brokers in the United States (in the United States—Futures Commission Merchants) with securities houses (in the United States—broker dealers) is required by the CAD, the overall structure of EEC regulation would be more prudent.

D. CONDUCT OF BUSINESS REGULATION, THE INVESTMENT SERVICES DIRECTIVE PROPOSAL AND OTHER EEC LEGISLATION

The ISD, under the rationale of *EC Commission v. Germany*,[294] is presumed to exempt investor protection from the scheme of home country control of branching.[295] This exception covering "conduct of business rules" may be so large as to swallow the rule of the ISD; Articles 10 and 11 concern the conduct of business rules that are in the control of the host country as discussed above.[296] Specifically, Article 10 requires adequate arrangements for funds belonging to investors to be safeguarded, monitoring requirements and requirements to protect clients' interests from conflict of interest. Article 11 even applies where appropriate to non-core services and includes additional conduct of business rules, including adequate disclosure, the avoidance of conflict of interest and the positive duty to act with due skill, care and diligence.

Article 12 requires that an investment firm inform investors which compensation fund or equivalent protection will apply with respect to transactions envisaged. This is a notable position given the complex conflict of laws which have traditionally applied in financial affairs.

A directive on Undertaking for Collective Investment Trusts (UCIT) (in US parlance, open ended mutual funds controlled by a trust indenture rather than by corporate governance) provides for EEC sale even if standards are more stringent in the country of the customer than in the home country of the Trust. Restrictions will not apply if the UCIT is headquartered in another member country.[297] Even if prospectus requirements are harmonized and eventually mandatory recognition is required, UCITs advertising would still have to be approved by an authorized person under the UK Financial Services Act and conform to host country marketing and advertising standards under the UCIT's directive. The difference between

marketing and advertising standards and conduct of business rules is obscure at best.[298]

Several problems remain unresolved under the ISD. Among the most important, addressed by the UK DTI are the issues of whether corporate finance and investment advice are covered by the directive.[299] The DTI further desires to limit the scope of the directive and finds it overbroad as currently drafted in that the ISD would cover investment advice given socially and by members of recognized professional bodies.[300] It also suggests that segregation of a client's money ought not be required for business and professional investors.[301]

Currently, TSA regulations do not cover investment services which advertise certain Euro-issues but are not permanently established in the United Kingdom. Part V of the FSA would cover these investment services by expanding the definition of prospectus in line with the EEC definition, which includes advertisement as well as offers, by requiring a prospectus to be issued before any advertisements (which must still be authorized) are permitted.[302] Ironically, the EEC regulation might provide greater protection for the investor. The time frame for coordination of conduct of business rules is unknown. However, the creation of European UCITs means, for example, that a Luxembourg Unit Trust may be sold in the United Kingdom even though it would not comport with fiduciary principles under UK law.

Whether the prudence or laxity of national regulators will attract business in the internal market is a matter of speculation, but it is clear that regulation which is a barrier to trade will lead to a loss of business while measures which are designed to promote investor confidence will not. The SIB's proposed Conduct of Business Rules (CBRs), which were secondary legislation under the Companies Act of 1989[303] (these rules replace a detailed SIB rulebook which was an additional layer of regulation between the FSA and the SROs), are of the latter variety and, with the Bank of England directly authorizing EEC investment services, the London market might prevail; but individual SRO rulebooks might still prove too cumbersome.

In general, the single market program is bound to lead to a growth in European investment services and securities business. While EEC Directives ensure adequate regulation in broad outline, national authorities will be the enforcers of investment protection measures in the near term. The Chairman of the TSA, who is also the Chairman of Merrill Lynch Europe Ltd., believes that CBRs will lead to a loss of business by UK markets to other centers in the EEC. He suggests that the advantages of a more highly regulated market are lost on sophisticated institutional investors because they believe that investments entrusted to universal banks which conduct securities business on the continent are effectively guaranteed by the prudential banking safety nets in those countries.[304]

While the need for segregation of clients' money and securities might therefore be obviated (under the latest ISD draft, credit institutions need only segregate non-institutional clients' securities),[305] there are other CBRs such as cold calling, advertising (particularly cross-border advertising), proper and timely execution of trades, and soft commission arrangements that drive up the cost of other commissions and tie-ins that are unrelated to solvency. Many CBRs can be harmonized internationally as David Walker, the Chairman of SIB, remarked at an IOSCO meeting in 1989.[306] Examples of specific problems posed by the international organization of securities markets are, according to Walker: (1) advertising and cross-border selling techniques, (2) proper prioritization of client business, (3) higher risks of market manipulation and (4) preferential soft-commission arrangements.[307] Also, stabilization practices vary widely between exchanges. The amenability of these problems to EEC and international cooperation is questionable.

The UK Financial Services Act of 1986 creates the most advanced structure for securities regulation in Europe; and London today is the center of the Euromarket. The Act goes one step beyond the First Banking Directive and provides for automatic authorization of any member state investment firm "carrying on business in the UK" not "having a permanent establishment in the UK."[308] While member state investment firms are thus "authorized" they also become subject to all rules of the SIB or relevant SRO whether or not they are members of the SRO.[309] While it is quite clear that investment firms are able to be regulated by either the SIB or the relevant SRO, according to their preference,[310] foreign banks and investment companies have chosen to be regulated by SROs as opposed to the SIB.[311] One possible explanation for this preference is that the common fund for compensation to investors is spread out over the several thousand members of a particular SRO and must be absorbed by the 60 or so members that are directly authorized by the SIB, and the SIB members include UK clearing house banks and building societies which, of course, have a phenomenal potential exposure.

It is unclear even from the discussion in the SIB's document *A Forward Look* as to whether other member states' investment service companies, and particularly banks, will be subject to the jurisdiction of the SIB or SROs.[312] The UK argument that they should be subject to the jurisdiction of these regulatory agencies is founded on the concept that such firms are subject to UK conduct of business rules and thus should be subject to the organizations that administer these rules. However, this logic seems to violate the freedom of establishment, the foundation on which the SBD and the ISD build. It appears that the anomalous result might ensue whereby other member states' firms would be subject to UK conduct of business rules but not to the regulatory agencies that administer such rules. A more likely result would be that member state firms were to be subject

to the SIB and various SROs—both of which, under the ISD, would already have certain host member responsibilities. However, an argument could be made that credit institutions are subject only to the regulatory authorities provided by the SBD, and the SIB's pamphlet *A Forward Look* hints at this idea.

There is certainly a problem regarding the regulation of banks in the United Kingdom after 1992. While banks could be regulated directly by the Bank of England, a suggestion put forward in the SIB document *A Forward Look*, there appears to be concern that foreign EEC institutions, where regulated by the Bank or by the SIB or an SRO, would not be subject to the direct authority of these institutions because the premise behind regulatory control exercised by these institutions is authorization,[313] a power that will devolve to the home member state under the ISD.

The ISD allows branching for investment services defined broadly. Services are defined as (1) reception and transmission of orders on behalf of investors in relation to one or more of the instruments listed in Section B and the execution of such orders other than for one's own account; (2) dealing in any of the instruments listed in Section B for the brokers' own account; (3) managing portfolios of investments in accordance with mandates given by investors on a discretionary client-by-client basis where certain instruments are included; or (4) underwriting in respect of issues of any of the instruments or the placing of such issues.[314]

Many of the key provisions of the ISD are contained in the "conditions" for taking up business[315] requiring each member state to make access available to the investment firms subject to authorization granted by the home member state.

Article 4 requires that the identities of the shareholders or members be known by the competent authorities of the home member state. The ISD requires approval for "qualified holdings" which means direct or indirect holdings in investment firms representing 10% or more of the capital or the voting rights—additional thresholds include 20%, 33% or 50% under Article 9, regardless of what approval is required for SROs.

In the case of branches of investment firms that have registered home offices outside the community, member states shall not apply provisions that result in treatment more favorable than that accorded to branches of investment firms that have registered home offices in member states.[316] The directive contains rigorous provisions relating to the treatment accorded to community investment firms in third countries mirroring those in the SBD.[317]

A Forward Look remarks that the hostility of continental financial institutions, which are primarily banks, to the ISD is due to the fact that investment services play such a small part on the continent.[318] Moreover, the document also finds the future of SROs dubious because of the additional requirements which they impose on other EEC member state finan-

cial institutions and considers the prospect that the Bank of England would directly regulate all activities of banks in the future. The document also notes an earlier draft of the ISD that would have denied regulator status to the SRO and delves into the question of whether SROs violate EEC anti-competition laws.

Part V: Conclusion

Trade surplus countries and capital markets countries operate fundamentally incompatible systems. But a truly international system is becoming increasingly inevitable because of the high degree of international interdependence. The only viable proposal is a harmonization of corporate legal structures involving a compromise between investment portfolio strategies principally employed in low leverage countries (the United States and the United Kingdom) and the cross-ownership position most commonly found in high leverage countries (such as Germany and Japan).

EEC directives including the listing particulars and prospectus requirement directives, the banking directives and the investment services directives will hasten the creation of a single market in financial services; they will also allow for linkage of European exchanges and branching of banks and investment services, thereby creating truly European enterprises and will facilitate the capital flow without regard to nationality of origin. Particular national interpretation of EEC directives (such as concepts of securitization and prudential supervision of consolidated or affiliated entities within the grey area of definition) will prove something of an obstacle but may eventually wither away. The harmonization of national interpretation will depend upon the creation of a European Central Bank, the continued expansion of the area of activities over which the European Community and the ECJ have jurisdiction and the consequent evolution of EEC financial law.

The trading book option contained in the proposal for the Capital Adequacy Directive highlights the problem that the single market for financial services envisions. By lowering capital requirements for banks on their trading book, the CAD would contravene the G–10 Agreement to which France, the United Kingdom, Germany and Belgium are signatories and that is the focal point of the international banking safety net.

An even broader and related issue is consolidation. Consolidation exists in three contexts: Financial reporting (i.e., the Eighth Directive on Company Law), consolidated supervision and consolidation of capital ratios, the latter two forms being contained in the 1983 and 1992 consolidation supervision directives, the SRD and the CAD. The CSD applies to groups with at least one bank, although it makes reference to the Capital Adequacy Directive and preserves the trading book option. As the work of IOSCO demonstrates, consolidated supervision becomes more, rather than less,

important as firms are governed by different capital adequacy regimes for their investment and trading books.

It is apparent that valid international agreements in the area of financial regulation involve the loss of national sovereignty. As the chairman of the SIB concludes, "The areas in which national regulators can act wholly independent of each other is being rapidly eroded by technology and other market developments."[319] This observation is also true with regard to national insolvency proceedings insofar as market charges are concerned. Within the EEC, the continued role of SROs and their Conduct of Business Rules (CBRs) will hamper the creation of a single market by prolonging disparate regulatory regimes and marketplaces. While CBRs are bound to be culturally sensitive and difficult to directly incorporate into statutory law, harmonization of CBRs is a *sine qua non* of a successful single market.

Financial liberalization in Europe is part of a global movement. The geometric increase in complexity of world financial markets receives divergent reviews as to its effects on financial market volatility—different organs within Bank for International Settlements reach opposite conclusions.[320] Nonetheless, this increase and the growing interdependence of global markets necessitates increased coordination of securities and monetary authorities and enhances the case for EEC and global regulation.

NOTES

1. The principal directives relating to Eurofinancial Integration are the Consolidated Supervision of Financial Institutions (*see infra* note 267), the Second Banking Directive (O.J. Eur. Comm. L.386, p. 1, *et seq.*), the Own Funds Directive (O.J. Eur. Comm. L.124, p. 16 89/299/EEC) and the Solvency Ratio Directive (O.J. Eur. Comm. L.386, p. 14 [1989]); the Investment Services Directive (*see infra* note 137) and its corollary, the Capital Adequacy Directive (*see infra* note 226). *See also* the Mutual Recognition of Prospectus Requirements (*see infra* note 189) and Mutual Recognition of Listing Particulars (*see infra* notes 187 and 188). The Second Banking Directive (SBD) and the Investment Services Directive (ISD) are the core of the Single Market in Financial Services. Liberalization in the insurance sector has not kept pace with that in the financial sectors. The Second Non-Life Directive (87/357/EEC, 31 O.J. Eur. Comm. [No. L. 172] [1988]) and the Second Life Directive (Comm [88] 729 Final [December 23, 1988]) did not provide for communitywide branching. The Second Non-Life Directive enabled a single market in insurance (*see* Sydney Key, "Financial Integration in the European Community," Federal Reserve Board of Governors, International Discussion Paper No. 349, pp. 120, 123–24 [1989]), while the Life-Directive affected only those customers who take the initiative (Proposed Second Life Directive, Com (88) 729 Final, *supra* this note, Article 13).

The Third Directive on Life Assurance 92/96 EEC (November 1992), which amends the Second Life Directive and the Third Directive on Non-Life Assurance 92/96 EEC (June 1992), which amends the Second Non-Life Directive establish the right of communitywide branching for assurance undertakings whose head office

is in the community. While provisions of these directives are broadly similar to the SBD and utilize authorization as a touchstone, these directives are specifically crafted to the particulars of the insurance industry.

2. The Investment Services Directive and the Capital Adequacy Directive do not come into effect until 1996.

3. Treaty of Rome, Article 52, Common Mkt. Rep. (CCH) ¶ 1402.

4. *Ibid.*, Article 59, *et seq.* Common Mkt. Rep. (CCH) ¶¶ 1502–1541.

5. *Ibid.*, Article 7, Common Mkt. Rep. (CCH) ¶ 191.

6. Single European Act, Articles 13 and 16. Treaties Establishing the European Communities (Luxembourg, Office of the Official Publication of the European Communities, 1987).

7. *Ibid.*, Article 18 (voting is weighted by population of the member state with 54 [out of 72] required). Also cited as Single European Act, Article 18 adding Article 100A to the Treaty of Rome, Common Mkt. Rep. (CCH) ¶ 21070.

8. *Ibid.*, Article 18 (2), *see also* Article 8 (4) and (5).

9. *Ibid.*, Article 6 ¶ 21050, Article 7 ¶ 21066.

10. *Ibid.*, Article 20, ¶ 21190, adding a new Article 102A to the Treaty of Rome.

11. In *Cassis de Dijon* the court found that Germany could not prohibit the import of liquor that was lawfully produced and sold in France solely because its alcoholic label was too low for it to be deemed a liquor under German law (Case 120–78 [1979] ECR 649). Common Mkt. Rep. (CCH) ¶ 8543 [1979].

12. Z. Costa, Ente Nazionale Per L'Energia Elettrica (Case 6/64) (1964) ECR 585, CMLR 425. Common Mkt. Rep. (CCH) ¶ 8023.

13. Treaty of Rome, *supra* note 3, Article 187, Common Mkt. Rep. (CCH) ¶ 4712; Article 192, Common Mkt. Rep. (CCH) ¶ 4915.

14. See *infra* notes 84, 85, 265, 266, and accompanying text.

15. *EC Commission v. Germany* (Case 205/84), (1987 Common Mkt. L. Rev. 69). *See also EC Commission v. France* (Case 220/83) (1987 Common Mkt. L. Rev. 113). *Insurance Services v. EC Commission v. Denmark* (Case 252/83) (1987 Common Mkt. L. Rev. 169).

16. *See* Part IV § D.

17. Michael S. Raab, *The Transparency Theory: An Alternative Approach to Glass-Steagall Issues*, 97 YALE L. J. 603, 607 (1988). *See also*, letter of Brian Smith, Chief Counsel of the OCC (April 12, 1983) Rep. 1M [1983–1984 Transfer Binder] Fed. Banking L. Rep. (CCH) § 88.421 at 77.544 granting approval for bank's sale of pass through certificates backed by FHA-insured mortgages. Donald Langevoort, *Statutory Obsolescence and the Judicial Process: The Role of the Courts in Federal Banking Regulation*, 85 MICH. L. REV. 672, 690–691 (1987).

18. Treaty on European Monetary and Economic Union (printed in full by Agence Europe, No. 1759/60, Feb. 7, 1992), Article 3(b), which states that in areas which do not fall within the exclusive competence of the community, it shall take action "in accordance with the principles of subsidiarity only if and insofar as the objectives of the proposed actions cannot be sufficiently achieved by the member states and can therefore by reason of the scaled efforts of the proposed action be better achieved by the community."

19. *See* Chapter 2, *infra* note 13, and accompanying text.

20. See George Zavvos, *Banking Integration in 1992: Legal Issues and Policy*

Implications, 31 Harv. Int'l. L. J. 463, 481 (1990). Zavvos says that France, Greece and Belgium have subjected banks to strict limitations against involvement in the securities business. He is incorrect when he states that the EEC does not have non-bank securities houses comparable in size to those in the United States and Japan. UK securities houses such as Warburg and James Cappel are internationally prominent. Furthermore, international banks in London tend to function primarily through securities affiliates.

21.

Ratios of Gross Debt to Total Assets (market value*):

Countries	1970	1975	1980	1985	1986	1987
Low leverage						
United States	.45	.52	.50	.50	.49	.51
United Kingdom	.51	.64	.63	.52	.48	.48
High leverage						
Japan	.86	.83	.84	.73**	.63	.59
Germany	.72	.76	.81	.71	.70	.77

*Private non-financial corporations (all producing enterprises for Germany) with total assets calculated as gross debt plus equity at market value.

**Break in the series.

Sources: National flow-of-funds statistics and BIS estimates. BIS, *58th Annual Report* at 85.

The high leverage of Germany, Japan, France and Italy as opposed to the United States is in large measure indicative of the predominant universal banking system employed in these countries. The United Kingdom and the United States are the only countries employing capital market systems, although Japan has a few aspects of the capital market system, including a Glass-Steagall type separation. *See* Chapter 4, note 76 and accompanying text.

22. M. Clarich, *German Banking System: Legal Foundation and Recent Trends*, European University Institute Working Paper: 87/269, p. 5.

23. *Ibid*. Organization of Social Insurance in German Penalized Non-banking Pension Funds—*see also* monthly report of the Deutsche Bundesbank August 24, 1984.

24. *See* notes 47–49 *infra*, and accompanying text.

25. Deutsche Bank, for example, owns 25% of the equity of Daimler-Benz.

26. *See infra* note 71.

27. *See* Financial Times, March 13, 1990, at 1, and Securities and Investments Board, *A Forward Look* (1990).

28. Several years ago Deutsche Bank moved all of its non-DM securities operations to London and a major part of its 1992 strategy involved the acquisition and subsequent integration of Morgan Grenfell into the *Zeit-Geist* of this German bank.

29. Alfred Steinherr and Christian Huveneers, *Universal Banking: The Prototype of Successful Banks in the Integrated European Market? A View Inspired by the German Experience*, Center for European Policy Studies (1990).

30. For a detailed discussion of leverage in Japan, *see* Chapter 4, *infra* notes 11–15, 22, 23, and accompanying text.

31. Bank for International Settlements (hereinafter BIS), *59th Annual Report*, June 12, 1989, at 85.

32. *Ibid.*

33. *Ibid.*, at 84–85.

34. *Ibid.*, at 85.

35. In Japan the "main bank" of a typical group of non-financial enterprises ("*Kereitsu*") nowadays provides between one-fifth and one-third of the group's borrowings (*Ibid.*, at 87). For detailed description, *see* Chapter 4.

36. Carl Kester, "Banks in the Board Room: The American Versus Japanese and German Experiences," Harvard Business School Research Colloquium, May 27–28, 1992, p. 9, citing David Shireff, "Bankers as Moral Molopolists," *Euromoney*, (March 1987) pp. 71–79.

37. Kester, "Banks in the Board Room," *supra* note 36, at 10.

38. Rolf Ziegler, Donald Dender, and Herman Biehler, *Industry and Banking in the German Corporate Network*, in NETWORKS OF CORPORATE POWER, A COMPARATIVE ANALYSIS OF TEN COUNTRIES, 91–111 (Franz Stockman, et al., eds., 1985).

39. High leverage countries are characterized by extremely high price/earnings ratios which are estimated at over 60 for Japan (about 4 or 5 times as high as would prevail in the US or UK markets). (*Ibid.*, at 81.) One reason for this high leverage is that companies in Japan own considerable amounts of land (*Ibid.*) which given the current capital gains rate and low real estate taxes means that few parcels of land are actually sold, and, when they are sold, are at an exorbitant price. A leverage buyout will typically involve a debt/asset ratio of 80% to 95% (*Ibid.*, at 88) but all bondholders will be arm's-length portfolio investors. But the risk inherent in the structure involves the new financial instruments such as resets, p.i.k.s., swaps, interest rate caps, futures and options. The Bank for International Settlements, 1989 annual report states that, "[a]t the level of the financial system, the main concern is the risk exposure of the US banking system. It has been estimated that by end June 1988 some 10% of the outstanding shares of commercial and industrial bank loans was LBO related." (*Ibid.*, at 89.)

40. Amended Proposal for a Thirteenth Directive on Company Law. O.J. Eur. Comm. C. 240/7 (September 14, 1990).

41. Julian Franks and Colin Mayer, *Capital Markets and Corporate Control: A Study of France, Germany and the UK*, ECONOMIC POL. 191, 197 (1990).

42. *Ibid.*, at 205.

43. *Ibid.*, at 207.

44. *Ibid.*, at 207.

45. Foreign loans of US banks went from $14 billion in 1970 to $405 billion at the end of 1982 (Robert Triffin, *The Paper Exchange Standard: 1971–19??* in INTERNATIONAL MONETARY COOPERATION: ESSAYS IN HONOR OF HENRY C. WALLACH, Princeton Essays in International Finance No. 69, 70, 81 (1987) because of OPEC deposits and capital inflows created by the rising deficit. One consequence was the necessity of US banks to relend funds placed on deposit). When US bankers awoke to discover the illiquidity of their loans they decreased their lending from $110 billion in 1982 to $1 billion in 1985 (*Ibid.*). In 1986, to avoid suspension of interest payments by debtors, they increased lending by $59 billion (*Ibid.*).

Default by sovereign debtors beginning in 1981 was caused by the prevailing high rate of interest which resulted from inflation caused by the tripling of oil prices in

1979–1980. Here the relation of commodity prices to currency and the relation of both to the soundness of the international banking system is brought into relief.

See Jack M. Guttentag and Richard Herring, *Accounting for Losses on Sovereign Debt: Implications for New Lending*, Princeton Essays in International Finance No. 172, 19 (1989), where the authors show an increase in outstanding loans to public borrowers and banks for Latin America from $49 billion in June 1982 to $61 billion in December 1987 in US banks' exposure. Meanwhile, the statistics of the IMF (appearing in the report of the Deutsche Bundesbank) show a growth to $477 billion at the end of 1988 (*Report of the Deutsche Bundesbank for the Year 1988*, 77). These figures are mismatched from the beginning but may be explained by loans made by unconsolidated subsidiaries. Exposure to Brady 15 loans was over 100% of stated capital in 1982 and has been reduced to approximately 70% for 9 money-centered banks on the more favorable statistics (Guttentag and Herring, *supra* this note, at 19).

Banks internationally and American banks in particular were frantic to raise capital in 1982. Devices included the sale-leaseback of corporate headquarters so as to realize the market value of property that was held at book value. J. Guttentag and R. Herring, *Disaster Myopia in International Banking*, Princeton Essays in International Finance No. 164, 29–30 (1986).

46. There have been many explanations of why US and UK bankers led the way in making loans to developing countries, most of the explanations tending toward the psychological rather than the economic. Broadly, these explanations can be grouped under the rubric of "moral hazard." If several of the major money center banks make a certain type of loan of sufficient magnitude, bankers become aware that the national government will be the de facto insurer of such loans. Furthermore, bankers in the United States share the propensity of other corporate executives to look at a very short-term horizon given the mobility within the US corporate structure. Second, like investment bankers, the *primum mobile* for bankers is not the long-term quality of the loans made but rather the fees generated and paid up front by the transactions. An additional contributing factor may be "disaster myopia"—the temporal distance between bankers and the last experience of a financial panic. It is important to note that financial crises develop in financial markets, that is, London and New York as well as Singapore and Hong Kong.

47. For a description of the decline of the FRN market and the rise of ECP, *see* BIS, *58th Annual Report* at 108–109; 127–128.

48. *Ibid.*

49. J.G.S. Jeanneau, *Structural Changes in World Capital Markets and Euro-commercial Paper*, Bank of England, Discussion Paper No. 37, at 2, 7, and 19 (February 1989).

50. *Ibid.*, at 21 and 33.

51. *Ibid. See also* Ralph Bryant, *International Financial Intermediation* 6–10 (Brookings Institution, 1987).

52. *Ibid.*, at 33. In 1988, net new issues of Eurobonds showed a 25% increase over 1987 at $138 billion, below the peak of $160 billion in 1986 (BIS, *59th Annual Report, supra* note 31, at 122); however, this picture is vastly distorted by the part played by Japanese Euroequity warrants. By 1989, over 50% of bonds floated in the first half of the year were Japanese and 60.3% of dollar issues were Japanese. Deutschemark issues expanded from 12.9 to 22.2 billion DM (*Ibid.*). Together the

Swiss Franc, the Yen and the DM accounted for 32% of the currency denomination of Eurobond issues (*Ibid.*, at 123).

The Eurobond market has been shrinking steadily in terms of its truly international dimension and has become transformed at least partially into an offshore market for Germany and Japan. However, the denomination of Japanese Euroequity warrants in US dollars raises interesting questions about the nature of the word "offshore" as contrasted with the word "international." Although dollar equity warrants are not permitted in Japan (FINANCIAL TIMES, March 10, 1990), the intricate network of Euromarkets serves to repatriate Japanese trade surplus to Japan; the period of heavy US activity on the Euromarket took place because of the need to finance foreign subsidiaries of US corporations.

The US International Lending Supervision Act of 1983 required banks to establish Allocated Transfer Risk Reserves (ATRRs) for countries if the government determined that a country's loans were value impaired (49 Fed. Reg. 5591 [1984]). In practice, in part because of the unfavorable tax treatment of such reserves, ATRRs were never imposed for major debtor countries. (*Ibid.*, Guttentag and Herring, *supra* note 45, at 10–12. Substantial discretion is allowed and ATRRs have never been established for the larger debtors.) Citibank's $3 billion special reserve in 1987 was allowed as a deduction yielding a tax-deferred write-off provided the loss was realized over a several-year period thereafter (*Ibid.*, at 36). Tax benefits might be as much as $600 million where the loss is charged off against income for the year it is realized, and the Bank of England has imposed a forbidding matrix system requiring provisioning of up to 70% against LDC loans (*The Bank of England Sets New Debt Provisioning Guidelines: 35%–50% Provisioning*, FIN. REG. REP. 19 [February 1990]).

53. BIS, *Developments in International Banking*, Q. REP. 33 (February 1990).

54. *Ibid.*, at 34.

55. BIS, *59th Annual Report*, *supra* note 31, at 108.

56. Japanese predominance in international banking assets is undercut by US predominance in off-balance sheet financing discussed *infra*. For example, 65% of interest rate swaps are denominated in dollars. Nearly 90% of Eurocommercial paper is denominated in dollars. *Developments in International Banking*, *supra* note 53, at 33.

57. Committee on Banking Regulation and Supervisory Practices, *International Convergence of Capital Measurement and Capital Standards* (July 1988). Banking Law Rep. (CCH) ¶ 5403.

58. *See* Bryant, *supra* note 51, at 140–144.

59. The Capital Adequacy Agreement adopted at Basle is only one of several regulatory frameworks that might have been adopted. These standards were developed in the United Kingdom and Basle in 1981. Traditionally, a capital to assets solvency ratio was used without regard to risk. (Richard Dale, *Regulation of International Banking* 131 (1986). *See also* William Lovett, *Moral Hazard in International Banking*, 49 OHIO ST. L. J. 1365 [1989].) The general loan loss provision had, however, been the mainstay of national banking systems. While the United Kingdom had employed reserve requirements for domestic banking purposes, it did not do so with regard to international banking, a field in which it was and has continued to be, the world's leading host. In 1978–1980, Paul Volcker, newly appointed head of the Federal Reserve Board (FRB), voiced a great deal of concern

about solvency in Eurobanking and urged an international banking reserve requirement (*Ibid.*). However, the United Kingdom did not oblige, fearing the loss of international business. The result was the establishment of the US International Banking Facilities (IBF) allowing US businesses abroad to compete on equal terms with other banks in the Euromarket (*Ibid.*), i.e., without reserves.

60. G. Zavvos, *The Integration of Banking Markets in the EEC. The Second Banking Directive*, 2 J. INT'L BANKING L. 53 (1988); M. Gossling, *The Capital Adequacy Framework—An Introduction*, 6 J. INT'L BANKING L. 243 (1988).

61. *Supra* note 1.

62. G–10 Agreement, *supra* note 57, § 2.11 (35), and SRD directive, *supra* note 1 at Article 6(2) and (4).

63. *Ibid.*

64. Own Funds directive, *supra* note 1 at Article 6 1–A.

65. *Ibid.*, § B.

66. G–10, *supra* note 57, Annex 1(C), and Own Funds Directive, *supra* note 1, Article 2(10).

67. G–10 Agreement, *supra* note 57 at Article 1(b)(iii)(21), and SRD, *supra* note 1 at Article (2)(1)(4), originally included without restriction but subject to additional limitation, presumably in keeping with G–10.

68. Interview with FRB staff.

69. *See* Chapter 2, *infra* notes 217–218.

70. Own Funds Directive Article 2(2).

71. G–10, *supra* note 57, at Article 1(b)(ii)16–17.

72. *See* Chapter 2, *infra* note 216 for a discussion of Germany's proposal to allow the inclusion of these kinds of revaluation reserves for banks with a tier-one capital ratio of at least 5%, and with other reserves.

73. Within the meaning of Article 3 of Council Directive 78/660/EEC O.J. No. L.222, August 14, 1978 pp. 11, 22.

74. Within the meaning of 37(2) of Directive 86/635/EEC OJ Eur. Comm. No. L.372 (December 31, 1986), p. 1. Articles 35, 36.

75. *Ibid.*, Article 35.

76. Part IV, section C.

77. G–10, *supra* note 57, at Article 1(c)(24)(ii).

78. Own Funds, *supra* note 1, at Article 2(1)(12–13).

79. Council Directive of 13 June 1983 on the supervision of credit institutions on a consolidated basis (83/350/EEC), 26 *O.J. Eur. Comm.* (No. L. 193) (1983), p. 18.

80. *See* note 267, *infra*.

81. O.J. No. L. 372, 1 (1986).

82. *See* note 208, *infra* and accompanying text. Member state banks which currently have subsidiaries in other member states may well close them down as they would then be subject to the full regulatory requirements one more time than is necessary, and branches may become comparatively more advantageous.

83. Bank of England, Banking Supervision Division/1986/3.

84. *See infra* notes 237 and 238.

85. Bank of England, "Consolidated Supervision of Credit Institutions" authorized under the *Banking Act of 1979, Notice*, March 1986. *See also*, Richard Dale, INTERNATIONAL BANKING DEREGULATION 112 (1992). *See* Chapter 2, *infra*

notes 60–62 for the US approach to consolidation of capital ratios which is more ambiguous than the UK approach.

86. SRD, *supra* note 1, Article 3(iii).

87. *Ibid.*, Article 3(5).

88. BIS and Committee on Banking Regulations and Supervisory Authority of the Group of 10 Countries, *Basle Concordat of 1975*.

89. BIS and Committee on Banking Regulations and Supervisory Authority of the Group of 10 Countries, *Basle Concordat of 1981*.

90. SBD, *supra* note 1, Article 12(1).

91. *Ibid.*, Article (10). Other thresholds for qualified holdings requiring the holder to inform competent authorities about increases and decreases in position are reached at 20%, 33% and 50% (*Ibid.*, Article 11).

92. *Ibid.*, Article 12(2). But member States are not required to apply limits to holdings in insurance companies (*Ibid.*, Article 12(3)).

93. *Ibid.*, Article 12(7).

94. *Ibid.*, Article 12(6).

95. The transitional period is seven years and will end in 2001 ("Communication from Commission to the European Parliament") pursuant to Article 149.2(b) of the Treaty of Rome, relating to the current position adopted by the council with a view to the adoption of the directive on monitoring the control of large exposures of credit institutions. Article 4(1).

96. *Ibid.*

97. Graham Penn, *Banking Supervision: The Banking Act of 1987: Regulation of the UK Banking Sector Under the Banking Act of 1987* 14–15 (Butterworth's Legal Pub., 1989).

98. *Ibid.*

99. *Ibid.*

100. SBD, *supra* note 1, at Article 11.

101. Penn, *supra* note 97, at 14–15.

102. *See* Part 3(c) which is the European System of Central Banks. *See also* Ernst Baltersperger, and J. Dermine, *European Banking: Prudential and Regulatory Issues* in EUROPEAN BANKING IN THE 1990's 17 (J. Dermine, ed., 1990).

103. Baltersperger and Dermine, *supra* note 102.

104. *Ibid.*

105. *Supra* note 1, at Annex 1, and G–10 *supra* note 57, at Annex 3 (1).

106. Under Article 11, subparagraph 4 of the SRD, *supra* note 1, Germany, Denmark and Greece may apply a 50% weighting to assets secured by mortgages and completed residential property, and on office or multipurpose commercial property provided that the sum borrowed does not exceed 60% of the value of the property in question.

107. *Supra* note 1, Annex 2, and G–10, *supra* note 57, at Annex 3.

108. *Supra* note 1, Article 6(a)(5) and (d)(1) and (3); G–10 *supra* note 57, Annex 2.

109. Baltersperger and Dermine, *supra* note 102.

110. R. Levich, *The Euromarkets After 1992*, citing Morgan Guaranty Trust World Financial Markets 1988 in EUROPEAN BANKING, *supra* note 102, at 392.

111. *Ibid.*, at 393.

112. Council Directive of 24 June 1988 for the Implementation of Article 67 of the Treaty (88/361/EEC), 31 O.J. Eur. Comm. (No. L 178) 5 (1988).

113. Commission of the European Communities, "Proposal for a Council Directive on A Common System of Withholding Tax On Interest Income," (89) 60 Final, imposing a 15% withholding tax on portfolio income throughout the European communities.

114. G–10 Agreement, *supra* note 57, at Annex 3.

115. In the United States, approximately $769 billion in mortgage-backed securities as of 1989, primarily government insured ("Asset Securitization: A Supervisory Perspective," 75 Fed. Reserve Bull. 658, October, 1989) and a rapid growing market on consumer loan receivables (*see* Chapter 2, *infra* note 48 and accompanying text).

116. Ian Falconer, *Securitization in the United Kingdom, Part I*, 5 J. INT'L BANKING FIN. L., 105, 109 (March 1989).

117. *Ibid.*

118. *Ibid.*

119. Companies Act of 1989, Clause 5, inserting a new § 227 in the Companies Act of 1985 and Clause 19 inserting a new § 257 in the 1985 Act. *See also* Bank of England, Banking Supervision Division, (BSD 1989/1/1 "Loan Transfers and Securitization").

120. *Supra* note 81.

121. In the United States, commercial banks are monitored by Federal Financial Institutions and Examination Councils. *See* "Asset Securitization," *supra* note 115, at 664.When asset sales involve recourse such sales are treated as on-balance sheet liabilities except for mortgage backed securities which are government-insured. (Actually, they are on-balance sheet but receive a 0% risk weight. [Ibid.]) If the securities representing the indebtedness are interest only or principal only strips, the strips will be treated as 100% risk. Final Rule Amendment to Regulations H and Y, 75 Fed. Reserve Bull. 157 and Appendix (1989). Capital Adequacy Guidelines for Risk Based Measures. Bank holding companies are governed by GAAP (Generally Accepted Accounting Principles), and thus asset transfers involving recourse and sales or financing treatment are determined by Financial Accounting Standards Board Statement No. 77 (FASB 77), which provides more lenient terms to treat asset sales as sales if: (i) transferor surrenders future economic control of the future economic benefits relating to the receivables; (ii) transferor can reasonably estimate its obligation under the recourse provisions; or (iii) the transferee cannot return the receivables to the transferor except pursuant to the recourse provisions. (*Ibid.*)

122. J. B. Devade, and P. Boys, *Securitization: Another Step Towards Developing the French Market*, 5 J. INT'L BANKING FIN. L. 218, 219 (1989).

Another interpretation of the SBD by the Banking Supervision Division of the Bank of England is worthy of notice. Cash collateral will receive a 100 percent risk weighting where the cash depositor is not of the same local domicile as the branch or subsidiary of the bank (BSD 1989/1, note 10), presumably because the charge of the bank over the deposit may be subject to collateral attack in the domicile of the cash depositor. Because other factors such as choice of law and floating jurisdiction must be evaluated, the regulation appears simplistic.

123. G–10 Agreement, *supra* note 57, at Introduction (8).

124. For a description of the conventional interest rate swap transaction and the credit risk involved transaction, *see* BIS, RECENT INNOVATIONS IN INTERNATIONAL BANKING 37 (1986).

125. *A Survey of Interest Rate Futures*, 29 BANK OF ENGLAND Q. 388, 397 (1989).

126. RECENT INNOVATIONS IN INTERNATIONAL BANKING, *supra* note 124, at 249.

127. *Ibid.*, at 244.

128. *Ibid.*, at 244, and BIS *59th Annual Report, supra* note 31, at 143–147.

129. RECENT INNOVATIONS IN INTERNATIONAL BANKING, *supra* note 124, at 199.

130. *Ibid.* at 229 *but cf., supra* note 128.

131. *Implementing the Second Banking Coordination Directive in the UK: A Consultative Document issued by HM Treasury and the Dept. of Trade Industry* (July 1992).

132. *Ibid.*, at 8.

133. *Ibid.*, at 12.

134. Amending the Banking Act of 1987 deals with the definitions of subsidiaries undertaking and parent undertaking. Regulation 23 requires that in a direct subsidiary undertaking the parent must actually hold 90% of the subsidiary undertaking. The main provisions dealing with the "inward passport" include limitations on the SIB's powers under the Financial Services Act and address specific areas of market risks where the host state has a duty of cooperation with the home state under Article 14–3 of the Directives. Regulation 32(1) implements Article 1 (10, 5 and 11 of the Directive) by adding to the existing shareholder notification thresholds triggered at shareholdings of significant influence—10%, 20% and 33% or "such that the institution shall become subsidiary." (Article 11-[1]). Regulation 54 (2) extends the reference in Section 25 (2) (A–D) of the Consumer Credit Act which currently refers to things done in the United Kingdom including corresponding things done in other member states. The Consumer Credit Act Rules and Regulations will be required to be changed to allow for a mechanism for certain activities forbidden in the home state regulatory regime to be disapplied for individual European institutions under Regulation 57.

Amendments of the Financial Act: There are two general categories: first, changes that are necessary to make sure that the SIB/SRO's relationship with European institutions does not trespass on areas which are appropriated for the home member state; second, there are provisions to ensure that EEC institutions which can use the passport for new investments in the United Kingdom are not able to circumvent the passport procedure; third, there are a number of provisions which ensure that European institutions are treated in the same way as an authorized person under the FSA where this is appropriate. European institutions cannot derive their ability to undertake home-regulated investment business from their membership in a self-regulatory organization (Schedule A, ¶ 3). Rules regulated under the General Good Provisions of host member states are contained in Schedule A in ¶¶ 17–23 and include cancellation rules, notification regulation, indemnity rules, rules concerning the compensation fund, client money rules, restrictions on investment advertisements and directions prohibiting the employment of persons who are designated not "fit and proper." The rules for the regulatory regime for a collective investment scheme are amended to treat a European institution as if it were an authorized person (Schedule A, ¶¶ 29–34). Of course, European institutions carrying on passport investment business are on the same

footing as authorized persons (Schedule A, ¶¶ 44 and 45). Additional rules of SROs must be scaled back so as not to trespass on matters that are appropriated for the home state (Schedule A, ¶¶ 53 and 54).

135. Eur. Comm. 715 Final (87), Article 7.

136. SBD, *supra* note 1, Article 7.

137. "Common Position Adopted by the Council of Ministers on 21st December, 1992 With a View to Adopting a Directive on Investment Services in the Securities Field." Article 7(4).

138. In the context of the midterm review of the Uruguay Round of GATT negotiations held in Montreal in December 1988, the concept of effective market access relating to host country treatment of foreign financial institutions emerged. (*See* the statement by Trade Ministers of the Trade Negotiations Committee of the GATT Uruguay Round [Montreal, December 8, 1988] p. 2). Effective market access appears to encompass two different concepts: national treatment and "progressive liberalization" (*Ibid.*).

139. SBD, *supra* note 1, Article 9(4).

140. Interest Equalization Tax Act, U.S. Code § 1970, Title 26, 4911 (1970). Regulation Q, 12 CFR 217.3.1, which mandated a minimum interest rate to be paid by domestic banks created an unregulated Eurodollar market.

141. *See* FINANCIAL TIMES, March 10, 1980.

142. International Banking Facilities Deposit Insurance Act, Act of December 26, 1981, Public Law 97–110. 95 Stat. 1513.

143. *See generally*, K. Osugi, "Japan's Experience of Financial Deregulation Since 1984 in an International Perspective," BIS Economic Paper No. 26 (1990).

144. The resolution officially called for the ECU to be used (a) as a denominator (numeraire) for the exchange rate mechanism, (b) as the basis of a divergence indicator, (c) as the denominator for operations in both the intervention and credit mechanisms and (d) as a means of settlement between monetary authorities of the EEC (Resolution of the European Council on 5 December 1978 on the establishment of the European Monetary System and Related Matters).

Short-term monetary support was extended to 14 billion ECU and medium term financial assistance to 11 billion ECU. The weighted composition of the ECU was to be reviewed every five years. EEC members were required to deposit 20% of their current dollar and gold holdings with the European Central Monetary Fund (ECMF).

145. *Ibid*. Pursuant to the Brussels agreement and the attendant agreements, a Very Short Term Credit Facility (VSTCF) was created enabling obligatory interventions under the ERM. The Basle-Nyborg Agreement of 1987 made the VSTCF under certain circumstances available for intramarginal (non-obligatory) intervention. *See* David Folkerts-Landau, and Donald Mathieson, "The European Monetary System in the Context of the Integration of European Financial Markets," IMF Occasional Paper No. 66, at 4.

146. Henry Nau, *The Myth of America's Decline: Leading The World Economy into the 1990s* 175–179 (1990); Hyman Minsky, *Stabilizing an Unstable Economy* 17–22 (A Twentieth Century Report, 1986).

147. *See* note 157, *infra*.

148. Committee for the Study of Economic and Monetary Union, *Report on Economic and Monetary Union* (1989).

149. European Economic and Monetary Union (EMU) may be said to refer to three distinct concepts: (1) a currency union, (2) monetary union and (3) financial integration.

The monetary component of EMU is an aggregation of several existing and proposed laws and agreements of the Board of Governors of European central banks, the Council of Europe and the Commission of the European Community. In April 1989, pursuant to the European Summit at Hanover, the Delors Committee composed of Jacques Delors, the President of the European Commission, and the Presidents of the European Central Banks, issued a report on economic and monetary union in the European communities. (Committee for the Study of Economic and Monetary Union, *Report on Economic and Monetary Union* [1989]). The report set three stages for monetary union: the first, beginning in June 1990, provides for full participation by all member states in the Exchange Rate Mechanism (ERM) of the European Monetary System (EMS) and a movement toward the end of realignments among currencies (*Ibid.* at 30). This first stage also grants the EEC Central Bank governors the right of making proposals directly to the European Council (*Ibid.* at 33). The second stage establishes a system of central banks and would allow realignment only as a last resort and sets rules for national budgets and their financing (*Ibid.* at 35). The final stage fixes exchange rates irrevocably with their eventual replacement by a single currency and grants the European system of central banks sole authority for the conduct of monetary policy (*Ibid.* at 36).

150. *Id.* at 36.

151. "Secondly, the Committee considered the possibility of adopting a parallel currency strategy as a means of accelerating the pace of the monetary union process. Under this approach the definition of the ECU as a basket of currencies would be abandoned at an early stage and the new fully-fledged currency, called the ECU, would be created autonomously and issued in addition to the existing Community currencies, competing with them. The proponents of this strategy expect that the gradual crowding-out of national currencies by the ECU would make it possible to circumvent the institutional and economic difficulties of establishing a monetary union. The Committee felt that his strategy was not to be recommended for two main reasons. Firstly, an additional source of money creation without a precise linkage to economic activity could jeopardize price stability. Secondly, the addition of a new currency, with its own independent monetary implications, would further complicate the already difficult endeavor of coordinating different national monetary policies." (Committee for the Study of Economic and Monetary Union, Report on Economic and Monetary Union (1989), *supra* note 148, at 29.)

152. Otto Pohl, "Basic Feature of a European Monetary Order," Lecture Organized by *Le Monde*, Paris, January 16, 1990.

153. *Ibid.*

154. *Supra* note 18.

155. *Ibid.*, Title 6.

156. *Ibid.*, Title 6, Chapter 4, Transitional Provisions, Article 109E, F.

157. *Ibid.*, Article 109J, ¶ 4.

158. *Ibid.*, Protocol on the Excessive Deficit Procedure.

159. *Ibid.*, Title 6, Economic and Monetary Policy, Article 104C, ¶ 11.

160. *Ibid.*, Protocol on Certain Provisions Relating to the United Kingdom and Northern Ireland and Protocol on Certain Provisions Relating to Denmark.

161. *Ibid.*, Article 104, ¶ 1.

162. *Ibid.*, Article 105A, ¶ 1.

163. Protocol on the Statute of European System of Central Banks and of the European Central Bank, Article 7.

164. *Ibid.*, Article 10.

165. *Ibid.*

166. *Ibid.*, Article 25.

167. *Ibid.*, Article 105. Additionally, Article 25 of the Statute establishing the ECB says the ECB "may" offer advice which is less than previous drafts would have accorded. One commentator has noted, "No one could have built a higher set of hurdles." Peter Kennen, *EMU After Maastricht* (Group of Thirty), Washington DC, 1992), p. 23.

168. Kennen, *supra* note 167, at 54.

169. *Ibid.*, p. 67.

170. One study found that net changes in federal receipts amount to 40 cents per dollar. (X. Sali-i-Martin, and Jeffrey Sachs, "Fiscal Federalism and the Optimum Currency Area," NBER Working Paper No. 3855, Cambridge: National Bureau of Economic Research, 1991) but other authors take issue with this study. *See also* Kennen, *supra* note 167, at 66–67.

171. *See* note 158, *supra*, and accompanying text.

172. *Treaty on Economic and Monetary Union*, *supra* note 18, Article 104b.

173. *See* C. Wyplosz, *Monetary Union and Fiscal Policy Discipline in* "The Economics of EMU," European Economy, Special Edition 1 (1991).

174. *See also* Kennen, *supra* note 167; *see also supra* notes 160 and 161, and accompanying text.

175. European Economy, Commission of the European Communities, Directorate-General for Economic and Financial Affairs, *One Market, One Money: An Evaluation of the Potential Benefits and Costs of Forming an Economic and Monetary Union*, No. 44 (October, 1990).

176. *Ibid.*, at 196.

177. *See supra* note 9, and accompanying text.

178. Treaty on Economic and Monetary Union, *supra* note 18, Article 109.

179. *See* D. Folkerts-Landau, *Systematic Financial Risk in Payments Systems*, in "Determinants and Systematic Consequences of International Capital Flows," International Monetary Fund, Occasional Paper No. 77 (1991), and D. Folkerts-Landau, and P. M. Garber, "The European Central Bank: A Bank Or a Monetary Policy Rule," NBER Working Paper No. 4016 (1992).

180. P. A. Chiappori, C. Mayer, D. Neven, and X. Vives, *The Microeconomics of Monetary Union in* MONITORING EUROPEAN INTEGRATION: THE MAKING OF MONETARY UNION, (1991).

181. *See infra* Part IV, section C, discussing whether conduct of business rules ought to be instituted at the regulatory or exchange level.

182. ISD, *supra* note 137, Title 5, Article 14.

183. *Ibid.*, Title 5, Article 14, ¶ 3.

184. *Ibid.*, Article 15, ¶ 3.

185. *Ibid.*, Article 21.

186. *Ibid.*, Article 16.

187. 87/345 EEC, O.J. Eur. Comm. L. 185 (1987), p. 81.

188. 79/279/EEC.

189. Directive Coordinating The Requirements For The Drawing Up, Scrutiny And Distribution of The Prospectus To Be Published When Transferable Securities Are Offered To The Public. (Mutual Recognition of Prospectus Requirements Directive), 90/211/EEC, O.J. Eur. Comm. L. 112 (1990).

190. Harriet Creamer, *Regulatory System Controlling the Issue of Foreign Securities in the UK,* 4 J. INT'L BANKING L. 171, 271 (1988).

191. Department of Trade and Industry, "Listing Particulars and Public Offer Prospectuses, Implementation of Part V of the Financial Services Act (FSA) of 1986 and Related EC Directives," July 1990.

192. *Ibid.*

193. *Ibid.*, at 18.

194. *Ibid.*, at 18, 19.

195. *Ibid.*, and Financial Services Act § 58–3 A–D and Sec. 161 A–D except Section 160 which limits advertisements of secondary offers.

196. *Ibid.* The relevant sections of US law are § 4/1 or § 4/2 of the US Securities and Exchange Act of 1933, or under the Safe Harbor of Rule 144.

197. *Ibid. See also* FSA § 160.

198. *Ibid. See also* MRP, *supra* note 189, Article 1.1.

199. *Ibid. See also* Companies Act of 1985, § 79–2.

200. *Ibid.*, at 27–28.

201. *Ibid.*, Annex F.

202. A) Where securities are offered to persons in the context of their trade or occupations, B) where securities are offered to a restricted circle of persons, C) where the selling price of transferrable securities does not exceed 40,000 ECU, D) where the transferrable securities offer can be acquired only for a consideration of at least ECU 40,000 per investor and to transferrable securities of the following types: (1) to transferrable securities offered at individual denominations of at least ECU 40,000, (2) to units issued by collective undertakings other than those of the closed-end type, (3) to transferrable securities issued by the State or regional authority, (4) to transferrable securities offered in connection with a take-over bid, (5) to transferrable securities offered in connection with a merger, (6) to securities allotted free-of-charge to the holders of shares, (7) to shares and transferrable securities equivalent to shares offered in exchange for shares of the same company, (8) to transferrable securities offered by employers for the benefit of employees, (9) to transferrable securities resulting from the conversion of convertible debt securities or warrants to shares, (10) to transferrable securities issued with a view to obtain the means necessary to achieve their disinterested objectives by non–profit-making bodies recognized by the State, (11) to U.S. securities which are not the subject of a generalized campaign of advertising or canvassing.

203. The minimum contents of the prospectus includes information regarding (a) those responsible for the prospectus' names of the functions, (b) the number of securities being issued and the rights attached to them, income withheld at source, date of entitlement to dividends, person underwriting or guaranteeing the offer, restrictions on free transferability, establishments serving as paying agents and the price of securities or the method of payment, procedures for the exercise of rights

of preemption, (c) information about the issuer, including place of incorporation, applicable legislation, capital, groups of undertakings to which the issuer belongs, in the case of shares—any shares not representing capital, the amount of authorized capital, duration of the authorization, and indication of shareholders who directly or indirectly exercise or could exercise control of the management of the issuer, (d) the issuer's principal activities, description of its principal activities (dependence on patents and licenses and contracts of these are of fundamental importance, and any legal proceedings having an effect on the issuer, (e) the issuer's assets and liabilities, financial position, profits and losses, audited and consolidated accounts, interim accounts, name and person responsible for auditing, (f) issuer's administration, management and supervision, (g) to the extent that such information will have an impact on the issuer, recent developments on its business and prospects (the most significant recent trends concerning the issuer's business since the end of the preceding financial year and information on the issuer's prospects for at least the current financial year). (MRP Directive, Section 3, Article 11.)

204. *Ibid.*, Article 21, 1 and 2.

205. *Ibid.*, Preamble.

206. Listing Particulars Directive 80/390/EEC, Section 2, Articles 8, 9.

207. 78/660/EEC.

208. 83/349/EEC.

209. Gerhard Mueller, *1992 and Harmonization Efforts in the EC*, in Frederic Choi, HANDBOOK OF INTERNATIONAL ACCOUNTING, Chapter 12.1 (Frederick Choi, ed., 1991). This section draws heavily on this article.

210. The expenditure format, Article 23—vertical form Article 24—horizontal form and the operational format—Article 25—vertical form and Article 26—horizontal form.

211. Fundamental accounting choices include historical costs, growing concern, prudence, accrual accountancy and consistency. Each category of assets and liabilities is to be valued separately. Consistency must be present and departure from basic principles is permitted only in certain cases and must be specified.

The most important specific measurement requirements of the Fourth Directive include: (1) property, plant and equipment: fixed assets with limited useful economic life must be depreciated by systematic annual charges to operations. If a member country allows any special tax incentives that result in excessive depreciation, the companies must disclose the nature and amount of the charge; (2) intangible assets; (3) intercorporate investments; (4) inventories to be valued at the lower of cost or market—lifo or fifo or weighted average may be used; (5) current assets—to be valued at the lower of cost or market; (6) liabilities—long-term debt, if issued at a discount, a reasonable amount of amortization is required; (7) organization; (8) inflation accounting—either (a) reevaluation of tangible fixed assets or (b) replacement cost for plant equipment and inventory or (c) valuation of all financial statement items. Article 47 (2)(a)(b) of the Directive allows member states the option to permit preparation of publication of only abridged balance sheets and abridged notes; and all EEC member states have used this option in whole or in part. (Fourth Directive, *supra* note 207, Article 47/2(a)(b).) *See also*, Ernst and Whinney, International Series "The Fourth Directive European Company Law" (1980); Deloitte, Haskins and Sells (Europe) "The Fourth Directive

Company Accounts (1978) and Price Waterhouse, E. C. Bulletin, Special Issue "Fourth E. C. Directive" (1987).

212. Article 13 includes (1) an undertaking that is of negligible importance; (2) severe long-term restrictions, such as currency control; (3) disproportionate expenses or undue delay unavoidable with regard to the information; (4) shares of enterprise held exclusively for subsequent resale. (*supra* note 109, at Chapter 12.16.)

213. Under the following circumstances, exemption from subconsolidation is possible: (1) annual financial statements of the exempted undertaking and of all its subsidiaries are consolidated in the financial statements or a larger undertaking; (2) consolidated financial statements of larger undertakings are drawn up in accordance with the Seventh Directive; (3) such consolidated statements are published in a manner prescribed by the law of the member country that governs that undertaking; and (4) notes to the financial statement of the exempted undertaking discloses the name and registered offices of the parent that draws up the consolidated financial statement and indicates that it is exempted from the requirements of the Seventh Directive.

214. Exemptions may be allowed if (1) the annual statements of the exempted undertaking and all of its subsidiaries are consolidated in the financial statement of a larger undertaking, (2) the consolidated financial statements are drawn up in accordance with the Seventh Directive or an equivalent manner (this would include U.S. GAAP) and (3) such consolidated financial statements are audited by appropriately authorized persons.

215. The following are essential requirements: (1) line by line consolidation, (2) conformity to the requirements of the Fourth Directive, (3) specifying applicable accounting principles, (4) disclosure of purchase accounting methods and pooling of interest methods, (5) application of the equity method of accounting to investments and associated affiliated companies, (6) allowing positive good-will to be either amortized over five years or written off directly to owner's equity. Article 31 addresses negative good-will.

216. 86/635 EEC. This directive was implemented in 1991. (*See generally* Price Waterhouse, E. C. Bulletin, Special Supplement "EEC Seventh Directive—Consolidated Financial Statements" [1983].)

217. *See* Lee Radebaugh, *Segmental and Foreign Operations Disclosure, in* HANDBOOK OF INTERNATIONAL ACCOUNTING, Chapter 23 (Frederick Choi, 1991).

218. *Ibid.*

219. Companies Acts of 1989, §§ 159–163.

220. Offshore Offers and Sales, Securities Act Release No. 6779, (1987–88 Transfer Binder Fed. Sec. L. Rep. (CCH) Sec. 84,242 [June 10, 1988]).

221. Section 230.144A Private Resale To Institutions Fed. Sec. L. Rep. (CCH) 84,523 (May 5, 1990).

222. *The Economist*, July 2, 1990, "Capital Markets: Stormy Past, Stormy Future."

223. *See* Section D of this Part V.

224. ISD, *supra* note 137, at Article 10.

225. *See supra* notes 189, 202, 203, and accompanying text.

226. "Common Position Adopted by the Council With A View to the Adoption of the Directive on Capital Adequacy of Investment Firms and Credit Institutions,"

July 27, 1992; *see also* Communication From the Commission to European Parliament Pursuant to Article 149.2(b) of the EEC Treaty, September 9, 1992, SEC (92, 1638 Final—SYN 257), Annex 1—Position Risk.

227. CAD, *supra* note 226, at Article 3, (1) and (3).

228. Securities Investor Protection Act (15 USC § 78aaa–78111) 1988, and Proposed Rule Securities and Exchange Commission 17 CFR Part 140, Release No. 34–272249, 54 Fed. Reg. 40395. October 1989.

229. *Ibid.*, Article 2(ii).

230. 92/30/EEC.

231. *Ibid.*, Article 7, ¶¶ 3–6.

232. *Ibid.*, ¶¶ 4–6.

233. *Ibid.*, ¶¶ 12 and 13.

234. CAD, *supra* note 226, Article 9.

235. *Ibid.*, Article 13.

236. *Ibid.*, Article 14. A simplified approach for risk on derivative instruments particularly applicable to small firms is set forth in Annex 1, ¶ 9.

237. *Ibid.*, Article 2(f).

238. *Ibid.*, Article 4(1)(iii).

239. *Ibid.*, Annex 5, (6) and (7).

240. *See supra* note 96.

241. CAD, *supra* note 226, Annex 6, (8)(ii).

242. *Ibid.*

243. *Ibid.*, Annex 6, (8)(iii and iv).

244. A long-term loan will have interest rate risk under the trading book option but not under the SRD, therefore it may be propitious to keep such a loan in the banking book.

245. Although an adjustable rate mortgage, which is prevalent in Europe, would be preferable to hold in the trading book.

246. *See supra* notes 74–76.

247. Own Funds, *supra* note 1, Annex 5, (2)(ii).

248. Own Funds are defined in Directive 89/270/EEC; O.J. Eur. Comm. No. L. 124, Annex 5, (1989) p. 16.

249. Securities and Investments Board, *Rule Book*, Chapter 2, Financial Regulation "The Financial Supervision Rules 1990."

250. *Ibid.*, Part 5, ¶ 5.04.

251. This is equal to 13 weeks' expenditures. This requirement is roughly comparable to the 2% of gross indebtedness which securities firms in the United States are required to maintain. Alternately, if firms are carrying margin transactions, the requirements, if higher, are 3.5% of the aggregate of these individual margin requirements.

252. *Ibid.*, Schedule 2, Part 2.

253. *Ibid.*, Schedule 2, Part 2, § 1, "Subtotal Equity, Method 2" ¶ 1.12 and "Subtotal Equity, Method 3," ¶ 1.14.

254. The calculations in Methods 2 and 3 take account of the size of the position relative to the overall size of the portfolio to allow for the degree to which the volatility and the price of the whole portfolio will be affected by movements in the price of a single stock rather than by the movement in the whole market. Methods 2 and 3 also take account of the effect of holding long and short positions on the

overall price volatility of the portfolio. Only certain equities known as "qualifying equities" may be treated under equity Methods 2 and 3, and they include only major stock markets of about 10 to 15 countries. Otherwise, non-qualifying equities are treated under Equity Method 1, where a "position risk requirement" is mandated. Equity Methods 2 and 3 require a diversification test, which mandates at least 10 long or short positions in qualifying equities in the United Kingdom, United States and Japan. A complex set of calculations is required to determine the position risk under Equity Methods 2 and 3 and include country factor and country adjustment.

255. *Ibid.* ¶ 2.12 defining qualifying debt instruments and ¶ 2.14 defining by exclusion, non-qualifying debt instruments. Non-qualifying debt instruments and discounts required on them are as set forth under Position Risk Factor, Debt Method 1 and Debt Method 2.

256. *Ibid.*, § 4, Position Risk Requirements Relating to Offerings of New and Existing Securities and Note Issuance Facilities, ¶ 4.3 "International Offerings," ¶ 4.4 "Domestic Offerings," ¶¶ 4.5 to 4.7 "Note Issuance Facilities."

This requirement applies to positions by lead managers and co-managers from commitment day to allotment day (and also other capital requirements begin at commitment day and extend to the earlier of closing day or 28 days after allotment day. After 30 days after closing day, concentration position requirements are activated). Section 5, treatment of concentrated positions relative to an issuer or an issue covers any exposure of any issuer if the total value of its exposure to that entity exceeds 25% or a concentrated position in one issue if it exceeds 5%.

257. CAD, *supra* note 226, Annex 1, Position Risk, (4) and (5).

258. *Ibid.*, Annex 1 (35–38). Stock Index Futures which are perfectly matched with underlying equities attract no general risk, depending on the extent of diversification (an S&P 500 index versus an oil index) will attract a specific risk of 2% or 4%. Positions which are not offset will, like any other long or short position, attract an 8% general risk weighting (as well as a specific risk weighting).

259. *Ibid.*, Annex 2, Settlement and Counterparty Risk.

260. *Ibid.*, Article 5 applying the Large Exposure Directive, *supra* note 95, to securities firms, except that exposures to clients which arise on the trading book are calculated by including the excess of institutions' long positions over short positions in all the financial instruments issued by the client, plus underwriting of equity for the client deducting subunderwriting position and the exposures to other transactions and agreements for counterparty risk. *Ibid.*, Annex 6, (2).

261. *Ibid.*, Annex 6 (8) (1 and 2).

262. *Ibid.*, Annex 6, Large Exposures.

263. *Ibid.*, Annex 5, (6).

264. Interview with staff of Bank of England, Banking Supervisory Division.

265. C. D. Deboissieu, *The French Banking Sector in Light of European Financial Integration in* European Banking, *supra* note 102.

266. *See* Part II, Financial Systems in the United Kingdom and Germany.

267. 92/30/EEC April 6, 1992; O.J. Eur. Comm. No. L. 110 52 (1992).

268. *Supra* note 95.

269. Excluded are those banking groups in any of the following situations: (1) an undertaking is included and situated in a third company where legal impediments exist to the transfer of information; (2) the undertaking that should be included is

of negligible interest (i.e., smaller than ECU 10 million or (1%) of the total balance sheet); (3) in the opinion of the competent authorities responsible, consolidation would be misleading. *Ibid.*, Article 3(3).

270. *Ibid.*, Article 3(8).

271. *Ibid.*, Article 8(9).

272. *Ibid.*, Article 4(2).

273. *Ibid.*, Article 4(2).

274. *Ibid.*, Article 5(1–2).

275. *Ibid.*, Article 5(4).

276. *Ibid.*, Article 8(1).

277. Consolidated Supervision Directive, *supra* note 267, Article 6(1)(2).

278. CAD, *supra* note 226, Article 7 (7).

279. *Ibid.*, Article 7 (9).

280. *Ibid.*, Article 7 (10).

281. *Ibid.*, Article 7 (11).

282. *Ibid.*, Article 7 (4). Own Funds defined in Annex 5 (9).

283. *Ibid.*, Article 7 (4).

284. *Ibid.*, Article 7 (5).

285. *See* Chapter 3, *infra* notes 71–74, and accompanying text.

286. International Organization of Securities Commissions, *Principles for the Supervision of Financial Conglomerates*. The eight principles are: (A) Group based risk assessment: where a regulated firm which is part of a financial conglomerate and subject to supervision on a solo basis is vulnerable to the risk of contagion, supervision of the regulated firm should be complimented by group-based risk assessment; (B) investment in other groups: where a regulated firm has an investment in another group company or has provided regulatory capital to another group company, these amounts should be patrolled by appropriate regulations; (C) intragroup exposures: effective risk assessment of financial conglomerates requires careful monitoring of intragroup exposures and, where necessary, limits on such exposures in the regulated entity; (D) structure of financial conglomerates: the corporate and managerial structure of financial conglomerates should be fully understood by the regulator and should not create undue difficulties for effective regulation; regulators should consider whether it is feasible or practical to acquire powers to prevent the manipulation of group structures which make effective regulation difficult; (E) relationship with shareholders: regulators should seek as far as possible to identify shareholders with a stake in a financial conglomerate which enables them to exert material influence on a regulated firm: the regulator should seek to ensure that these shareholders meet applicable fitness standards; (F) management: regulators should ensure managers who directly or indirectly exert control on a regulated entity are subject to appropriate regulatory standards; and should seek as far as possible to be able to impose sanctions on managers who have influenced the policy and decision of a regulated entity in ways which are inconsistent with those regulatory standards; (G) supervisory cooperation: where possible, regulators should seek to cooperate to improve the effectiveness of supervision of financial conglomerates. In many cases, where more than one regulator has responsibility for some part of the financial conglomerate, it may be desirable to identify one regulator who would have primary responsibility for group-based risk assessment. This regulator is likely to emerge as the lead regulator when serious

concerns arise about a particular financial conglomerate. Each regulator will continue to be responsible for the sole entity in its jurisdiction and the lead regulator will have no authority to seek to take over or interfere with the exercise of that responsibility. The lead regulator's main role should be to ensure that relevant regulatory information about the conglomerate is shared properly among all the regulators concerned to inform their actions; (H) external auditors: regulators should recognize the importance of the role of external auditors of regulated firms and the possible contribution that they may be able to make to group-based risk assessment. Auditors should be encouraged where they have serious concerns regarding the financial or operational condition of the regulated entity or the group to ensure that such concerns are brought to the attention of the supervisor.

The Report sets forth four examples of full consolidation and the deduction method for capital:

Case 1: The securities subsidiary is unregulated and is subject to no capital requirements and the parent meets the capital requirement.

Case 2: The subsidiary is regulated but subject to a different, that is, lower capital requirement for the parent bank and the parent bank meets the capital requirement using the deduction method, but does not do so if the security subsidiary is consolidated.

Case 3: The securities subsidiary is regulated and subject to the same capital requirement as the parent bank.

Case 4: The securities subsidiary is regulated but subject to different, that is, higher capital requirements from the parent.

Annex 2: Comparison of full consolidation and the deduction method.

287. *Ibid.*, at 5.

288. *See* Chapter 3, *infra* note 72, and accompanying text.

289. *Principles for Supervision of Financial Conglomerates*, *supra* note 286.

290. *See supra* note 75.

291. Geoffrey Fitchew, Director General, D G. XV, Commission of the European Communities, "The Regulation of International Financial Conglomerates." Paper presented at the 17th Annual Conference of the International Organization of Securities Commissioners, London, October 29, 1992.

292. The IOSCO report states that from 1985 through 1991 over 1,100 US banks failed and required funds from the Federal Deposit Insurance Corporation, the entity that protects depositors of failed banks. More than 720 of these banks were subsidiaries of bank holding companies, and thus subject to prudential supervision of the consolidated entities. By way of comparison, during the same seven year period, the Securities Investor Protection Corporation, the organization that protects customers from failed US securities firms, handled only 51 securities firm insolvencies. Securities firms in the United States have only recently been subject to holding company risk investment requirements and they are not subject to prudential consolidation. Moreover, from the Securities and Exchange Commission's perspective, prudential consolidation has not worked and creates unnecessarily high expectations and therefore risk along with unnecessary costs. Therefore, the SEC strongly believes that a regulatory environment with functional regulation focusing on the regulated firm with strong capital standards and with risk assessment is the appropriate regulatory model to deal with group oriented activities of financial conglomerates.

293. *See supra* note 286, and accompanying text.

294. *See supra* note 15.

295. This is a view derived from several components. *See* The Securities Association, *The Investment Services Directive*, (1990); SIB "Conduct of Business Regulation: The International Dimension." Speech given by David Walker, Chairman of the Securities and Investments Board at the 14th Annual Conference of IOSCO in Venice on Wednesday, September 20, 1989. *See also* Committee for the Study of Economic and Monetary Union, *supra* note 148, and accompanying text.

296. ISD, *supra* note 137, Article 10 and Article 11.

297. O.J. Eur. Comm. L. 375 (1985), 85/611/EEC.

298. *Ibid.*, Article 44. *See also* Key, *supra* note 1, at 119, but the marketing and advertising of UCITs remain under host country control.

299. Department of Trade and Industry, *The EEC Investment Services Directive* (July 1990).

300. *Ibid.*, at 12.

301. *Ibid.*, at 18.

302. *See* discussion of Mutual Recognition of Prospectus Requirements Directive, *supra* note 189, and accompanying text.

303. SIB, *Proposed Conduct of Business Rules* (1989) enunciates three kinds of rules, 10 principles and core rules of which there are 16, and third-tier rules, thus being the rules of particular SROs. These concepts are included in secondary legislation under the Companies Act of 1989, Part VIII, § 192.

304. Stanislas Yassukovitch, *The European Financial Services Industry After 1992—Regulation and the Competitive Challenge*, 5 J. INT'L BANKING FIN. L. 201, 203 (1989).

305. FINANCIAL TIMES, March 13, 1990, at 1.

306. Walker, *supra* note 295, at 7, 8.

307. *Ibid.*

308. Financial Services Act of 1986 § 31B.

309. The Securities Association, *supra* note 295.

310. *Ibid.*

311. Phone interview with staff member of SIB.

312. Securities and Investments Board, *supra* note 27.

313. The Security Association, *supra* note 295, at 36.

314. The instruments listed in Section B include: transferrable securities, units in collective investment trusts, money market instruments, financial futures contracts, forward interest agreements, interest rate currency and equity straddles and options on any of the above (ISD, *supra* note 137).

315. *Ibid.*, Title 2, Article 3.

316. *Ibid.*, Article 5.

317. *Ibid.*, Article 6.

318. *A Forward Look*, *supra* note 312.

319. Walker, *supra* note 295, at 9.

320. *See supra* note 129.

2

Judicial and Administrative Expansion of Bank Powers and Current Legislative Proposals

In 1991, the Department of Treasury submitted proposals regarding the modernization of the US financial system.[1] The House of Representatives considered a number of bills which were responsive to the Department of Treasury's proposal. Collectively, these bills are referred to as the Financial Institution's Safety and Consumer Choice Act of 1991.[2] In addition to considering recapitalization of the Bank Insurance Fund (BIF), several measures were considered which ultimately failed to pass during the 102nd Congress: (1) nationwide banking and branching,[3] (2) reregulation of foreign banks,[4] (3) financial services modernization, which would have enabled the establishment of diversified Financial Services Holding Companies (FSHC),[5] allowing securities activities of subsidiaries of banks and commercial firm investment in financial service companies through FSHCs. The Senate likewise considered financial reform of the banking system in its bill entitled "Comprehensive Deposit Insurance Reform and Taxpayer Protection Act of 1991."[6] This bill contained roughly analogous provisions enabling interstate banking and branching[7] and bank affiliation with securities firms,[8] but did not allow, unlike the House bill, commercial affiliation with banks. Congress did pass the Federal Deposit Insurance Corporation Improvement Act which included provisions to ensure the safety and soundness of the banking system but did not expand banking powers. Part I of this chapter will consider the circumstances which led to the consensus that banking reform in the United States was necessary. Part II of this chapter will explain the degree to which the Glass-Steagall Act (GSA), which separates banking activities from most securities activities, has been eroded by judicial interpretation of the GSA. Part III—Regulation of Derivative Instruments—will consider the degree to which certain activities of banks are essentially securities-like activities and the extent to which it is impossible to separate securities-eligible from securities-ineligible activities. Part IV will con-

sider the role of interstate branching and its importance to the competitiveness of US financial firms. Part V considers legislative initiative for reforming the GSA. Part VI considers the role that the 1991 Federal Deposit Insurance Corporation Improvement Act plays in the supervision of banks. Part VII considers broad policy perspectives. The conclusion in Part VIII favors a more expansive and complex regulatory system, expanding the definition of bank to include money market funds and finance companies and allowing limited underwriting powers for a group of "narrow banks."

Part I: Decline of the US Banking System Sector at Home and Abroad

In a report (the "Report") presented to the Congressional subcommittee by the Economic Advisory Committee of the American Bankers Association entitled "International Banking Competitiveness—Why It Matters," dated March 1990,[9] the Banker's Committee argued that decreasing international competitiveness of US financial institutions will have a substantial effect on the economic life of the United States.

If American banks become less important suppliers of financial services, more and more financial business will be conducted by foreign institutions in overseas markets. The Report says:

Losing our financial leadership will reduce the competitiveness and market share of other US industries, especially export-oriented industries. At the same time, the increasingly dominant position of foreign banks will enable them to provide stronger international support to compatriot businesses. Again, the result will be a loss of jobs, declining profitability for US businesses and a worsening of the balance of payments situation.[10]

The Report concludes that US banks operate under more costly and restrictive regulations than do institutions in other industrialized countries. The Report notes that the US financial firms, particularly banks, have not fared well in today's sophisticated environment and supports this statement with the following facts:

As recently as 1983, two of the top three world banks ranked by assets were US banks; now the largest US bank ranks 24th.

Ranking by market capitalization yields the same result—no US banks are among the top twenty financial firms in the world. The largest US financial firm, American Express, ranked 21st;[11] the largest US banking organization, Citicorp, ranked 32nd.

US banks accounted for less than three percent of the assets of the top thirty banks at the end of 1988, down from 16.5 percent in 1983.[12]

A focus of attention of the banking industry in its desire to remove restrictions on its freedom of action is the GSA.[13] The GSA, enacted in

1933, limited the kind of activities in which commercial banks could engage, but the advent of financial innovation has placed many of the original principles of the GSA in question. The extent to which banks should be permitted to underwrite and deal in securities has been considered by Congress, the judiciary and bank regulators. Currently, commercial banks are regulated by several regulatory agencies, but all are subject to GSA.[14]

Robert Litan, former fellow at the Brookings Institute, has written a pamphlet entitled "The Revolution in US Finance," in which he shows the radical movement towards the development of non-bank financial institutions and the tendency toward "securitization" of assets.[15] Litan emphasizes that commercial banks represent only half of this country's financial assets, approximately $3.2 trillion in assets, while life insurance companies have approximately $1.2 trillion, pension funds $1.2 trillion and mutual funds, including money market mutual funds, approximately $1 trillion in assets; additionally, finance companies have considerable assets. Banks have faced competition from money market mutual funds (MMFs), which exploded in assets in the late seventies and early eighties and gained their prominence at a time when Regulation Q allowed banks to offer small denomination deposit interest rates of only 5.25%. Although banks were able to offer competing money market type funds,[16] these new forms of deposits eroded bank profits. The advent of "securitization" resulting from MMF's willingness to hold pools of securities secured by mortgages and, later, consumer loans had a positive side for banks in that it enabled them to remove assets from their balance sheet, earning fees in the process, and thereby freeing up capital with which to invest in other assets. An even more important challenge to banks than securitization has been the boom in the Commercial Paper market. With the crisis of the early 1980s resulting from loans to lesser developed countries, several well-capitalized companies found themselves in a position whereby they were able to go directly to financial markets without the intermediation of banks and to sell commercial paper (usually with a 30- to 90-day duration) for which they had to pay a significantly lower rate than that for bank loans. Although banks participate in the commercial paper market by offering issuance credit facilities (such as note issuance facilities [NIFs] and revolving underwriting facilities [RUFs], the marginal profit on such instruments is extremely thin.

As of late 1990, two finance companies—GMAC and GE Capital—had more equity capital than all banks except Citicorp, and top finance companies earned 12.7% on equity in 1989, far more than the 7.8% return on equity recorded by the entire banking system that year.[17]

Part II: Judicial and Administrative Agency Erosion of the Glass-Steagall Act

Much of the GSA has been eroded by judicial decisions as well as administrative regulations promulgated by the Office of the Controller of the

Currency (the OCC) and the Board of Governors of the Federal Reserve System of Banks (the FRB). The process of erosion has concentrated on the definition of what is a security. Several related concepts allowing banks to undertake non-traditional activities and to utilize new financial instruments and innovations have been approved.

The following sections of GSA are particularly relevant to this discussion: (1) GSA Section 16 permits a bank to deal in securities and stock, but only if such dealing is "limited to purchasing and selling such securities and stock without recourse, solely upon the order, and for the account of, customers, and in no case for its own account . . . ,"[18] (2) GSA Section 16 also provides that banks "shall not underwrite any issue of securities or stock,"[19] (3) GSA Section 20 prohibits the affiliation of any bank regulated by GSA with any corporation or other business entity "engaged principally" in the issuance, underwriting or distribution of securities.[20] A "Section 20 subsidiary" is a securities' affiliate of a bank that is allowed, under judicial construction of GSA Section 20, to engage to a limited extent in the underwriting of securities that banks are generally ineligible to underwrite, and (4) GSA Section 21 prohibits any organization "engaged in the business of issuing, underwriting, selling, or distributing . . . securities" from engaging at the same time in the business of receiving deposits.[21]

Also relevant are certain sections of the Federal Reserve Act (FRA) which govern the relations of bankholding companies, their affiliates and subsidiaries and require that such relations be at arm's-length. Currently, Sections 23(a) and 23(b) of the FRA limit commercial bank exposure to non-banking activities and control in general the terms of arrangement between banks, subsidiaries and parent companies.[22] In general, Section 23(a) prohibits a member bank from extending credit to or purchasing assets from an affiliate in excess of 10% of the bank's capital, and an aggregate cap of 20% of capital is established for bank loans to affiliates.[23] Section 23(b) requires that covered transactions by a bank with an affiliate or a person with whom the affiliate has business relationships be on the same terms, including credit standards with substantially the same as those prevailing at the time for comparable transfers with or involving non-affiliates.[24] There are other provisions that are basically similar to those contained in the European community's Large Exposure Directive (LED) and Second Banking Directive (SBD),[25] but these are determined by state law[26] and the OCC.[27]

The process of change in the GSA has been led by the judiciary which has constantly expanded the freedom of regulators, particularly the FRB to allow further investment services activity by commercial banks. While in *Investment Company Institute v. Camp (ICI 1)*[28] the Supreme Court refused to allow a bank to offer an open-ended mutual fund,[29] in *ICI 2*,[30] the Court did allow the non-bank subsidiary of a bank holding company to act as an investment advisor to a closed-end mutual fund because "the

subtle hazards" enunciated in *ICI 1* did not exist in a closed-end mutual fund, particularly given the additional restrictions placed on the banks by the FRB order. In *Securities Industry Association v. Board of Governors* (the "Schwab Decision"),[31] the Supreme Court held that a bank holding company was free to enter the brokerage business because GSA Section 20 reaches only those entities principally engaged in activities traditionally associated with the distribution of securities, and brokerage was not held to be such an activity. An administrative decision in this line was rendered by the OCC in *Seligman and Company* and *Dreyfus and Company* allowing full service brokerage securities companies acting through a bank holding company to acquire control of National Banks.[32]

The tendency to allow greater range of freedom is pronounced in the area of commercial paper. In three cases, *Bankers Trust 1, 2 and 3*, the Supreme Court and the Court of Appeals for the Second Circuit sanctioned the ability of the Board to allow underwriting of commercial paper and debt and equity securities by commercial banks.

In *Bankers Trust 1*,[33] the Securities Industry Association (SIA) brought suit when Bankers Trust, a state member bank, began acting as an agent by placing corporate customers' commercial paper with institutional investors, pursuant to a Board order. The Supreme Court on appeal determined that commercial paper was a note or security within GSA Sections 16 and 21 but remanded regarding determination of whether or not Bankers Trust placement activity constituted underwriting.[34] In *Bankers Trust 2*,[35] the Court of Appeals determined that acting as agent in the placement of commercial paper does not constitute underwriting. In *Bankers Trust 3*,[36] the SIA challenged the Board's decision to allow bank holding company subsidiaries to underwrite securities previously deemed ineligible and endorsed the Board's view of *Agnew*[37] defining the "engaged principally" language of GSA Section 20. The court rejected a market share limitation imposed by the FRB, but it upheld a gross revenue limitation on such activities. In *J.P. Morgan and Co., Inc., Chase Manhattan Corp., Bankers Trust New York Corp., Citicorp, and Securities Pacific Corp.* ("J.P. Morgan")[38], the FRB rejected the contention of SIA and the Investment Company Institute (ICI), a trade association of the mutual fund industry, which contended that the proposed activities would violate GSA Section 20 and did not meet the "closely related and proper" incident to banking standards of Section 4(C)8 of the Bank Holding Company Act (the BHCA).[39] First, the Board investigated compliance of GSA Section 20 which prohibits affiliation of a member bank with a company that is "engaged principally" in underwriting or dealing in securities.[40] The FRB determined that (1) the 5% to 10% revenue limitation does not include US government and other securities that a member bank is expressly authorized to underwrite, and (2) a company that derives no more than 5% to 10% of its gross revenues from underwriting and dealing in ineligible securities would not

be engaged principally in underwriting or dealing.[41] The Board held that the closely related banking test is met if (1) banks generally provide activities or services operationally and functionally similar to those activities proposed, and (2) that the proposed activities are integrally related to the existing activities of the bank and further noted that banks have been involved in securities underwriting by active participation of foreign offices of US banks and bank holding companies overseas.[42] Pursuant to the Board's Regulation K,[43] a bank holding subsidiary may write and deal in any kind of debt and equity securities outside the United States subject to limitation on the size of their position.

The Orders also established operating limitations to regulate transactions by an affiliate bank or thrift with, or for the benefit of, an underwriting subsidiary in order to prevent the transfer of risk to federally insured affiliates, conflicts of interest and other adverse effects. In general, these limitations:

—preclude the holding company and any affiliate from purchasing ineligible securities from the underwriting subsidiary during the underwriting and for 50 days thereafter or while the underwriting subsidiary is making a market in the security;

—prevent a bank or thrift from lending to issuers to enhance the creditworthiness of securities underwritten by the underwriting subsidiary, or to pay off the principal and interest on such securities;

—prohibit banks from knowingly making loans to customers secured by or for the purpose of purchasing securities underwritten by the underwriting subsidiary during the underwriting or in which it makes a market;

—require disclosure by the underwriting subsidiary to ensure that the public will not confuse the underwriting subsidiary with its federally insured affiliates and will know that the instruments purchased from the underwriting affiliate are not federally insured deposits or guaranteed or otherwise backed by a bank or thrift affiliate (unless such is the case);

—prohibit an affiliated bank and thrift from acting as agent for, or engaging in marketing activities on behalf of, the underwriting subsidiary;

—limit self-dealing transactions between the underwriting subsidiary and its bank and thrift affiliates acting in a fiduciary capacity; and

—prohibit the transfer of confidential customer information between the bank or thrift and underwriting subsidiary without customer consent.[44]

One theory of interpretation of the GSA holds that a bank is not negotiating in securities if the process involves the transformation of assets into securities which are "legally transparent" as the holders of the securities have essentially the same rights, liabilities and risks as if they were direct owners of the underlying asset; banks would thus be able to enhance their liquidity by securitizing, in addition to mortgages, low-risk assets such as auto loans, credit card receivables and high-quality commercial loans.[45]

Generally, the process of securitization is not considered one requiring the same kind of prudential restraints as other forms of off-balance sheet financing. "Securitization" is the name given to the process whereby loans or receivables are pooled and then sold. Securitization is not addressed by the G–10 Agreement[46] on capital adequacy or the SBD in part reflecting the fact that the United States is so far ahead in financial innovation in general and securitization in particular.[47] Receivables in order to be securitized must have a cash flow that is reasonably ascertainable such as mortgages and credit card receivables. The market is vast, approximately $769 billion in mortgage-backed securities, primarily government insured, and from January 1989 to November 1990, the securitization of consumer lending has skyrocketed from $29 billion to more than $70 billion.[48]

Certain situations allow more favorable treatment of mortgages. In the United States, commercial banks are monitored by Federal Financial Institutions and Examination Councils (FFIE).[49] When asset sales involve recourse, such sales are treated as on-balance sheet liabilities except for mortgage-backed securities which are government-insured. (Actually, mortgage-backed Government Insured Securities are on-balance sheet but receive a 0% risk weight.)[50] Bank holding companies are governed by Generally Accepted Accounting Principles and thus balance sheet treatment of asset transfers involving recourse and sales or financing treatment is determined by Financial Accounting Standards Board Statement No. 77, which provides more lenient terms to treat asset sales as sales if: (1) the transferor surrenders economic control of the future economic benefits relating to the receivables; (2) the transferor can reasonably estimate its obligation under the recourse provisions; and (3) the transferee cannot return the receivables to the transferor except pursuant to the recourse provisions.[51]

Under this criterion (FFIE), the OCC did permit Security Pacific National Bank's sale of mortgage-backed pass-through certificates. The OCC held that the proposed issuance by Security Pacific would not violate the prohibitions of either Section 16 or 21 of GSA even if the certificates were securities within the meaning of GSA. The OCC noted that "underwriting" refers to the process of purchasing *another* company's newly issued securities for distribution and sale to investors and that "dealing" involves the purchase and sale of *another* company's securities in the secondary market. Since Security Pacific wanted only to participate in the initial sale of instruments backed by *its own* mortgage loans, the OCC held that the proposed transaction involved neither "underwriting" nor "dealing."[52] The District Court to which the SIA appealed the OCC administrative decision held that Security Pacific by assigning its mortgages to a trust for which it received a pass-through certificate—when taken together with the description of its role as described in the prospectus had been involved in the

forbidden activity of underwriting securities.[53] On appeal, the US Court of Appeals for the Second Circuit ruled that Security Pacific was not engaged in the activity of underwriting, enunciating a very similar argument to that made originally by the OCC.[54]

Aside from the FRB's expansive discussion in *J.P. Morgan* regarding the expertise of banks in the area of distribution, dealing, origination and structuring of securities transactions, the FRB remarked at that time that certain kinds of securities are of the ineligible variety, including municipal revenue bonds, one to four family mortgages and consumer receivable securities and commercial paper.[55] It is a question of magnitude as to whether restricting these activities to 5% (or 10%) of the gross revenues of a subsidiary of a bank holding company is in fact an unnecessary constraint on commercial banking activity. Some of the philosophy of the FRB concerns the financial resources of the bank holding company and refers to a previous statement that banking organizations contemplating major expansion proposals should maintain strong capital levels substantially above the minimum levels specified in the FRB's capital adequacy guidelines.[56]

In addition to the specific prudential limitations surrounding an underwriting discussed above, the FRB also instituted a prohibition on lending by a bank or thrift affiliate to the underwriting subsidiary as well as a prohibition on the purchase and sale of financial assets between these institutions for their own account subject to a limited exception for clearing US government and agency securities.[57] The FRB did not prohibit bank lending in connection with financing arranged by the underwriting subsidiary or limit the ability of the subsidiary to market securities for the purpose of repaying affiliate bank lending because Section 23(b) would cover bank lending under these circumstances, and continued to allow these transactions subject to the establishment by banks and their affiliates of appropriate limits to control concentration of credit and overall exposure to individual underwriting clients and aggregate exposure to borrowers.[58] It is important to consider whether this accounting limitation together with the 5% to 10% of gross revenue limitation for ineligible securities revenue is such that commercial banks will be discouraged from properly funding securities activities. The FRB also prohibits any member of an underwriting subsidiary from being an officer, a director or employee of a bank or bank holding company and vice versa.[59]

Furthermore, the FRB requires that each applicant deduct from its consolidated primary capital its investment in the underwriting subsidiary and exclude from its total consolidated assets the assets of the underwriting subsidiary.[60] Whether bank holding companies engaged in securities underwriting are subject to consolidated bank capital ratios is in some doubt. Investment in subsidiaries must be deducted; but capital ratios are not

consolidated.[61] Interviews with staff of the FRB have not yielded any certainty about current practice. Perhaps this uncertainty provides healthy discipline.[62] Apparently, the FRB considers both an unconsolidated ratio of parent companies which have securities affiliates and a consolidated ratio.

In the *Bankers Trust Order*[63] approving an application to act as agent in the private placement of securities and to act as principal in buying and selling securities, the FRB created an entirely new category of securities-eligible as opposed to securities-ineligible activity. Bankers Trust contended that these proposed private placement activities were not the kind of securities activities described in GSA Section 20.[64] The rationale was garnered from *Bankers Trust 2*[65] where the court had determined that private placement of commercial paper does not constitute underwriting, distribution, or impermissible selling of such securities for purposes of GSA Sections 16 or 21. Let us recall that it was only as of March, 1989—neolithic time in regulation of the securities business of banks—that banks were allowed to engage in securities-ineligible activities through subsidiaries.[66] This December 1989 *Bankers Trust Order*[67] was fundamentally concerned with allowing the private placement to be conducted through a securities affiliate and not to be subject to the 5–10% limitations on gross revenue.[68] The Board, in allowing this activity, makes use of the rationale of the court that placing new issues of securities with a limited number of purchasers in transactions that do not involve a public offering is not underwriting for purposes of the GSA, because there are none of the various attributes of a public offering, including general solicitation, small denominations, or individual as opposed to institutional investors.[69] Thus, the Board allows such activities not to be viewed as a securities-ineligible activity "for purposes of the 10% revenue test,"[70] to the extent that a bank acts as agent rather than firm commitment underwriter.

In *J.P. Morgan II*,[71] the FRB, building on its own prior decision in the *Bankers Trust Order*[72] allowed banks affiliated with a GSA Section 20 subsidiary to extend credit to the issuer of debt securities which were privately placed in order for the issuer to repay the principal amount of such securities.[73] Furthermore, the Board allowed the GSA Section 20 subsidiaries to place debt securities with an affiliated parent holding company or a non-bank affiliate but not equity securities or any unmarketable debt security (i.e., those that cannot be resold because of Securities and Exchange Commission private placement restrictions).[74] It is not evident how Rule 144A[75] allowing a pathway for private sales by banks will affect this restriction. The Board will monitor aggregate exposure of a bank holding company on a consolidated basis to any single customer whose securities are dealt in by the bank holding company.[76]

On September 20, 1990, the FRB approved an application by J.P. Morgan to trade and engage in the underwriting of corporate equities.[77] The

logic behind this decision is contained in the January 1989 *J.P. Morgan* decision cited above.[78] While allowing underwriting of equities is the next step after underwriting of debt securities, and equities are considered part of all Section 20 subsidiary activities which must be limited to 10% of gross revenue, allowing underwriting equities is the final philosophical, break from the GSA. The move is known to have outraged different members of Congress, including Henry Gonzalez, Chairman of the House Banking Committee.[79] Most important, in allowing Morgan to be the only triple-A rated bank company to underwrite equities, the FRB promotes the separation of banking regulation into two categories: the highly rated banks and the more troubled banks, thereby perhaps contributing to the erosion of the latter.

Part III: Regulation of Derivative Instruments

At this juncture, it will again be necessary to delve into the interrelation between securities and banking regulation. Rule 144(a),[80] which allows privately placed securities under the Securities and Exchange Act Section 4 exemption to be freely resold to institutional investors in the international marketplace and elimination of registration requirements, may galvanize the international marketplace.[81] (Note that under *Bankers Trust I*,[82] commercial paper is a security [it has always been treated as such in Europe] and is also subject to Section 5 of the Securities and Exchange Act, despite particular exemptions under the Act.)[83] One of the possible logical progressions is allowing banks to underwrite corporate debt and even equities in private placements as securities-eligible activities. In fact, this is one reading of the FRB *J.P. Morgan* decision. Thus, the mileage that could actually be gained under GSA without reformation is really quite extraordinary. However, the issue of allowing banks to privately place commercial paper as a securities-eligible activity and concerns about consequent bank failure are Janus-faced because the emergence of the commercial paper market in the early 1980s was itself largely a result of the credit problems created by the global debt problem and the realization by private companies that their ratings were in fact higher than those of most commercial banks, and that they would, by issuing commercial paper, be able to borrow money at *Sub-Libid.* levels.[84] And it is widely noted that the commercial paper market has caused a deterioration of the creditworthiness of the banking system by withdrawing triple-A borrowers from the market and causing them to be replaced by less creditworthy borrowers.[85]

In addition to securitization and new securities activities, US banks have been involved in financial futures markets since their inception. The power of US banks to engage in futures transactions is to be found in the "Incidental to Banking Language of the National Banking Act."[86] Banks other than national banks will in this area be subject to state as well as federal

regulations. Thus, the legality of futures trading activities by banks will vary from state to state.[87]

In 1980 the OCC, the FRB and the Federal Deposit Insurance Corporation (the FDIC) jointly announced revised guidelines for banks that engage in futures forward and standby contracts on US government and agency securities.[88]

Generally, banks may take short and long positions with respect to their investment portfolio[89] and hedge against interest rate exposure associated with undesired mismatches in interest sensitivity and liabilities.[90] In accordance with several rules[91] certain criteria exist in determining whether an interest rate future will qualify as a hedge.[92] The importance of a hedge is that it will enable banks to offset losses against gains.

Part IV: Interstate Banking: And Other Deregulatory Regulations

A bank may currently extend the market it serves by establishing a new branch or combining with an existing commercial bank through merger or acquisition across state lines; and a bank holding company may acquire another bank as a bank subsidiary if permitted by state law.[93] A bank holding company may also acquire a non-banking subsidiary whose activities are closely related to banking under a test incorporated in the Bank Holding Company Act.[94] Banks may acquire thrifts under certain circumstances; most importantly where state law permits,[95] the Douglas Amendment of the Bank Holding Company permits interstate branching.[96] Recent legislative initiatives would allow nationwide branching.[97]

The current state of deregulation of commercial banks and thrifts, in particular, was created by the Monetary Control Act of 1980 and by the Garn–St. Germain Act of 1982.[98] The 1980 and 1982 Acts affected state chartered thrifts and commercial banks in the majority of states that had "wild-card" provisions authorizing state thrifts to engage in those activities permitted to their federally chartered counterparts.[99] (There are about 25 states that have such "wild-card" provisions.)[100] Another expanded banking power is the right of banks to establish networks for sharing of automatic teller machine facilities (ATM). The Supreme Court has held that an ATM is a branch and subject to particular state regulations in *First National Bank in Plant City v. Dickenson*.[101]

The Monetary Control Act provided for the elimination of interest rate ceilings on savings account balances[102] and granted to all federally insured commercial banks and thrift institutions the ability to offer consumers negotiable order of withdrawal (NOW) accounts[103] thus allowing accounts equivalent to interest bearing savings accounts to compete with money market mutual funds. The Monetary Control Act gave federally chartered thrifts the power to invest 20% of their assets in consumer loans[104] and

20% in approved non-residential real estate.[105] The Act also granted federally chartered thrifts trust and fiduciary powers[106] and the authority to provide credit card services.[107] The Garn–St. Germain Act expanded consumer loan authority to 30%[108] and non-residential real estate loan authority to 40% of assets.[109]

Part V: Legislative Initiatives

In 1988, the Senate passed the Proxmire Act.[110] In pertinent part the Proxmire Act would have allowed banks to affiliate with a securities firm. To maintain the integrity of the affiliated bank, the Act had a series of firewalls between the bank and the bank affiliate—prohibiting banks from: (1) extending credit or purchasing the financial assets of the securities affiliate; (2) enhancing marketability of securities underwritten by the securities affiliate; (3) knowingly extending any credit that would be used to purchase securities underwritten by the securities affiliate; (4) extending any credit that would be used to pay the principal or interest on securities underwritten by the securities affiliate; (5) having officers and directors who are also officers and directors of the securities affiliate; (6) giving investment advice to the securities affiliate.[111]

The Proxmire Bill inexplicably failed to pass the House of Representatives at the early end of the session. But it appears to have been highly regarded by legislators and banking and investment banking sources. The limitations which the Proxmire Act would have constructed when implemented may have been sufficient to stem the tide against speculative enterprises to be conducted by universal banks. In fact depending upon the interpretation of certain aspects of the proposed Proxmire Act by the relevant agencies, the firewalls may have even been more restrictive than is currently the practice under FRA Sections 23(a) and (b).[112]

Firewalls under the Financial Institution Safety Act were substantially similar to those under the Proxmire Act but more flexible. In particular, banks are allowed, with the approval of the FRB based upon proper capitalization, to engage in certain activities with securities affiliates. Such activities enable banks to extend a fraction of their capital to securities affiliates if unaffiliated lenders participate in the transaction demonstrating the arm's-length nature.[113] Banks are able to purchase government securities from affiliates and other investment-grade securities on a mark to market basis. Well-capitalized banks may extend credit to securities affiliates provided there is adequate collateral. Credit may, under certain circumstances, be extended with FRB approval to securities affiliates provided in accord with § 23(a) (calling for arm's-length transactions); however, the aggregate of such transactions may not exceed 5% of the bank's capital. Banks may, where certain prudential requirements are met, extend credit up to 40% of the bank's capital to the issuer of a security underwritten by

its securities affiliate. No credit can be extended for the purpose of purchasing securities underwritten by a securities affiliate to any underwriter
or member of a selling group with such securities affiliate.[114] Given the
deterioration of the banking system in 1991, only bank holding companies
(or under the Treasury and House proposals, financial services holding
companies) with high capital standards were permitted to have securities
affiliates,[115] thus following the rationale of the *Morgan* decision allowing
only well-capitalized banks to engage in equity underwriting.

Another important limitation on banks which does not currently exist is
on the investment services activities of banks which have not been here-
tofore regulated under the Investment Company Act. Banks which publicly
solicit securities brokerage business and receive commissions based on
executing securities transactions in excess of costs would be subject to SEC
regulation as broker dealers.[116] The financial modernization proposals
would require SEC registration of bank holding companies, securities affiliates or banks that engage in giving any investment advice.[117]

One feature of the 1991 financial modernization debate, which was not
present in earlier discussions, was the proposed repeal of BHCA provisions
that forbade commercial firm ownership of banks.[118] This provision was
endorsed enthusiastically by former SEC Chairman Breeden[119] and more
tentatively by FRB Chairman Greenspan.[120] It was endorsed by Breeden
because many large finance companies, such as Ford and Sears, already
have banks which were grandfathered by the relevant BHCA amendments
and because foreign financial entities involved such conglomerations. It
may be argued that such combinations make concentration of economic
and political power likely. The attempt to throw this wrench into the current
debate overturning 200 years of separation of commerce and banking[121]
indicates the absence of consensus as to how to resolve the banking regulatory dilemma.

In addition to prohibiting commercial bank affiliation, US legislation has
rigorously limited economic concentration by banks through other limitations on banking activity. The BHCA and the amendments to that Act
adopted in 1970 taken together have restricted banking organizations from
product-line expansion. The commonly voiced fear is that diversified financial firms would tie the sale of their various services together. Section
3 of the Clayton Anti-Trust Act of 1914 bars tieing arrangements involving
goods where the producer establishing the tie-in has substantial market
power in the tie-in goods market or where the tie-in will foreclose "not
insubstantial volume" of the sales in the tie-in goods market.[122]

Tie-in arrangements involving services are judged under the rigorous
standards of Section 1 of the Sherman Act and Section 5 of the Federal
Trade Commission Act. The Sherman Act has been construed to require
both proof of market power in the tying product and the foreclosure of a
substantial amount of commerce. It was in 1970 that Congress recognized

the unique importance of credit in the economy by amending the Bank Holding Company Act to prohibit any type of tying of bank credit to other services offered by a bank or its holding company.[123] According to Robert Litan, the practical ability of diversified financial organizations to engage in anti-competitive tying arrangements will depend on the market power held by these organizations, and most markets banks are but one of many providers of financial services. The exceptions are largely in rural areas or small communities.[124]

Part VI: FDICIA

A. BACKGROUND AND GENERAL PROVISIONS OF FDICIA

The present value of the cost to US taxpayers of bailing out the insolvent savings and loans (S&Ls) was estimated by the Congressional Budget Office to be approximately $215 billion in 1992.[125] This represents only the direct monetary cost to the government of upholding the deposit insurance system and it does not include the production and consumption that has been and will be foregone as the result of poor investments which creates an estimated total bill of 500 billion 1990 dollars.[126] In general, the costs of commercial bank failures are estimated to be about $30 billion and with indirect costs included are about $50 billion.[127] Nearly one-third of bank assets at the end of the third quarter of 1988 were being managed by institutions with capital ratios below 6%. Roughly $700 billion of these assets were concentrated in 13 of the nation's 15 largest banks.[128]

Bank regulatory policy, pursuant to the Garn–St. Germain Act,[129] removed statutory restrictions on permissible loan to value ratios (LTV ratios) governing the real estate lending of national banks which had previously ranged from 66.7% for unimproved land to 90% for improved land.[130]

Real estate loans in the United States as a percentage of the portfolio composition of commercial banks have risen from 21.8% in November 1985 to 28.7% in November 1992.[131] In December 1990 all commercial banks together held $384.8 billion in commercial real estate loans and had net equity capital of $222.5 billion or 6.57% of total assets. Since net equity capital was only 58.1% of the size of commercial real estate loans, every 1% write down in loans would produce a 1.72% write off of net equity capital. Current adverse conditions in commercial real estate markets indicate declines in property values of 20–25% in the period 1988–1990 and perhaps more since then, if commercial real estate loans were written down to value.[132] While a 25% fall in the market value of all real properties would not result in a 25% fall in the value of all real estate loans, significant decline would produce a significant fall in a bank's total net equity capital.

In 1991, Congress enacted the Federal Deposit Insurance Corporation

Improvement Act of 1991 (FDICIA).[133] FDICIA requires that bank regulators adopt uniform standards for real estate lending including construction finance and prescribes that such standards consider the risk posed to the deposit insurance fund by real estate lending.[134] An interagency notice of proposed rule making has been issued to classify real estate lending depending upon LTV ratios.[135] The category of real estate loans are divided as follows: raw land 50–65%, preconstruction development 55–70%, construction and development 65–80%, improved property 65–80%, 1–4 family residential property owner-occupied 80–95%, home equity 80–95%. Institutions may make real estate loans that do not conform with established LTV ratio limits up to an amount not to exceed 15% of the institution's total capital. The LTV ratio is the only aspect of real estate addressed by FDICIA; the most important aspects of real estate lending are not addressed by FDICIA, and banks are subject to regulatory guidance by bank regulators.[136]

In a March 1, 1991, statement, the Federal Reserve Board Comptroller of the Currency, OTS and FDIC issued a joint statement regarding the treatment of real estate loans. The statement clarified policies on a supervisory evaluation of real estate and also provided for enhanced disclosure to the public by (a) requiring disclosure of non-accrual loans and (b) requiring disclosure of highly leveraged transactions.

Clarifying the March 1, 1991 statement was an interagency policy statement dated November 7, 1991, which addressed the review and classification of commercial real estate loans by examiners of federal bank and thrift regulatory agencies, established indicators of troubled real estate markets and projects and related indebtedness providing a classification system for loans.[137]

Under Section 131 of the FDICIA, significant provisions are enacted to categorize institutions depending upon the degree of capitalization and enabling prompt corrective action.[138] Pursuant to Section 38 of the Federal Deposit Insurance Act (FDIA) as added by Section 131 of FDICIA, each banking agency was required to implement prompt corrective actions within the categorization as delineated in the statute. The regulations issued on September 29, 1992, provide a framework for prompt corrective action by explicitly defining capital required within the five categories established by the statute.[139] Any institution is well capitalized if it has a total risk base ratio of 10% or greater, a tier-one risk base capital ratio of 6% or greater, and a leverage ratio of 5% or greater.[140]

Several commentators suggested that the agencies eliminate one or more of the proposed capital measures.[141] One of the rationales for retaining a leverage ratio after the risk-based capital measure was that a risk-based capital measure is focused on credit-related risk and does not explicitly factor in other risks, particularly interest rate risks. However, once Section 305 of FDICIA discussed below is implemented to require agencies to

revise their risk-based capital standards to take into account interest rate risk, the agencies intend to lower or eliminate the leverage capital component from the definitions.[142]

Commentators noted that overall the standard for well-capitalized institutions would require an institution to hold 25% more total risk-based capital, 50% more tier-one capital, and 65% more leverage-based capital than an adequately capitalized institution.[143]

FDICIA Section 131 (FDIA Section 38) specifically limits regulatory initiative in determining the amount of capital distinguishing between an undercapitalized financial institution and a critically undercapitalized institution which in no event shall have tangible equity less than 2% of total assets and not less than 65% of the required minimum level of capital under the leverage limit.[144] Section 38 does not define tangible equity, and it is nowhere else defined. So, the issue faced by the regulators was whether to consider all forms of tier-one capital and, the agencies did recognize cumulative perpetual preferred stock, however not other types of instruments such as hybrids of equity and debt. Section 38 also enables agencies to take account of non-capital supervisory criteria in reclassifying institutions.[145] The agencies may reclassify an institution if such an institution is deemed to be engaged in unsafe or unsound banking practices. If the institution is well capitalized, it can be reclassified as adequately capitalized. If adequately capitalized, the institution can be deemed undercapitalized.[146] The agencies do not believe that the statute or the principle of fairness require a formal administrative hearing be afforded in reclassifications, because the courts have determined that the statutory language after notice and opportunity for hearing does not require a formal hearing.[147] An institution which has been reclassified to a different capital category as a result of an agency determination that the institution is in unsafe or unsound condition or engaged in a similar practice is required to submit a capital restoration plan.[148]

Under Section 132 of FDICIA (FDIA Section 39), standards for safety and soundness aside from capital are enumerated.[149] Federal agencies must prescribe standards relating to (a) internal controls, informational systems and internal audit systems; (b) loan documentation; (c) credit underwriting; (d) interest rate risk exposure; (e) asset growth; (f) compensation fees and benefits; and (g) other appropriate operational and managerial standards. Banking agencies have issued advance notice of proposed rule making regarding Section 132 (FDIA 39).[150] The very vagueness of this section shows an absence of concerted thought about what standards should supplement the prompt corrective action capital standards. The operational and managerial controls including internal controls, information systems, loan documentation, credit underwriting, interest rate risk exposure and asset growth and compensation in fees are so general as to defy description. It is certainly appropriate to take notice of internal controls and information

systems. However, where does this become so imprecise as to edge out of the area in which governmental supervision should be present? Certainly, it is important as far as interest rate risk exposure is concerned that there be additional safeguards compared to the rather mechanical framework of FDICIA Section 305.[151] Similarly, asset growth ought to be a consideration even where capital standards fit into a particular category. However, the delineation between Sections 38 and 39 is unnecessary as other vehicles exist for changing the category of an institution based on non-capital concerns in Section 38.[152]

Section 39(b) of the FDIA requires each of the agencies to prescribe standards specifying a maximum ratio of classified assets to capital and minimum earnings sufficient to absorb losses without impairing capital and, to the extent feasible, a minimum ratio of market value to book value for publicly traded shares. The question of asset quality in terms of the concept of "classified assets" ought to be integrated with the current real estate classification provided in various bank circulars.[153] Earnings sufficient to avoid impairing capital are difficult to define, but the problem with the definitions in Section 39, as segregated from Section 38, is that this should simply be an additional standard with which to gauge institutions with impaired safety and soundness standards, although its capital has not fallen below the minimum. Defining market value as a criteria is difficult because most bank shares are not traded, and many of those that are traded are thinly traded, and many opportunities for manipulation exist. Again, this should simply be a non-capital based indication that should be an early warning trigger. Compensation standards should likewise be considered as a factor to the extent that this would impair capital or is inappropriate given the state of the institution. The drafting of the statute and concomitant advance notice of proposed rule-making seem to be vague as to when a salary is excessive. Once again, this ought to be another factor and may be one of even relatively more significance to indicate a problem even where capital is appropriate. It is indicative of the indecisiveness of regulators that the agencies request comment on the extent to which an institution's financial and managerial condition should result in different regulatory standards. It is quite apparent that limiting compensation of extremely well-performing banks is not the legislative intent.

In a more general and dispositive vein, one wonders whether the fear of throwing the baby out with the bath water in terms of providing inclusiveness for regulatory intervention has failed to create a definitive group of standards by which bank performance and safety and soundness can be gauged. The very high standards to which banks are held in the highest category (includes 95.8% of banks and 88% of assets)[154] state that most banks are well capitalized. It seems that distinctions in the legislation for the other 4.2% of banks should probably be closed or merged given the macroeconomic problems of concentration in real estate as such banks or

at least a large proportion of them, are not viable; thus, the legislation as enacted creates too many categories which balance obvious interest group concerns. At the other extreme, the vast number of banks that are well capitalized indicates that the credit crunch may be effectuated by regulatory overresponse and can have adverse effects on the competitiveness of US banks and the US financial system in general. These capital standards are in addition to the regulatory guidance in the form of regulations, particularly concerning real estate. A further regulatory burden imposed by FDICIA which polices capital adequacy and is an additional penalty for undercapitalized institutions is the risk-based assessment of federal deposit insurance.[155]

Section 122 of FDICIA[156] requires that banks annually submit information on small business and small farm lending. Regulations enacted pursuant to Section 122 and Section 477 of FDICIA[157] require the FRB to collect and publish information regarding loans to small businesses. The proposed schedule includes the number and amount of loans, fee income, and net charge-offs.[158] The general unpopularity of these regulations has been given credence by David Mullins, Vice Chairman of the FRB, who has suggested that these rules are onerous and are partly responsible for the credit crunch.[159] But, the rules as implemented are less inclusive than originally proposed.[160] The FFIEC did not propose to collect data on loans to minority owned businesses or to small businesses in existence for less than one year, yet it had requested comments on such reporting.

Although interest rate regulation is noticeably absent from the G–10 Agreement on risk adjusted capital,[161] under Section 305 of the FDICIA, bank regulators are required to review risk-based capital standards for insured depository institutions to ensure that these standards take adequate account of (1) interest rate risk, (2) concentration of credit risk, and (3) the risks of non-traditional activities.[162] Pursuant to Section 305, a joint proposal of banking regulators to incorporate interest rate risks into risk-based capital guidelines has been issued recently.[163] Specifically, the change in the institution's net economic value attributable to interest rate risk would be computed as a change in the present value of its assets minus the changes of present value liabilities and off-balance sheet positions for an assumed 100 basis point parallel shift in market interest rate. In other words, the exposure and threshold level of interest rate risk exposure would be set at 1% of assets so that an institution with a measured exposure of 1.50% of assets would be required to allocate to capital the dollar amount of capital equal to .50% of total assets. According to a study accompanying the proposal, the average American bank has an interest rate risk exposure of about 1%.[164] Prepayment assumptions must be made in measuring interest rate risks, including prepayment estimates for pass-through securities. Particular adjustments must be made for nonamortizing and deep discount risks.

Currently, the United States employs a leverage ratio that is not used in most G–10 countries. This ratio applies a minimal capital standards for all on-balance sheet assets regardless of risk rating. The impact of these rules is to bolster the required amount of capital and in essence act as a substitution for interest rate risk ratings.[165]

B. SYSTEMIC RISK REGULATIONS UNDER FDICIA

The failure of Continental of Illinois in 1984 occurred at a time when 67 banks had over 100% of their capital in interbank loans with Continental and 113 banks had over 50% of their capital thus invested;[166] further, the technical provisions of Sections 23A and B of the FRA were violated.[167] Thus the failure of Continental could have caused a national bank failure crisis of epidemic proportion. There have been other bank failures, however, that can be contained and do not create systemic risk.[168] Under the least cost resolution method of FDICIA,[169] a present value analysis and documentation is required.[170] In order to effectuate a bailout, a two-thirds majority of the FRB and the Secretary of Treasury (in consultation with the President) must determine that such systemic risk is present.[171]

Under Section 308 of the FDICIA, the FRB is required to develop regulations which limit the exposure of insured depository institutions to other institutions and require banks to develop internal procedures to evaluate and control exposure to the depository institutions with which they do business. The FRB has issued a proposed regulation,[172] establishing "benchmark" guidelines for overnight credit exposure to individual "correspondent banks." These guidelines are stated as percentages of the exposed bank's capital, so that higher levels of the bank's capital may be exposed to better-capitalized correspondents. Benchmarks are based on a measure of credit exposure that excludes certain relatively low-risk transactions and generally permit a bank to have credit exposure to an individual correspondent equal to 25% of the exposed bank's capital. For a bank that can demonstrate that it is "adequately capitalized" under FDICIA,[173] it would be allowed credit exposure equal to 50% of the bank's total capital, but no more than 25% of the bank's capital could be exposed through transactions that have a term to maturity of more than 30 days. Because it is difficult to monitor all credit exposure, and rigid limits would require banks to target a much lower level of credit exposure, these limits are not defined precisely.[174] Prudential limits take into account credit risk and settlement risk. For a bank that is well capitalized, there is no established benchmark. For well-capitalized correspondents, there is no established credit exposure. For adequately capitalized correspondents, the limit is 50% of the exposed bank's total capital, with a separate benchmark for a longer term credit exposure under which a bank should not have credit

exposure with a remaining term of 30 days over 25% of the bank's total capital. For other correspondents, the limit is 25% of a bank's total capital, and a bank must include the credit exposure of its subsidiaries. Off-balance sheet transactions, such as interest rate and foreign exchange rate contracts are included in credit exposure, but only to the extent of current replacement value, and netting contracts under FDICIA Sections 401–407 are permitted. Credit exposure does not include transactions that are fully secured by the US government or agency securities. Correspondents include foreign banks within the definition and imply capital equivalency standards based on the Basle Capital Accord.

Another aspect of systemic risk which is addressed by FDICIA is direct lending by the FRB to securities firms without intermediation by banks. This subject is considered later in this chapter and in Chapter 3, but the statutory basis is Section 473 which allows the FRB to provide emergency liquidity to broker dealers by discounting their obligations.[175]

C. THE FOREIGN BANK SUPERVISION ENFORCEMENT ACT CONTAINED IN FDICIA

Under early drafts of legislation implementing the 1991 Treasury Proposal,[176] foreign banks that wanted to engage in newly expanded bank powers were subject to a "branch roll-up provision," which would have subjected them to the requirement to incorporate a subsidiary to take advantage of these new powers.[177] The ambiguity of Section 214(a) could be construed as requiring any foreign branch bank with deposit balances to roll up its branch into an insured deposit subsidiary affecting a large number of foreign banks.[178] The Foreign Bank Supervision Enhancement Act of 1991 (FBSEA), as enacted, mandates two conditions for a foreign bank to maintain deposits of less than $100,000: (1) the foreign bank must obtain deposit insurance; and (2) the foreign bank must establish one or more subsidiaries for the purpose,[179] but grandfathered insured branches existing at the date of enactment. This section was supposed to apply only to retail deposits, as evidenced by the title of the subsection.[180] Until this error is resolved, the FRB and OCC have indicated that foreign banks would not be considered in violation if they restrict their depository activities to those permissible under existing FDIC and OCC regulations in effect on December 19, 1991,[181] but the FRB reserves for the future the right to promulgate rules on this subject.[182] FBSEA prohibits foreign banks from establishing a branch or agency without FRB approval, whether the branch is state or federally chartered.[183] FBSEA amends the BHCA by enumerating "managerial resources"—the competence, experience and integrity of officers and directors and shareholders the FRB may consider in determining whether to approve the establishment of new branches or agencies.[184]

Additionally, the FBSEA establishes discretionary standards which the FRB may consider in approving branches,[185] grants the FRB power to terminate operations of a foreign bank if it is not subject to comprehensive and consolidated supervision in its home country and has violated the law.[186] It imposes a litmus test of "sound banking practices" on permissible activities for state chartered banks that are prohibited to federal branches,[187] and subjects all state-chartered branches to the lending limits in respect of loans to a single borrower that are applicable to federally chartered foreign branches under the International Banking Act of 1978 (IBA)[188] which are the national bank lending limits.[189] Other enforcement provisions in FDICIA Section 202(a) include coordination by regulators in bank examinations, approval and supervision of representative offices, reporting of loans to foreign branches secured by bank stock, cooperation with foreign bank supervisors, new civil money penalties, new authority to issue subpoenas and require production of documents, and enforcement of consumer statutes.[190] FBSEA also applies BHCA provisions requiring FRB approval for the acquisition of more than 5% of a bank or bank holding company by foreign banks and their parents.[191]

Prior to the enactment of the IBA in 1978, a regime existed which enabled foreign banks to branch in the United States without any restrictions on the activities of these branches which could engage in securities-related and other commercial activities.[192] One major burden on a bank subsidiary was requiring the bank to obtain deposit insurance.[193] The most significant federal law restrictions on having one or more banking subsidiary was imposed by the Bank Holding Company Act (BHCA) which applied to foreign banks that owned a US subsidiary bank.[194] The principal restrictions included prohibition on a foreign bank (as a bank holding company) directly or indirectly owning or controlling any commercial enterprise, including a securities operation engaged in the United States in activities closely related to banking.[195] No restrictions were placed on a state licensed branch or agency presence in the United States so, neither the MacFadden Act[196] nor the FRA[197] prohibitions against interstate branching applied. A foreign bank whose operations in the United States did not include a bank subsidiary did not control a "bank" for purposes of the BHCA and accordingly was not generally subject to the non-banking provision of Section 4(c)8 of the BHCA.[198] Under the IBA, foreign banks are subject to various federal prohibitions and restrictions that they had been able to avoid through branches and agencies previously. Section 6 requires foreign bank US branches carrying FDIC deposit insurance if they accept any significant level of retail deposits.[199] Section 7 applies reserve requirements to branches and agencies of all except the smallest of foreign banks.[200] Perhaps most important, Sections 5 and 8 respectively impose interstate banking and non-banking restrictions on foreign banks. However, existing interstate and non-banking activities were "grandfathered"

by provisions in Sections 5 and 8.[201] A complicated compromise based on Section 2(h) of the BHCA[202] authorized foreign banks that own interests in commercial industrial concerns abroad to engage indirectly in those activities in the United States though subject to restrictions and conditions.[203] Two forms of full service banking are available in the United States to foreign banks, branches and subsidiaries, and since the IBA, the advantage of a subsidiary is that it can branch, and a branch can make use of its foreign parent's capital.[204]

According to one commentator BHCA Section 2(h) and the comparable provision in the IBA limiting US non-banking business of a foreign bank holding company, which has a US branch or subsidiary, is unduly restrictive as interpreted by the FRB.[205] Unfortunately the limitations in the IBA are an attempt to ensure competitive equality and are consequently wrought with difficulties when considering the entry of a foreign financial conglomerate which does have a large US presence in its non-banking business. The only way to effectuate a change in current policy without giving foreign financial conglomerates undue advantage is to continue a process of consolidated capital ratios and prudential supervision which had been developing in the IOSCO framework discussed in Chapter 1.[206]

At the time the IBA was passed, Congress was aware that non-US banks were permitted to hold investments in commercial properties under the laws of their national incorporation. Congress adopted a scheme (embodied in Section 2(h) of the BHCA) under which foreign bank organizations principally engaged in banking abroad are permitted to have both a banking presence in the United States and to retain their holdings in commercial industrial companies principally engaged in business outside the United States but doing business in the United States, as long as the US business of the off-shore non-banking company is in the same line of business.

According to one commentator, the FRB has taken a narrow view of the meaning of principally engaged in banking business abroad so as to define which non–US banking organizations qualify for the 2(h) exemption of their US non-banking business. In the Competitive Equality of Banking Act of 1987, Congress rewrote Section 2(h) by adding Section 2(h)(iii) stating that nothing in the special authorization shall authorize a foreign bank holding company to "hold more than 5% of the outstanding shares of any class of voting securities of a company engaged in banking, securities activities, insurance or other financial activities in the United States."[207]

Under Section 214(b) of the FBSEA of 1991 (included in FDICIA), the FRB and the Treasury are required to submit to the Committee on Banking, Housing and Urban Affairs of the Senate and the House Banking Committee, a report analyzing:

1. The capital standards contained in the Basle Accord for measurement of capital adequacy;

2. Foreign regulatory capital standards that apply to foreign banks conducting banking operations in the United States; and

3. The relationship of the Basle and foreign capital standards to the risk-based capital and leverage requirements applicable to US banks.

The report is also required to include guidelines to be used by the FRB in converting data on the capital of foreign banks to the equivalent risk-based capital and leverage requirements for US banks for purposes of determination under Section 3 and 4 of the Bank Holding Company Act of 1956 and Section 7 of the IBA as amended.[208]

The joint study by the FRB and the Treasury[209] reveals that banks from Germany, Sweden and Belgium have not issued cumulative preferred stock that would be included in tier-one capital, even though they are permitted to do so;[210] and Japanese banks face legal obstacles in issuing such instruments. Canada, France, Italy, Japan, the Netherlands and the United States allow the inclusion of current-year profit and mandate the deduction of current-year losses in tier-one capital. In Germany, Hong Kong and Switzerland, the inclusion of current-year profit is not permitted, nor is the deduction of current-year losses required.[211] Similarly, any non-qualifying, intangible asset is required to be deducted from capital. Although certain qualifying and intangible rights may be included in capital, limited amounts of purchased mortgage servicing rights and purchased credit card good receivables would constitute qualifying intangible assets. These kinds of intangible assets are generally not available in other countries, except in the United Kingdom to a limited extent, largely because these markets lack a developed market for securitization. Undisclosed reserves may be included in tier-two capital, however in Germany such reserves may be included only to the extent that they have been taxed.[212] Hybrid capital instruments may be included in tier-two capital provided (1) issuance is on an unsecured subordinated and fully paid-up basis; (2) they are not re-deemable at the initiative of the holder or without the prior consent of the supervisory authority; (3) they are available to participate in losses without the bank being obliged to cease trading; and (4) they may carry an obligation to pay interest that cannot be permanently reduced or waived, but service obligations should be deferrable when the profitability of the bank would not support payment. Hybrid instruments exist in the United States, Germany, France and the United Kingdom, and although traditionally prohibited by Japan, these prohibitions have recently been relaxed.[213]

Subordinated term debt may be carried in tier-two capital up to a limit of 50% of tier-one capital. Theoretically, bank regulators in all countries subscribing to the G–10 Agreement, except Germany, permit the inclusion of subordinated term debt in tier-two within the 50% limit. However, in practice banks in most countries, with the exception of the United States and the United Kingdom, have not issued such subordinated term debt.[214]

Countries in which banks have not issued limited, redeemable, preferred stock to date include France, Japan, the Netherlands and Belgium.[215]

Reevaluation reserves arise primarily in two ways: the first instance is with regard to the reevaluation of fixed assets, such as is permitted in Belgium, France, Italy, the Netherlands and the United Kingdom. However, this historically has not been permitted by accounting practices in the United States, Germany and Japan. A means to achieve the same result has been the sale leaseback in the United States. Another form of reevaluation is the latent reevaluation reserve which arises from long-term holdings of equity securities valued on the basis of their original cost. To date, only Japan and Hong Kong have permitted the inclusion of latent reevaluation reserves in tier-two capital. The German authorities at present have under consideration a proposal to allow the inclusion of latent reevaluation reserves within tier two but only for banks with a tier-one capital ratio of at least 5%. Such reserves would be limited to a maximum of one percentage point in tier-two capital.[216]

General loan reserves are included up to the full 1.25% of total risk assets permitted by the G–10 Agreement in the United Kingdom, France, Japan and the United States, although they are excluded in such countries as Canada, Belgium and Hong Kong. The existence and treatment of general loan loss reserves within tier two varies from country to country as does the distinction between specific, general and problem country loan loss reserves, in spite of a 1991 amendment in the definition of general loan loss reserves by the G–10 Basle Committee.[217] According to the US Treasury FRB study, these changes were in part directed at US practices with regard to the inclusion of country risk in general provisions.[218] US regulators concluded that the revised language was not in conflict with current US practices and announced that there would be no change in US requirements.

Under the G–10 Agreement, capital would be deducted where subsidiaries are not consolidated, provided that this type of investment constitutes more than 10% of the capital of the investee. The purpose is to avoid double-counting of capital. In the United States and Japan, such investments must be deducted only if the sole purpose of the investment is to increase the capital ratio. Under the EEC directive, only that part of the investment in excess of 10% is to be deducted.

The risk weight assigned to privately issued residential mortgage-backed securities varies from 50% in the United States to 100% in many countries, particularly members of the EEC. Supervisors in the United States view mortgage-backed securities as indirect holdings of the underlying mortgages, and thus US banks may assign a 50% risk weight (or if government backed, 0%), while most other countries do not have a market for mortgage bank securities, and banks generally hold residential mortgages on their books until maturity.

Pursuant to the FRB Treasury study, the FRB declined to impose a "hard wire test" for capital equivalents. Such a test may actually be impossible to employ. It is difficult to tell whether one financial system or another has higher capital requirements given the complexity of many factors, particularly the market for perpetual preferred and subordinated debt, the treatment of loan loss reserves, reevaluation assets and the market for securitization and treatment of current year profits and losses.

One commentator has remarked on the advantage of subordinated term debt in that it provides a means for banks to expand assets that are market-determined, rather than relying on a regulatory substitute.[219] The distinction between equity and loan loss reserves leaves room for ambiguity and is not a "hard" number. The absence of subordinated term debt in certain markets may nonetheless make bank capital more secure. Term debt with less than five years duration, even though discounted at 50%, may nonetheless have a deleterious affect on the safety and soundness of the banking system if its chances of renewal are less than clear, in spite of its inability to participate in any priority distributions. In general, subordinated term debt raises the slippery slope of the distinction between banking and securities activities. Subordinated term debt is quite common in securities markets and is permitted up to 250% of core capital under the EEC CAD,[220] and even more short-term capital is permitted under US broker/dealer capital requirements in an underwriting.[221] As banks securitize their assets and hold generally shorter maturity liabilities, subordinated debt is an appropriate form of capital, and certain types of cumulative preferred debt may be superior to other forms of tier-one capital. However, to the extent that banks hold long-term liabilities, capital must remain similarly long-term. Because securities firms' assets are marked to market, they pose inherently less distortionary possibilities.

Part VII: Policy Perspectives

One of the benefits which is claimed by proponents of bank entry into the securities business is portfolio diversity. What are the benefits and disadvantages of portfolio product diversification by banks? Certain pairwise combinations can, in fact, reduce risks by combining bank and non-bank activities. For example, underwriting of corporate equity securities was less risky between 1976 and 1983 than the underwriting of corporate bonds, based on variations and the spread between the issue price and secondary market price transactions during the underwriting period the securities were offered for sale.[222]

The fact that banks could reduce their risk exposure by entering certain individual non-banking activities does not address the number of different non-banking activities which could simultaneously offer opportunities to

reduce risks.[223] This shortcoming can be addressed by estimating activities.[224]

In the period 1973 to 1982, banking was the least risky and the least profitable activity, and at the other extreme an insurance agency was the riskiest and highest earning activity.[225] Portfolio theory suggests that potential gains will always exist if investment choices are widened.[226] However, accelerating the removal of financial product line restrictions may increase risks to the financial system, because deposits are federally insured and "moral hazard" may make bankers more willing to engage in risky activities given their ready access to funds. In a study of 324 thrifts that failed between December 1981 and October 1985, the Federal Home Loan Bank Board (FHLBB) investigators determined that the relative amount of direct investments was positively correlated to a statistically significant degree to the cost that the FHLBB incurred in closing failed thrifts and assisting in their merger with healthy institutions,[227] and this level of loss is far greater than the average loss of 15 to 20 cents on the dollar that Federal Savings and Loan Insurance Corporation (FSLIC) experiences on failed thrifts generally.[228] According to the Bank Board staff, of the 37 thrifts that have made direct investments exceeding 10% of assets in December 1983, 21 either failed or were near failure by October 1986.

Given the advantages of portfolio diversification by banks, taken together with the systemic risks of such diversification, there are few means of driving a wedge between the polarities. Litan has created a highly attractive model of narrow banks that would enable financial holding companies (FHCs) to diversify their holdings, while insuring the safety and soundness of the payment system by requiring them to isolate their federally insured deposits in a bank which has only a limited permissible range of lending.[229] This limited range includes treasury bills, federally insured bonds, federally guaranteed securities (such as Ginnie Maes and Fannie Maes) and also includes short-term commercial paper. The interest rate risk of long-term treasuries and the credit risks of commercial paper could be mitigated by the higher spread between interest rates on deposits and lending. Certainly, this proposal resolves many of the conventional problems of the banking industry. To the extent that banks remove their commercial real estate activities from the banking safety net, the Bank Insurance Fund will be in a better state. But what could induce them to do this?

The narrow bank proposal would prevent holding companies from using the resources of their depositories to bail out risky non-bank affiliates because the deposit-insured subsidiary or affiliate is limited to investing in high quality marketable instruments so it could not legally channel its funds to support affiliated corporations, and it may not be able to channel dividends to their parent holding companies.

The narrow bank proposal would ultimately allow for low deposit in-

surance premiums. The proposal generates extremely complex questions about the nature of banks, and whether banks are special. The proposal speaks extremely well to minimizing payment system risks. In other words, to the extent that the banking system is a payment system, the system would be protected. It may be necessary for the FRB to require that all intraday transfers of bank credit to non-bank affiliates be fully collateralized.[230]

Among the possible objections raised to the narrow bank proposal is that increased interest rates will result because FHCs will be forced to rely on uninsured deposits, but the process of financial disintermediation has reduced the differential between rates paid on CDs and those on commercial paper, and regulatory costs would be lower for FHC, also reducing the spread. One additional objection is that, as discussed above, the backup facilities (including NIFs and RUFs, which banks provide to the commercial paper market) are a large reason for commercial paper market stability. There is some possibility that a threatened failure of an FHC lender could cause contraction of economic activity, and the FRB may be enticed to organize a rescue.[231]

How to insulate the payment system from the expansion of banking activities remains an open question. In spite of the prudential effect of Sections 23A and B,[232] it is likely that bank holding companies will use various mechanisms to channel resources from their banks to their non-bank corporations by imposing higher fees for management services or by increasing depository tax reimbursements to affiliated companies or by making sole adjustments to interaffiliate pricing. Former Citicorp chairman Walter Wriston has observed "it is inconceivable that any major bank would walk away from any of its subsidiaries of its holding companies. If your name is on the door, all of your capital funds are going to be hiding in the real world. Lawyers can say you have separation, but the market place is pervasive and it would not see it that way."[233] Professor Hal Scott of Harvard Law School focuses the debate by insisting that prudential matters including limitations on underwriting activities by banks are necessary only insofar as these activities pose systemic risk to the payment system.[234]

The Fedwire settlement process is intraday[235] and all the rules requiring proper collateralization for loans may be insufficient in the event of a rapid market break. Thus, any process which expands bank powers, even through affiliates or subsidiaries, is rife with possibilities for creating unsustainable systemic risks in payment systems, because judgements required under Sections 23A and B are difficult to make (consider the term "collateralization") and would be particularly difficult to make in the event of rapidly deteriorating securities and derivative markets. The attempts by the FRB to transmit easing of monetary policy, as it did in 1987, may run into difficulties if banks lend to their own affiliates and subsidiaries as opposed

to independent brokers and dealers. Even the current degree of banks underwriting poses problems to interconnecting payment systems in the event of a market break.

One limitation of the narrow bank idea is that banks are inevitably exposed to systemic risk in the securities market. Even if the FRB can lend directly to broker-dealers,[236] it will not be able to make the necessary credit decisions.

The accelerating securitization of credit claims, ownership claims and derivative contracts is a fundamental phenomenon of financial markets according to David Folkerts-Landau of the International Monetary Fund. An important form of securitization has been the growth of negotiable, high quality, short-term, non-bank and corporate obligations (i.e., commercial paper and certificates of deposit) and the growth of exchanged, traded derivative products, such as interest rate futures. Also, a substantial portion of banks' illiquid assets have been securitized by the repackaging and sale of bank assets into tradeable securities, particularly mortgage-backed government insured securities. The extent of the "securitized assets" of the US banking system are substantially in excess of that of other countries. Additionally, wholesale money center banks may finance their assets/liabilities with bought funds, such as negotiable CDs, interbank funds and repurchase agreements. More important, a liquidity crisis may develop where non-bank–funded financial intermediaries rely on banks to provide credit. According to Folkerts-Landau "participants on organized futures and options markets, the heart of last-day case development in financial engineering, make intensive use of bank lines because of the requirement of nearly instantaneous delivery of cash needed to satisfy margin calls. Credit lines to banks are the only practical method of assuring such delivery."[237] By contrast, Germany's clearing of payments is effectively done internally in banking organizations or among a small group of tightly connected banks, and because of the absence of developed securities markets, few occasions will arise where funds are demanded on a large scale for unexpected settlements.

Perhaps the most telling objection to the narrow bank proposal is that it would frustrate the FRB's conduct of monetary policy. To the extent that the FRB conducts monetary policy through reserve requirements, the process of monetary policy will not be affected. However, to the extent that money creation results from diversified bank lending, there is a substantial likelihood that monetary policy will be affected.[238] And a ten-year transition period would be necessary to give the market time to absorb the increased demand that new narrow banks would place on treasury markets. What we know about monetary creation and monetary policy has been affected by the recent credit crunch. The diversion of bank liabilities from commercial and industrial loans to long-term treasuries has been one major factor of the inability of the FRB policy of monetary easing to be satis-

factorily transmitted, as discussed below. There are two components to this policy. To the extent that interest rate risks could be minimized in the narrow bank proposal, the remaining concern would still be the constriction of credit. Would FHCs be able to provide the credit that banks currently provide, or would overall credit diminish, particularly as the result of the higher price paid for uninsured deposits by FHCs?

The FRB's role as prudential supervisor has recently conflicted with its role in shaping monetary policy. The recent behavior of monetary aggregates has appeared to have reacted to the rechanneling of credit flows away from depository institutions.[239] Reduced depository intermediation, according to Greenspan, stems from emerging problems of asset quality, which prompted responses by regulators that reenforced those tendencies. The net effect of bad loans in the commercial banking industry has been a sharp decrease in funds supplied by private financial institutions from $536 billion to $337 billion between 1989 and 1991 with commercial banks falling even more—53% from $177 billion to $83 billion.[240] The S&L crisis caused the sharp contraction of lending by thrifts, which contracted in 1990 and 1991 by about $90 billion each year.[241]

Banks tightened their non-price lending term and credit standards appreciably and widened the spreads of lending rates relative to cost of funds.[242] Upward pressure on bank loan rates created by closer regulatory supervision was augmented as regulators, concerned about adequate bank capitalization, raised risk premiums on banks.[243] As intermediation costs rose because of greater costs of funding and closer regulatory supervision, banks continued to increase loan spreads and constrained their expansion in their balance sheets. Recent regulatory initiatives in the FDICIA[244] have further elevated the cost of intermediation. According to Greenspan's testimony, lending spreads have stayed relatively high, as suggested by a prime rate that as of July 1991 was a substantial 2-¾ points above the Federal Funds Rate.[245] Banks with little demand for funds have also lowered rates on retail time deposits more than market rates have declined[246] and have cut back on broker deposits. Consequently, a process of rechanneling credit flows away from depositories has ensued. As a result investors have chosen to pay down debts rather than to hold low-yielding monetary assets. Funds have also been rechanneled away from low-yielding deposits to take advantage of higher-yielding assets on longer term debt and equity instruments. Bonds and stock mutual funds, in particular, have recorded substantial inflows.[247]

The increased percentage of bank assets that are invested in treasuries may be correlated with the failure of the FRB monetary policy to stimulate the economy. The percentage of bank assets invested in US government securities has risen from 15.1% in 1985 to 27% in 1992, and commercial and industrial loans have fallen from 27.7% to 19.4% of all assets over the same period.[248] These increases in securities holdings are represented

largely by holdings of government securities. The capital adequacy rule, which the United States implemented pursuant to the G–10 Agreement,[249] has been partly responsible for reduced bank lending to the private sector, and the FRB's target range for growth of M–2 and M–3 was not met in 1991 and 1992. Litan notes that banks that were less well capitalized displayed little tendency to be more heavily invested in commercial real estate loans than those banks that were well capitalized, and that smaller banks showed no strong evidence of moral hazard behavior by increasing such investments and may have actually decreased their investment in commercial real estate.[250] The inevitability of bank entry into the securities business that stands behind the FHC proposal would stand on rather slim ground were it not for the EEC CAD.[251] The fact that the CAD directive provides for such capital standards for trading books of banks and credit institutions involves an inevitable tendency towards securitization of credit business and even more so towards conducting securities activity generally, rather than traditional lending activities. If traditional lending business cannot compete with securities business internationally, US banks, if not deregulated, may be subject to intensive foreign competition. One option is to require foreign banks to do business in the United States only in a subsidiary form. More probably, FHCs and the narrow bank represent an idea whose time has come, given trends in regulation, internationally.

The narrow bank's main attraction is to tighten the bank safety net and reduce the costs of deposit insurance to taxpayers; but the narrow bank may impinge on the effectiveness of monetary policy by shrinking the assets of institutions which have direct access to the federal funds rate (or the discount window) and impede monetary policy.

As the conduct of monetary policy has moved from the late 1970s through the 1980s into the exclusive arena of the FRB, the regulation of credit institutions ought to move away from Congress toward independent administrative agencies. Because the issues in banking regulation will always remain legitimately within the scope of congressional power, a process must be arrived at whereby consultation between Congress and an administrative agency concerned with regulating credit institutions and securities is ongoing. It may also be that the human capital required for regulating credit institutions differs fundamentally from that required for the conduct of monetary policy. If this is so, a new federal agency ought to be created to be directly responsible (or an existing one, such as the OCC, revamped) to have exclusive administrative authority to regulate financial institutions, including credit institutions as well as other financial institutions.[252]

A variant of the narrow bank idea is the core bank proposal that allows banks to perform functions that are traditionally bank activities, including lending to small businesses and small real estate concerns. This proposal has an advantage over the narrow bank proposal in that those borrowers whose loans are neither speculative, that is, large commercial real estate

development, nor capable of being securitized, are left out of the narrow bank arena, but both proposals are deficient in that they fail to explain how these "clean" banks can emerge.

The other extreme from a narrow bank proposal would be a proposal that would regulate non-bank finance companies and money market mutual funds as banks by broadening the definition or interpretation of deposit-taking under the National Banking Act of 1864.

The justification for regulating money market funds and finance companies as banks[253] is that these funds are able to secure backup facilities from banks that basically provide them with access to the payment system at minimal cost. Certainly the operating expenses of money market mutual funds are far lower than those of banks, and the unbundling of financial risks may suggest that commercial paper can lower the costs of borrowing to credit worthy borrowers. But this is an insulated view of the process of credit allocation. First, commercial banks must allocate assets between different sectors of the economy while the commercial paper market is a distinctly carved out part of this process; it is invested in triple-A companies (of course, some of these companies, like GM, Westinghouse and IBM are not triple-A any longer) and for periods of no more than 90 days. Second, commercial paper relies on the banking system for the guarantee underwriting facilities. The fact that banks have been unable to price these facilities appropriately does reflect part of the moral hazard endemic in an insurance deposit system. However, the commercial paper market would be impossible without this backup facility. Because banks aren't able to appropriately price these underwriting facilities indicates that in this and other ways banks must be protected from the vagaries of a deregulated market. Banks' inability to sufficiently price these backup facilities to reflect risk is an indication that some kind of legislation is required to protect the payment system.

It may be argued that if prompt, corrective action had been employed in the S&L crisis, commercial banks would have invested less in commercial real estate and would have had more of their portfolio in residential loans (because insolvent thrifts would not have made these loans). Regardless of what caused the precarious financial condition of commercial banks, they would be greatly aided by a new market for real estate loans. Such a market would evolve if money market mutual funds and finance companies were regulated as banks because regulatory costs would require them to expand into the commercial and industrial loans (and real estate) as the issuing of commercial paper would no longer be sufficient to cover the cost of money market funds, and finance companies (which are already in the commercial real estate lending business to a certain extent) would be forced to compete on a more level playing field with banks. Because none of the other categories of institutional investors (pension funds or insurance companies) would be likely to assume any more commercial real

estate lending in the future, providing a new entrant into commercial real estate lending would greatly alleviate the problems of the banking sector. Certainly the cost of commercial paper issuance would rise, but this is probably a necessary expedient. Although this would cause a rise in the cost of consumer lending, the long-term interest of the financial sector would be better served by measures to broaden the market for commercial real estate loans.

The consequence of this "parallel banking system" has been an extension of consumer credit, for example, factory to dealer incentives which pass through in terms of credit allocation by finance companies. The competition which banks faced from finance companies reduced their industrial loans substantially as a percentage of total loans throughout the 1980s, causing them to seek other kinds of borrowers, particularly real estate borrowers. The aggressive consumer credit programs offered by non-banks and finance companies led to cut-throat competition where banks extended credit to consumers in terms that may not have been appropriate.[254]

The growth of consumer lending in the 1980s proceeded on non-price lines and included the proliferation of credit cards and other channels of credit. Total credit increased from $5 to $10 trillion between 1985 to 1991, overshadowing monetary policy.[255]

The ratio of total liabilities to income cranked up by about 0.3% a year between 1961 and 1976. Between 1976 to 1990, that ratio grew by 1.5 points a year.[256] The fraction of households owning at least one bank credit card increased from 16% in 1970 to 54% in 1989.[257] The average down payment as a fraction of house value for first-time home buyers declined from 18% in 1976 to 11.4% in 1985.[258]

The percentage of individuals who were delinquent on mortgage payments tended steadily upward from the early 1970s to the 1980s.[259] Additionally, auto loans and bank credit cards showed higher rates of delinquency in the mid–1980s and early 1990s than any other time since 1955. Data on other delinquency rates, foreclosure rates, personal bankruptcies and other measures confirm the impression that from the mid to late 1980s, there was a substantial increase in debt repayment problems. Developments in information technology may have made it easier to swap information on prospective borrowers as the number of credit reports grew from $60 million in 1960 to $100 million in 1970 to $400 million in 1990.[260] The loosening of credit had either halted or began to reverse with the credit crunch of 1990 and the personal savings rate had gradually improved from that time, averaging 4% in 1989, 4.3% in 1990, 4.7% in 1991 and 5.2% in the first half of 1992.[261]

The conduct of monetary policy has been uppermost in the agenda of the FRB, certainly since Volcker's tenure and to a large extent since World War II. The failure to target credit as a policy objective has been intermingled with a lax policy of prudential supervision, and the two are not

unrelated. The expansion of finance companies and unregulated non-banks led to a proliferation of credit which borrowers generally accepted on non-price terms. The hostility of the FRB to credit rationing is pointedly observable in Volcker's account of the Carter credit rationing program. Volcker portrays himself as unable to stem the contraction of the money supply resulting from rationing, although the higher interest rates he had employed had been unable to accomplish the same results.[262]

Part VIII: Conclusion

The sting of the GSA appears to be eroding under the auspices of the judiciary and the FRB. However, other barriers such as the barrier separating banks from insurance companies may continue to pose a threat to the competitiveness of US banking institutions. In Europe, vast insurance banking conglomerates such as Alliance Dresner Bank (the French Bank Assurance, the West German Allfinanz and the Japanese Ginsei) are in the process of formation,[263] and the threat posed by finance companies such as American Express, which is the largest financial institution in the United States and other consumer credit organizations is quite overpowering, as is the commercial paper market which makes such finance companies possible. The regulation of non-bank banks has not received enough attention. The conditional credit facilities that banks supply to the commercial paper issuers may pose the largest single threat to the banking system.

Securitization of assets that are transparent ought to be considered as securities-eligible activities. The fact that banks did not share in the underwriting fees on $769 billion in securitized mortgages is extremely unfortunate, given the special role of banks in providing stability in the domestic and international financial system. That banks have only recently been allowed to underwrite commercial paper is also unfortunate, but to turn caution to the winds, as some regulators and the bank lobby would have us do, might only be to invoke a new "disaster myopia" similar to that evident in the global debt crisis of the 1970s or the thrift crisis of the 1980s. It may be that placing greater restrictions on investment banking would offset the risks of liberalization of the securities activities of banks, creating a universal banking safety net.

While it may be true that the dual system of the GSA is obsolete, and universal banking is a global trend, any attempt at deregulation of banks ought to impose stringent safety regulations, including limitations on exposure to loans in different sectors, perhaps with collateral requirements. Perhaps there should be stringent dollar limits on firm commitment underwriting and strict prohibitions of enhancement of credit of any securities by any bank affiliate of the underwriter of such securities. Furthermore, regulations as to the kind and grade of investment to be owned by pension funds, insurance companies, and S&Ls, ought to be restrictive and

perhaps be confined to triple-A bonds and annuities. Another view is that the marketplace serves as a better rating agency than the federal government, and that Moody's is more efficient than the FRB at providing ratings, particularly so because of the relevant regulators' monopolistic position, but this view is myopic because any threat of systemic risk will inevitably result in taxpayer bail-outs.[264]

The trend toward securitization will continue. Banks will always be necessary for small and medium-sized commercial borrowers, and such special circumstances cannot be pooled. Banks are also necessary to transmit monetary policy. If banks had been deeply involved in securities activities in 1987, would it have been possible to lower the discount rate or would banks' extension of credit to their subsidiaries have had the adverse effect, leading to complete collapse of the banking system? This question has not even been raised in the financial modernization debate.

Japanese banks have capitalization problems because the market value of equity ownership has slumped—the Nikkei has fallen 40% from its 1989 high—and have consequently retrenched foreign lending; thus, any immediate threat of Japanese domination of our banking system has been warded off; but strong capitalization of continental European banks will make them strongly competitive in the United States, although securitization is diminishing the relative importance of banks in Europe.

It is paradoxical that financial innovation leads to the predominance of securities financing over banking finance and that those countries with less developed securities markets have preeminent banks that will continue to capture a large share of the US banking market and impede the transmission of domestic monetary policy.[265] The diminishing power of banks may also disadvantage small businesses that only rarely, through venture capital firms, can access securities markets.

Current problems of the US banking system may be attributed to a regulatory lag between the realities of international banking and the inadequacy of contemporaneous legislation. Regulation Q made financial institutions uncompetitive with unregulated money market investment management companies. By the time these regulations were lifted, substantial losses had been suffered by regulated banks and thrifts. Despite this regulatory gap, thrifts would undoubtedly have been insolvent simply because their portfolio of assets was so heavily invested in long-term mortgages when interest rates skyrocketed in the mid–1970s.

Free market economists may oppose any form of governmental interference in a bank's determination of its portfolio of assets. But, as long as government deposit insurance is considered a public good, government must have a role in evaluating the long-term safety and soundness of bank portfolios. Deterioration of bank portfolios brought about the flourishing of the commercial paper market and finance companies in the early 1980s. The consequence of finance companies was to shift the center of gravity

of previous net lending by financial institutions. Not only did the lender change, so did the borrower. Funds which had previously been lent by banks are now lent by the commercial paper market, and these funds created a new source of consumer credit. In the quest for new business, banks greatly increased their portfolio of real estate loans, particularly in response to the Monetary Deposit Act and the Garn–St. Germain.[266] Furthermore, banks took on obligations to provide low profit margin guarantee underwriting facilities for the commercial paper market (such as RUFs and NIFs). Because finance companies were unregulated, and thus not subject to the costs of regulation, reserve requirements and deposit insurance premiums, they were able to capture and were in part responsible for the growing consumer credit market, and they were free riders of the underwriting facilities provided by banks. These circumstances would not have existed if finance companies were regulated as banks, which is functionally what they were. In order to regulate finance companies as banks within the current bank holding company restrictions, commercial companies would have to divest their holdings in such finance companies. However, they should be allowed to continue owning finance companies and making commercial loans that are incidental to their business (for example, GMAC should be able to make car loans).

Narrow banks answer some of the problems posed by the international movement toward securitization; but the Narrow Bank/FHC option will not induce most banks to move their assets out of insured depositories (where subject to certain write-downs, assets, particularly real estate, may be held at book value), at least in the short term. In the long term, narrow banks may be a viable option if their investing powers are better enumerated and inducements are offered to preserve small business lending (inside or outside the narrow bank); yet narrow banks, since they may be the only banks whose access to the discount window is viable, will still be exposed to risks posed by securities firms that require access to the payment system. Allowing full-scale underwriting by banks, without prudential limitation—at least an outright prohibition on lending to securities affiliates—is ill-advised.

NOTES

1. Department of the Treasury, *Modernizing Our Financial System: Recommendations for Safe and More Competitive Banks* (1991).

2. "Financial Institutions Safety and Consumer Choice Act of 1991," Report of the Committee on Banking, Finance and Urban Affairs, House of Representatives of the Committee of Banking, Finance and Urban Affairs, House of Representatives Report 102–157, Part 1–2 (June 23, 1991).

3. "Financial Institutions Safety and Consumer Choice Act of 1991," Title 3, reprinted in Banking Committee Report, *supra* note 2.

4. *Ibid.*, Title 2, Regulatory Improvement—Subtitle A—Diversified and Financial Services Holding Company.

5. *Ibid.*, Title 4, § 4.1, amending § 2 of the Bank Holding Company Act of 1956 (12 USC § 1841), amending §§ 2, 3, and 4 of the Bank Holding Company Act (12 USC §§ 1841, 1842, and 1843). Subtitle C, "Financial Activities of National Banks," § 431, Securities Activities of National Banks, amending the paragraph designated as the "seventh" of § 5136 of the Revised Statutes (12 USC § 24 [7th]) (as amended by § 234b of this Act) § 433, amendments to §§ 23A and 23B of the Federal Reserve Act (12 USC § 371).

6. "Comprehensive Deposit Insurance Reform and Taxpayer Protection Act of 1991," Report of the Committee on Banking, Housing and Urban Affairs, United States Senate to accompany § 543 together with additional news, October 1, 1991.

7. *Ibid.*, Title 3.

8. *Ibid.*, Title 7.

9. *International Banking Competitiveness—Why It Matters*, A Report of the Economic Advisory Committee of the American Bankers Association, March 1990, p. 1.

10. *Ibid.*

11. *Ibid.*, at 7.

12. *Ibid.*

13. Public Law 73–66; 48 Statute 188; *See infra* notes 18–20 for citation to sections of the Glass-Steagall Act.

14. National banks, that is, those banks with federal charters, are regulated by the Office of the Controller of the Currency (OCC). Banks with state charters which are members of the Federal Reserve System are regulated by the Board of Governors of the Federal Reserve Bank and by state regulatory agencies. State-chartered banks that are not members of the Federal Reserve System are regulated by state regulators and, if they are federally insured, by the Federal Deposit Insurance Corporation (FDIC). Savings and Loan Associations (S&Ls) were regulated by the Federal Savings & Loan Insurance Corporation (FSLIC), but since the beginning of 1989 they are regulated by the successor to FSLIC, the Office of Thrift Supervision (OTS). The regulation of S&Ls differs fundamentally from that of commercial banks. For example, S&Ls had at one time 20% of their capital invested in junk bonds, whereas commercial banks were not allowed to undertake such investments and have only recently been allowed to purchase high-grade securities. The difference in regulatory schemes was originally justified by the fact that mortgage loans tended to be made by S&Ls, whereas this no longer seems to be the case.

Bank holding companies are regulated by the FRB, no matter which agency regulates their commercial bank subsidiaries. Bank holding companies have been used to create financial conglomerates that could conceivably serve to fuse securities underwriting and commercial banking activities.

15. Robert Litan, *The Revolution in US Finance*, The Frank M. Ingall Lecture in Economic Security presented on April 30, 1991, at the American College, Bryn Mawr, Pennsylvania (Brookings Institution, Washington, D.C., 1991).

16. Money Market Deposit Accounts and Negotiable Order of Withdrawal Accounts (NOWs).

17. Litan, *supra* note 15, at 18.

18. 7th Provision of 12 USC § 24 made applicable to state member banks by 12 USC § 335 (1985).

19. *Ibid.*

20. 12 USC § 377.

21. *Ibid*, and § 378(a).

22. Federal Reserve Act, Chapter VI, § 23(a)–(b), 38 Stat. 251, 272–273 (1913) codified as amended in different sections of 12 USC.

23. 12 USC § 371(c).

24. 12 USC § 371(c)(1).

25. O.J. Eur. Comm. L. 386, p. 1 (1989).

26. 12 USC § 84.

27. *See* for example, N.Y. Jur.2d § 4823, Banking and Financial Institutions, limiting loans to one borrower to 10% of capital although such loans may not include affiliates of corporations.

28. 401 U.S. 617 (1971).

29. *Ibid.*, at 630–633.

30. 450 U.S. 46 (1981).

31. 468 U.S. 207 (1984).

32. *Seligman* (1982–1983 Transfer Binder) Fed. Banking L. Rep. (CCH) 99,463 (Feb. 2, 1983) Dreyfus (1982–1983 Transfer Binder) Fed. Banking L. Rep. (CCH) 99,464 (Feb. 7, 1983). Normally, bank holding companies are regulated by the FRB under the Bank Holding Company Act, but the bank in question was structured to accept demand deposits but not make commercial loans. Therefore, the FRB lacked jurisdiction. The Bank Holding Company Act (12 USC § 1842 (1982)) requires that approval be obtained from the FRB whenever a company acquires control of a bank; one of the criteria that the Board considers is the financial resources of the proposed holding company.

33. 468 US 137 (1984).

34. *Ibid.*, at 160.

35. *Securities Industry Association v. Board of Governors*, 807 F.2d 1052 (D.C. Cir., 1986), *cert. denied*, 403 U.S. 1005 (1987).

36. 839 F.2d 47 (2d Cir.), *cert. denied* 108 S. Ct. 2830 (1988).

37. *Board of Governors, Federal Reserve System v. Agnew*, 329 U.S. 441, 67 S. Ct. 411 (1947).

38. *J.P. Morgan and Co., Inc., Chase Manhattan Corp., Bankers Trust New York Corp., Citicorp, and Securities Pacific Corp.* (75 Fed. Reserve Bull. 192 (March 1989)).

39. 12 USC § 1843 (1982).

40. *J.P. Morgan, supra* note 38, at 196.

41. *Ibid.*, at 195–196.

42. *Ibid.*, at 212–213.

43. 12 CFR 211(5)(D)(13) as revised June 20, 1979, in 44 Fed. Reg. 36,007.

44. These prudential prohibitions were in addition to other prohibitions contained in an earlier FRB order allowing banks to underwrite a narrow range of eligible securities (*Citicorp/Morgan/Bankers Trust*, 73 Fed. Reserve Bull. at 485), and preclude the holding company or any affiliate from purchasing eligible securities from the subsidiary during the underwriting and for 60 days thereafter (*J.P. Morgan, supra* note 38, at 202). The J.P. Morgan decision changes this to 30 days (*Ibid.*

at 208), and prevents banks from lending to issuers to enhance the creditworthiness of securities underwritten by underwriting subsidiary.

45. Michael S. Raab, *The Transparency Theory: An Alternative Approach to Glass-Steagall Issues*, 97 YALE L.J., 603, 607 (1988). *See also*, letter of Brian Smith, Chief Counsel of the OCC (April 12, 1983) rep. 1M (1983–1984 Transfer Binder) Fed. Banking L. Rep. (CCH) § 88.421 at 77.544 granting approval for bank's sale of pass-through certificates backed by FHA-insured mortgages. Donald Langevoort, *Statutory Obsolescence and the Judicial Process: The Role of the Courts in Federal Banking Regulation*, 85 Mich. L. Rev. 672, 690–691 (1987).

46. Committee on Banking Supervision, Convergence of Risk-based Capital Adequacy Standards (July 1988).

47. Official Journal of the European Committee L. 386, p. 1 *et seq.* (Dec. 31, 1989).

48. Litan, *supra* note 18, at 14 to 15 (Source: Fed. Reserve Bull., various issues).

49. "Asset Securitization: A Supervisory Perspective," 75 Fed. Reserve Bull. 658, 664 (1989).

50. Final Rule Amendment to Regulations H and Y (75 Fed. Reserve Bull. 157 and Appendix 164, 165). Capital Adequacy Guidelines for Risk Based Measures. If the securities representing the indebtedness are interest only or principal only strips, the strips will be treated as 100% risk because of the interest rate risk (*Ibid.*, at 180).

51. *Id.*, at 664.

52. *Ibid.*

53. 703 F. Supp. 256, 260 (S.D.N.Y. 1988).

54. *SIA v. Clarke* 885 F.2d 1034 (2d Cir.), *cert. denied*, 493 U.S. 1070 (1989).

55. *J.P. Morgan, supra* note 38, at 193.

56. *Ibid.*, at 214. At that time set out in Capital Adequacy Guidelines 50 Fed. Reg. 16,057 (1985) and 71 Fed. Reserve Bull. 445 (1985).

57. *J.P. Morgan, supra* note 38, at 206–207. The Board also adopted two other provisions: (1) bank holding companies may not enter into agreements to engage in reciprocal transactions with other bank holding companies for the purpose of evading the operating limitations in this order and other limitations; (2) a bank may not directly or indirectly treat unaffiliated securities firms less favorably than an affiliate underwriting subsidiary, unless the denial is based on objective criteria.

58. *Ibid.*, 207–208.

59. In order to arrive at its decision, the Board rejected SIA's argument that the market for corporate debt and the equities securities market are much more volatile than the market for non-corporate income securities and that US banks suffered large losses in London in 1986 and 1987 thereby demonstrating ineptitude in these markets. *J.P. Morgan, supra* note 38, at 211.

60. *J.P. Morgan, supra* note 38 at 202. Note also that applicants may deduct 50% of the amount of the investment in the underwriting subsidiary from tier-one capital and 50% from tier-two capital. (*Ibid.*)

61. Federal Reserve System, "Report to Congressional Committee Regarding Differences in Capital and Accounting Standards Among the Federal Banking and Thrift Agencies." Banking L. Rep. (CCH) ¶ 5412. *See* Chapter 1, *supra* note 84, for the UK approach to consolidation of capital ratios.

62. Interviews with staff of the FRB, November and December 1992.

63. 74 Fed. Reserve Bull. 829 (1989).

64. *Ibid.*, at 833.

65. *Supra* note 35.

66. *See supra* note 38, and accompanying text.

67. *Supra* note 63.

68. *Ibid.*, at 829–830.

69. *Ibid.*, at 831 and 832.

70. *Ibid.*, at 833.

71. 76 Fed. Reserve Bull. 26 (1990).

72. *Banker's Trust, supra* note 63.

73. 76 Fed. Reserve Bull., at 28.

74. *Ibid.*

75. § 230.144A Private Resale To Institutions, Fed. Sec. L. Rep. (CCH) 84,523 (May 5, 1990).

76. *Ibid.*

77. New York Times, September 21, 1990, p. 1.

78. *J.P. Morgan, supra* note 38.

79. Wall Street Journal, September 21, 1990, p. 1.

80. *Supra* note 75.

81. *J.P. Morgan, supra* note 38, at 192.

82. *Bankers Trust I*, 408 U.S. 134 (1984).

83. The application of § 5 (registration requirements) of the Securities Exchange Act has been known to result in US persons being excluded from investment opportunities. (*See* The Division of Market Regulatory Securities and Exchange, *Commission Summary of Internationalization Roundtable* on February 17, 1987, p. 21. *See also*, Note, *Moving Away from Section 5*, 102 U. Pa. J. Int. Bus. L. 225 (1988). Traditionally, restrictions against sale to US persons are often included in offering documents for non–US persons to ensure that the offerings are not sold to US persons until they have come to rest abroad within the definition of Security Act Release #4708 (1964 Transfer Binder) Fed. Sec. L. Rep. (CCH) §§ 1361–63 (1964). One of the complicated results from this act is the security of a US issuer is more likely to return to the United States and therefore such issuers are required to take more precautions. The Commission has made a proposal to the effect that any offer or sale that occurs within the United States is subject to Section 5 and any offers or sales that occur outside the United States are not. The safe harbor for this proposal would require that the buyer be offshore at the time of the buyer's order and that the transaction be consummated overseas, that the sale not be prearranged for persons in the United States or be made on or through the facilities of an established foreign security exchange. Offshore Offers and Sales, Securities Act Release # 6779 (1987–88 Transfer Binder) Fed. Sec. L. Rep (CCH) § 84,242 (June 10, 1988).

84. J.G.S. Jeanneau, "Structural Changes in World Capital Markets and Eurocommercial Paper," Bank of England, Discussion Paper Number 37, February 1989, at 2, 7 and 19, and Bank for International Settlement, *58th Annual Report*, June 1988, pp. 108–109, 127–128.

85. Ralph Bryant, *International Financial Intermediation* (Brookings Institution, 1987). *See also* Moody's report in 48 Banking Rep. 152 (BNA) (January 19, 1987).

86. As of June 3, 1964, Ch. 106, 13 Stat. 99 (codified in scattered sections of 12 USC).

87. Some state banking statutes such as New York include incidental powers language similar to the provisions of the National Banking Act. New York Banking Law §96(1) (McKinney Supp. 1981); *compare with* 12 USC § 24 (7).

88. The OCC guidelines were published as Banking Circular No. 79, 45 Fed. Reg. 18116 (March 20, 1989). The Federal Reserve Board (FRB) policy statement was published at 45 Fed. Reg. 18120 (March 20, 1980). The policy statement of the FDIC, PR–27–80, was published at 45 Fed. Reg. 18116 (March 20, 1980). The OCC regulations are at Banking Circular No. 79 (2d rev.), 45 Fed. Reg. 18116, reprinted in (1979–1980 Transfer Binder) Fed. Banking L. Rep. (CCH) ¶ 98, 190 at 84,275 (March 28, 1980).

89. OCC Banking Circular, *supra* note 88, Item 1A.

90. *Ibid.*, Item 1B.

91. Thomas Russo, *Regulation of Commodities Future and Options* §§ 7–12, 13 (1992).

92. AICPA, Accounting Research Bulletin No. 43, Statement 5 (1953); *see* AICPA, Accounting for Forward Placement and Standby Commitments and Interest Rate Futures 15016 (1980).

93. 12 USC § 1842a (1982).

94. Section 4c(8) of the Bank Holding Company Act (BHCA), Pub. Law 84–511, 70 Stat. 135, as amended. First, a non-banking function must be incidental to banking under the National Banking Act of 1864; second, activities must be closely related to banking. A "laundry list" is set forth in Regulation Y (12 CFR § 225.4).

95. In *Department of Banking and Consumer Finance v. Clarke* ["*Deposit Guarantee*"], 809 F.2d 266 (5th Cir.), *cert. denied*, 107 S. Ct. 3240 (1987). Restrictions were eased on branching by national banks by the Court's finding that state chartered thrifts were carrying on banking businesses for the purposes of the McFadden Act. (Act Chapter 199, Section 7, 44 Stat. 1244 [current version at 12 USC § 36(c) (1982)]). *Deposit Guarantee* thus allows a national bank to establish a branch at a location authorized for a state chartered thrift even though state banks are subject to more restrictive branching provisions. It is important to note that *Deposit Guarantee* only applies to intrastate branching and would not affect rights under the Douglas Amendment, *infra* note 96.

96. 12 USC § 1842(d). *See also Northeast Bankcorp., Inc. v. Board of Governors of the Fed. Reserve Sys.*, 472 U.S., 159, 163, 174–178 (1985) (upholding the constitutionality of a popular type of interstate banking statute—a regional, reciprocal interstate compact—if permitted by a target bank's state). (The Douglas Amendment does not limit the permissible location of banking subsidiaries.)

97. *Supra* note 3. Banc One believes separate subsidiaries with separate corporate structures are actually more appropriate to capitalizing on the opportunities in local markets. Litan, *supra* note 15, at 51.

98. Monetary Depository Institutions and Regulatory Control Act of 1980, March 31, 1990, Pub. Law 96–221, 94 Stat. 132. Garn–St. Germaine Depository Institutions Act of 1982, Pub. L. No. 97–320, 96 Stat. 1469, current version in scattered sections of 12 USC.

99. *See* Lisa Broome, *Commercial Bank Market Expansion; The Influence of Enhanced Thrift Institution Powers*, 67 N.C. L. Rev. 795 (1989).

100. The Bank Merger Act sets forth the procedure for review of a proposed bank merger. The Federal Banking Agency must determine whether the effect of the proposed bank merger "may be substantially to lessen competition." 12 USC § 1828(c)(5)(B) (1982). These decisions must be made in light of the Supreme Court's product market definition enunciated in *United States v. Philadelphia National Bank*, 374 U.S. 321, 356 (1963) where the court found a single broad product market consisting of "a cluster of products (various kinds of credit) and services (such as checking accounts and trust administration) denoted by the term commercial banking." In *United States v. Connecticut National Bank*, 418 U.S. 656 (1974), the Court refused to include savings banks in the same product market (*Ibid.*, at 662).

101. 396 U.S. 122 (1969). In a decision reminiscent of the contemporaneous *Camp* decision (*supra* note 28), *ICI* 2 (*supra* note 30) and other liberalizing decisions of the 1980s relating to the GSA, the court has sanctioned the use of shared ATMs in *Independent Bankers' Association v. Marine Midland Bank* 727 F.2d 453 (1985), *cert. denied*, 106 S.C. 2926 (1986).

102. Current version at 12 USC § 3503(a)–(b).

103. Broome, *supra* note 99, at 815. *See also*, Miss. Code Ann. § 81–12–49(r) (Supp. 1987) ("wild card" law that permits a Mississippi savings association to engage in any activity permitted a federally chartered savings and loan association located in Mississippi). The Fifth Circuit acknowledged that the Garn–St. Germaine Act of 1982, while expanding the powers of savings and loan associations, preserved the principal difference between commercial banks and thrift institutions—that being "the limits placed on the commercial and consumer loans and investments of the savings institutions, designed to protect their capacity to make needed home loans." *Deposit Guarantee, supra* note 95, at 217. But the court found that the legislative distinction "neither proscribes the functional analysis made by the Comptroller nor militates against his interpretation of 12 USC § 36(h)" (*Ibid*).

104. 12 USC § 1464 (c)(2).

105. *Ibid.*

106. *Ibid.*

107. *Ibid.*

108. 12 USC § 1464(c)(2)(B).

109. *Ibid.*, and § 1464 (c)(1)(b).

110. S. 1886, 100th Congress, 2d Sess. 1988 (the Proxmire Act). *See also Glass Steagall Reform: Time to Replace a Crumbling Wall*, J. Corp. L. 973 (Summer 1989).

111. *Ibid. See also Legislative Proposals to Restructure our Financial System, Hearings before the Senate Committee on Banking, Housing and Urban Affairs*, 100th Congress, 1st Sess. 152 (1987). *See also Modernization of the Glass Steagall Act: Hearings Before the Senate Committee on Banking, Housing and Urban Affairs*, 100th Congress, 1st Sess. 138, 140 (1987) (Statement of Thomas S. Dodson, President of Chemical Bank testifying that ten investment banks hold over 50% of pretax profits of the entire US securities business).

112. *Supra* notes 23 and 24.

113. Senate Banking Committee Report, *supra* note 2, at 159–161.

114. Financial Institutions Safety and Consumer Choice Act, *supra*, note 3, Title 7, § 716.

115. Treasury Proposal, *supra* note 1, at 162.

116. *Supra* note 3, Title 7, Subtitle B.

117. *Ibid.*, Title 7, Subtitle C.

118. *See supra* note 5, and the Treasury Proposal, *supra* note 1.

119. Testimony of Richard Breeden. "Restructuring of the Banking Industry," *Hearings before the Subcommittee on Financial Institutions Supervision and Regulation and Insurance.* Pub. L. 102–23, p. 15, April 30, 1991.

120. Testimony of Alan Greenspan—"Strengthening the Supervision and Regulation of the Depository Institution," *Hearings before the Committee on Banking, Housing and Urban Affairs, US Senate*, Pub. L. 102–355, pp. 1318, 1356, April 23, 1991.

121. *Senate Hearings, supra* note 6, Appendix, reprint Bernard Shull, The Separation of Banking Commerce, Origin, Development, Antitrust Bull. 25 (Spring 1983).

122. *Times-Picayune Publishing Company v. United States*, 345 U.S. 594 (1953). *See also* Robert Litan, *What Should Banks Do?* 131–135 (Brookings Institution, 1987).

123. *Ibid.*, at 133.

124. *Ibid.*, at 135.

125. Congressional Budget Office, "The Effects of the Savings and Loan Crisis" (January, 1992).

126. *Ibid.*

127. *See* Litan, *supra* note 15, at 6, citing Treasury Proposal, *supra* note 1.

128. R. Brumbaugh, Dan Andrew, S. Carron, and Robert E. Litan, "Cleaning Up the Depository Institution Mess," *Brookings Papers In Economic Activity* No. 2, p. 243 (1989).

129. *Supra* note 98.

130. Robert Litan, "Banks and Real Estate: Regulating the Unholy Alliance." Paper prepared for the Federal Reserve Bank of New England Conference on Real Estate Lending (1992).

131. *See infra* note 248.

132. Anthony Downs, "Banks and Real Estate: How to Resolve the Dilemma," 20 (National Realty Committee and the Urban Land Institute, 1991). By the first quarter of 1992, nearly 15% of all construction and development loans made by US banks were on a non-accrual status, while almost 6% of all bank commercial mortgage loans were in a similar condition. A study by Goldman Sachs reported in the spring of 1992 that $93 billion in bank loans for commercial real estate still had to be "repriced" in order to reflect a projected average deterioration of 30% in the underlying value of real estate. The report estimated that such write-downs would occur as more than $300 billion in construction loans rolled over, translating into additional losses of $12 to $21 billion. (Ibid.)

133. Pub. Law 102–232 (December 19, 1991) (12 USC § 1811).

134. *Ibid.*, § 304 amending § 18 of the Federal Deposit Insurance Act, 12 USC § 1828.

135. Department of the Treasury, Office of Comptroller of the Currency 12 CFR Part 34, Board of Governors of Federal Reserve System 12 CFR Parts 208 and 225, Federal Deposit Insurance Corporation 12 CFR Part 365, Department of the

Treasury, Office of Thrift Supervision 12 CFR Part 563 "Real Estate Lending Standards."

136. The notice also clarified questions regarding the recognition of income on loans that are partially charged off. The release also contains guidance on (1) cash basis income recognition, (2) multiple loans to one borrower, (3) acquisition of non-accrual assets, (4) treatment of formally restructured debt, and (5) allowance for loans and lease losses.

137. Indicators include (1) an excess of similar projects under construction, (2) construction delays, (3) lack of a sound feasibility study, (4) changes of concepts and plans, (5) rent concessions and discounts, (6) concessions on finishing tenant space, etc. Additionally, another focal point was created around unsound projects that arose in connection with the origination of loans and included such factors as minimal borrower equity. The classification guidelines are (1) classification of troubled project pendant commercial real estate loans, (2) guidelines for partially charged off loans and (3) guidelines for classifying formally restructured loans. A review of the allowance for loan and lease losses is also included and requires (a) effective systems and controls for identifying and monitoring asset quality problems and (b) analysis of all significant factors linked to collectibility of the portfolio. Attachment 1 includes the treatment of guarantees in the classification process. Attachment 2 is the valuation of income producing real estate and the valuation which involves a general classification approach including (a) a cost approach, (b) a market data or direct sales comparison approach, and (c) an income approach. Among the distinctions discussed are (1) between a discount and cap rate: a discount rate is based on a required rate of return (discount rate) based on stabilized net operating income and a cap rate reflects expected increase in future prices, and (2) between holding period and marketing period which is extremely consequential in determining returns on assets.

138. FDICIA Section 131 amending the Federal Deposit Insurance Act, by adding a § 38 (12 USC § 1831) which classifies insured depository institutions into five categories according to their capital: (1) well capitalized, (2) adequately capitalized, (3) undercapitalized, (4) significantly undercapitalized, and (5) critically undercapitalized. There are two relevant measures for capital: (1) the leveraged limit relating an institution's capital to its total assets, and (2) the risk-based capital requirements relating an institution's capital to its risk-adjusted assets; and these approximate the Basle standards. The two forms of determining capitalization are intended to be cumulative. The leveraged limit requires that tangible equity not be less than 2% of total assets or more than 65% of the required minimum level of capital under the leveraged limit. Thus, if the required minimum level is 4% of total assets, the critical capital level cannot exceed 2.6%. If the institution is undercapitalized, it cannot make capital distributions, which are broadly defined to include dividends, including stock, and may not pay stock redemptions or other transactions which are broadly similar, although this last restriction is discretional with the regulator under certain exceptions. Furthermore, management fees are restricted and undercapitalized institutions are closely monitored for compliance with capital restoration plans that require detailed information and also require a guaranty of the bank holding company of the institution that must be equal to 5% of the institution's total assets or the amount necessary to bring the institution in compliance with capital standards. Asset growth may be restricted unless the federal

banking agency has accepted the institution's capital restoration plan and the increase in total assets is consistent with that plan. Undercapitalized institutions must also have prior approval from their appropriate regulator for branching and commencing new lines of business. In addition to these detailed guidelines, the regulator may make any determinations which are for the purpose of § 38. Under § 133 of the Act, a conservator or receiver may be appointed for an undercapitalized institution. A detailed list of significantly undercapitalized institutions requires certain mandatory safeguards to be employed including (a) the requirement that the institution recapitalize by selling shares or become acquired by another entity, (b) denying the institution the exemption under § 23A(d)(1) of the Federal Reserve Act and (c) restricting interest rates the institution pays on deposits. Furthermore, the institution may be required to divest itself of a subsidiary or to divest itself of any interest in an affiliate. Additionally, a wild-card authority enables the agency to deal with extraordinary cases for which other safeguards are ill-suited. Senior executive officer compensation can be restricted for a significantly undercapitalized institution. Furthermore, § 38 permits the appropriate federal banking agency to act against an insured depository institution based on non-capital criteria, including the other CAMEL rating criteria (capital, asset quality, management, earnings and liquidity). § 132 of the Federal Deposit Insurance Corporation Improvement Act adds a new § 39 to the Federal Deposit Insurance Act requiring banking agencies to establish operational, managerial, quality earnings, stock valuation and compensation standards for all insured depository institutions. This is a "trip wire" standard. *See generally*, "Prompt Corrective Action under the FDIC Improvement Act of 1991," Richard Carnell, Senior Counsel, Committee on Banking, Housing and Urban Affairs, US Senate. Lecture delivered at Columbus School of Law, Catholic University of America, April 6, 1992.

139. Department of the Treasury, Office of Comptroller of the Currency, 12 CFR Parts 6 and 19 (Docket #92–19 Federal Reserve System) 12 CFR Parts 208 and 263 (Docket #R–0763; Regulation H) Federal Deposit Insurance Corporation 12 CFR Parts 308 and 325, Department of the Treasury, Office of Thrift Supervision 12 CFR Part 565 Prompt Corrective Action, "Rules of Practice for Hearings." 57 Fed. Reg. 44,866 (September 29, 1992).

140. The leverage ratio is the ratio of tier-one capital to total average assets (*Ibid.*, at 44,867). An institution is adequately capitalized if it has a total risk-base capital ratio of 8% or greater, a tier-one capital ratio of 4% or greater, and a leverage ratio of 4% or greater, or leverage ratio of 3% or greater if the institution is rated composite one in its most recent bank examination. An institution is undercapitalized if (1) it has a total risk-based capital ratio that is less than 8%, (2) tier-one risk-capital ratio that is less than 4% or (3) a leverage ratio that is less than 4% or a leverage ratio that is less than 3% if the institution is rated composite one. An institution is significantly undercapitalized if it has a total risk-based capital ratio that is less than 6%, a tier-one risk-based capital ratio that is less than 3% or a leverage ratio that is less than 3%. An institution is critically undercapitalized if the institution has a ratio of tangible equity to total assets that is equal to or less than 2%.

141. 57 Fed. Reg., *supra* note 139, at 44,870.

142. 57 Fed. Reg. *supra* note 139, at 44,870. *See also infra* notes 161–164.

143. *Ibid.*, at 44,871.

144. FDICIA, *supra* note 133, § 131; FDIA § 38(c)(3)(B)(i), and (ii).

145. *Ibid.*, FDIA 38(g), 12 USC § 1831(o)(G).

146. *Ibid.*, at 38(g). Reference is made to subjecting adequately capitalized institutions to subsections (d) and (e); since these generally refer to payments made that would render an institution undercapitalized, these sections are likely to seriously affect not well-capitalized institutions that are recategorized, but adequately capitalized institutions will be significantly affected, having the additional burden over undercapitalized institutions of addressing its unsafe or unsound banking practices.

147. *See, e.g., United States v. Florida, East Coast Ry.*, 410 U.S. 224, 240 (1973).

148. FDICIA Section 131, *supra* note 144, amending FDIA by adding § 38(g).

149. FDICIA § 132 amending FDIA (12 USC § 1811 *et. seq.*) by adding after § 38, 39.

150. Department of the Treasury, Office of the Comptroller of Currency, 12 CFR Chapter 1, Docket No. 92–11, Federal Reserve System 12 CFR Chapter 2, Docket No. R–0766, Federal Deposit Insurance Corporation 12 CFR Chapter 3, Department of the Treasury Office of Thrift Supervision, 12 CFR Part 563, 57 Fed. Reg. 31,366.

151. *See supra* note 139.

152. *See supra* notes 145 and 146, and accompanying text.

153. *See supra* notes 136 and 137, and accompanying text.

154. Federal Financial Institutions Examination Council, *Consolidated Reports of Condition and Income* (December 1992).

155. FDICIA, *supra* note 133, Title 3(a) § 302 amending § 7(b) of the Federal Deposit Insurance Act (12 USC § 1817b). The assessment system is based on different categories and concentration of assets and liabilities both insured, uninsured and contingent and non-contingent claims. *Ibid.*, at § 302[b][1][C].

156. FDICIA, *supra* note 133, § 122 requiring reporting information on small business (12 USC § 1817) and FDICIA § 477 Modified Small Business Disclosure (12 USC § 251), requiring the FRB to collect and publish information on loan to small business.

157. Federal Financial Institutions Examination Council Reporting of Information on Small Business Lending, 57 Fed. Reg. 54, 235 (November 17, 1992).

158. Of the 537 comments received on the proposed regulation, 438 commentators explicitly expressed their opposition to the proposal where only 4 indicated they were in favor of the proposal (*Ibid.*).

159. Conference on FDICIA: Banks and Regulatory Responses, December 16, 1992, Brookings Institution, Remarks by David Mullins.

160. The Federal Financial Institutions Examination Council decided to delete the proposed items on estimated income and net charges on loans to small businesses and small farms. (FFIEC Notice, *supra* note 157.)

161. *See* Chapter 1, *supra* notes 123–125.

162. The risk-based standards must also reflect the actual performance and expected risk of loss of multifamily dwelling mortgages. (Because this risk is minimal it is likely that multifamily dwelling mortgages will not be affected substantially by risk-based capital standards.) FDICIA, *supra* note 133, Title 3A § 305 amending § 18 of the Federal Deposit Insurance Act (12 USC § 1828). This section further requires the Federal Banking Agencies discuss the development of comparable

standards with members of the Supervisory Committee of the Bank for International Settlements. (*Ibid.*, § 305 b(2)).

163. Federal Deposit Insurance Corporation, 12 CFR, Part 325; Department of the Treasury, Office of the Comptroller of the Currency, 12 CFR, Part 3; Federal Reserve System, 12 CFR, Part 208 and 225; Risk-based Capital Standards: Joint Advance Notice of Proposed Rule Making (July 30, 1992).

164. *Ibid.*

165. *See* Office of the Treasury, Secretary of the Department of the Treasury, Capital Equivalency Report, pursuant to Section 214B of the Foreign Bank Supervision Enhancement Act of 1991 (June 19, 1992).

166. Jack Guttentag and Richard Herring, "Disaster Myopia in International Banking," Princeton Essays in International Finance No. 164, pp. 29–30 (1986).

167. The case of Continental Illinois and its First Options subsidiary has cast renewed doubts on the ability of 23A- and 23B-style restrictions to insulate a bank from its affiliates. Although in this case First Options was a direct subsidiary of the bank and not of the holding company and was not strictly subject to 23A and 23B restrictions, the bank had in effect agreed to similar lending restrictions with regulators at the time of acquisition of its First Options subsidiary. When on October 19, 1987, the Options subsidiary got into financial difficulty, Continental Illinois, as the parent, extended loans to this affiliate beyond the agreed lending ceilings, thereby technically violating its agreement with the regulators. Anthony Saunders, *Bank Holding Companies, Restructuring Banking & Financial Services in America* 156, 167–168 (William S. Haraf, and Rose Marie Kushmeider, eds., 1988).

168. *See* Chapter 1, *supra* note 97, and accompanying text for a discussion of a comparable situation in the United Kingdom with the failure of Johnson Mathey.

169. FDICIA, *supra* note 133, Title 1(e) § 141 amending § 13c of the Federal Deposit Insurance Act (12 USC § 1823c).

170. *Ibid.*, at 141B.

171. *Ibid.*, at 141G Systemic Risk.

172. Federal Reserve System 12 CRF, Part 206 (Regulation M; Docket No. R–0769), 57 Fed. Reg. 31,974.

173. *See supra* notes 138–140.

174. *Ibid.*, Section 206.4, "Guidelines for Credit Exposure."

175. FDICIA Section 473 amending Section 13 of the Federal Reserve Act (12 USC § 343) in the third paragraph by "striking of the kinds of maturities made eligible for discount for member banks under other provisions of this Act."

176. *See supra* notes 2, 3 and 6.

177. S.543, 102d Congress, First Sess. § 214(a) and HR1505 (1991). *See* S.543, etc.

178. Cynthia Lichtenstein, *U.S. Restructuring Legislation: Revising the International Banking Act of 1978, for the Worse?* 60 FORDHAM L. REV. 537 (1992).

179. FDICIA, *supra* note 133, § 214 (a)(1)(B) (amending IBA Section 6, 12 USC § 3104(c)[1]).

180. Daniel Gail, Joseph Norton, and Michael O'Neal, *The Foreign Bank Supervision Act of 1991: Expanding the Umbrella of "Supervisory" Reregulation*. 26 INT. LAW. 993 (Winter 1992).

181. 57 Fed. Reg. 12,992 and 12,997 (April 15, 1992).

182. *Ibid. See also* Michael Whitener, *New Federal Reserve Board Regulations Regarding Foreign Banks in the United States.* 26 INT. LAW. 1007 (Winter 1992).

183. FDICIA, *supra* note 133, § 202(a).

184. FDICIA, *supra* note 133, § 210 adding Bank Holding Company Act. § (3)(c)(5), 12 USC § 1842(c)(5).

185. FDICIA, *supra* note 133 § 202(a).

186. *Ibid.*

187. *Ibid.*

188. Pub. Law 95–369; December 17, 1978; 92 Stat. 607 § 41, 12 USC § 3102(b), (1978).

189. 12 CFR § 211.29. *See also* Gail, *supra* note 180, at 1000.

190. *Ibid.*, at 1000–1005.

191. FDICIA, *supra* note 133, § 207 amending IBA Sec. 8(a) 12 USC § 3106(a).

192. *See generally* Note, *The Non-Banking Activities of Foreign Banks and the International Banking Act of 1978*, 80 U. ILL. L. F. 325 (1980).

193. 12 USC § 1842 (e) (1982) (Subsidiary banks of bank holding companies must obtain deposit insurance).

194. 12 USC §§ 1841–1849.

195. 12 USC § 1843.

196. 12 USC § 36(c).

197. 12 USC § 321 applied to foreign banks.

198. 12 USC § 1843(a).

199. 12 USC § 3104.

200. *Ibid.*, § 3105.

201. *Ibid.*, §§ 3103–3106.

202. *See supra* note 94.

203. 12 USC § 1841 (h)(2). *See generally* John Carr and John H. Moore, *Developments in the Regulation of Foreign Bank Operations in the United States*, 88 U. ILL. L. F. 225 (1988).

204. Once a bank establishes either type of full service US banking operation (an unrestricted branch or a US bank subsidiary), it will have far fewer opportunities for subsequent interstate expansion through additional full service banking operations. A foreign bank's establishment of the banking subsidiary will trigger application of BHCA § 4 non-banking restrictions to that bank. Moreover, establishment of an unrestricted branch or added establishment of an unrestricted branch will also subject a foreign bank to BHCA § 4 non-banking restrictions as made applicable by § 8 of the IBA. Section 5(a) of the IBA requires a foreign bank that has an unrestricted branch or subsidiary to select a state in which such full service operation is located as its "IBA home state." Except for grandfathered operations, the IBA prohibits a foreign bank from having an unrestricted branch outside the cited IBA home state, and a foreign bank cannot acquire control of a banking subsidiary outside of its IBA home state absent the expressed statutory permission of the state it desires to enter. It is possible to have an unrestricted branch which would have a lending limit based on a foreign parent's bank capital, not the US bank subsidiary, as well as a subsidiary which would have other advantages. The principal regulatory advantage of the commercial bank subsidiary is the ability to branch. A bank may determine whether to have a state or national charter, and as a consequence of *Conference of State Bank Supervisors versus*

Conover 715 F.2d 604 (D.C. Cir., 1983), *cert. denied*, 466 US 927 (1984), state limitations such as those requiring reciprocity between a state and the foreign country are not applicable to federally licensed branches and agencies because they are not outright prohibitions and entry. Moore, *supra* note 203, at 233–242.

Choosing a limited service operation such as a restricted branch or an agency will not limit a bank's geographic expansion opportunity. However, their limitations on restricted branches enable it only to accept those deposits that an Edge Act corporation can accept (§ 5 of the IBA, 12 USC § 3103(a) (1982)). Under an agency authorization, a bank is not entitled to accept deposits but they may be freely funded in the interbank market. Under § 4 of the IBA, a foreign bank without a home state may establish a federal agency with the approval of the comptroller where not prohibited by state law. An agency is subject to fewer regulatory requirements than a restricted branch. Another option is a New York wholesale agency which has no lending limits (whereas a federal agency is subject to federal lending limits). Moore, *supra* note 203, at 251, 252.

205. Lichtenstein, *supra* note 178.

206. *See* Chapter 1, *supra* note 286, and accompanying text.

207. Competitive Equality Banking Act of 1987 (codified as amended at 12 USC § 1841 [h][iii] (1988)).

208. Section 3 of the Bank Holding Company Act requires, subject to certain exemptions, applications to the Board in relation to the formation and merger of bank holding companies. Application is also required for acquisition of subsidiary banks or bank assets and acquisition of control of bank or bank holding company securities. Section 4 requires application to the Board with regard to the acquisition of permissible non-banking activities or engaging directly in such non-banking activities. Section 7 of the International Banking Act requires the approval of the Board prior to foreign banks establishing a federal or state licensed branch or agency or acquiring ownership or control of a commercial lending company.

209. Secretary of the Department of the Treasury, Board of Governors of the Federal Reserve System, "Capital Equivalency Report" (June 1992) considers tier-two capital to provide a "menu" of internationally agreed upon items that supplement core capital.

210. *Ibid.*, at 22.

211. *Ibid.*, at 24.

212. *Ibid.*, at 28.

213. *Ibid.*, at 28.

214. *Ibid.*, at 31.

215. *Ibid.*, at 31.

216. *Ibid.*, at 32.

217. Committee of Banking and Supervisory Practices, Bank for International Settlements, *Amendment to the Convergence Agreement of the Group of Ten Countries Regarding Loan Losses* (November 1991).

218. In the United States, country risk is dealt with partly through Allocated Transfer Reserve Requirements that are not mandatory. *See* Chapter 1, *supra* note 52, and accompanying text.

219. Litan, *supra* note 130, at 24.

220. *See* Chapter 1, *supra* note 248, and accompanying text.

221. *See* Chapter 3, *infra* note 70, and accompanying text.

222. Ian Giddy, *Is Equity Underwriting Risky for Commercial Bank Affiliates in Deregulating Wall Street, in* COMMERCIAL BANK PENETRATION OF THE CORPORATE SECURITIES MARKET 145–170 (Ingo Walter, ed., 1985).

223. Litan, *supra* note 122, at 89.

224. *Ibid.*, at 89–91.

225. *Ibid.*, at 91.

226. *Ibid.*, at 97.

227. Litan, *supra* note 122, at 111, citing James R. Barth, R. Dan Brumbaugh, Jr., and Daniel Sauthert, "Failure Cost of Government Regulated Financial Thrifts: The Case of Thrift Institutions," Research Working Paper, 123, Federal Home Loan Bank Board (FHLBB), October 1986.

228. *Ibid.*

229. Litan, *supra* note 122, at 164–198.

230. *Ibid.*, at 174.

231. *Ibid.*, at 184.

232. *See supra* notes 22–24, for citation and discussion.

233. Litan, *supra* note 122, at 137 citing *Financial Institutions Restructuring and Services Act of 1981*, Hearings Before the Senate Committee on Housing, Banking and Urban Affairs, 97th Congress, 1st Sess., 587–590 (1981).

234. Hal Scott, *Policy Essay: Deregulation and Access to the Payment System*, HARV. J. ON LEGIS. 337 (1986).

235. *See generally* David Folkerts-Landau, *Systemic Financial Risks In Payment Systems*, in DETERMINANTS AND SYSTEMATIC CONSEQUENCES OF INTERNATIONAL CAPITAL FLOWS, Occasional Paper No. 77 (International Monetary Fund, 1991).

236. *See supra* note 175.

237. David Folkerts-Landau, and Peter M. Gerber, "The European Central Bank: A Bank or a Monetary Policy Rule," National Bureau of Research, Working Paper No. 4016 (March 1992).

238. Litan proposes that consideration could be given to expanding the investment authority of the Federal Reserve, *supra* note 122, at 187.

239. Testimony by Alan Greenspan, Chairman of the Board of Governors of the Federal Reserve System, before the Committee on Banking, Housing and Urban Affairs, United States Senate (July 21, 1992) (Humphrey Hawkins Testimony).

240. Fed. Reserve Bull., July 1992; *see also* Litan, *supra* note 15 at 22.

241. Fed. Reserve Bull., October 1992, A–41, p. 9.

242. Greenspan Testimony, *supra* note 239.

243. *Ibid.*

244. *See* Part VI, above.

245. Greenspan Testimony, *supra* note 239.

246. *Ibid.*, at 11.

247. "1992 FRB Monetary Policy Objectives" (July 21, 1992) at 10. Consequently, the FRB has determined that the slowdown in M–2 and M–3 has been offset by an increased velocity of these monetary aggregates. The decline in the usefulness of monetary aggregates may possibly also indicate a decline in the efficacy of monetary policy. This possibility was first discussed by the G–10 and Bank for International Settlements in the Report on Financial Innovation in 1986. *See* Chapter 1, *supra* note 127.

248. In March 1985, commercial banks had total assets of $1.758 trillion, of which $266 billion was invested in US government securities, $488 billion in commercial and industrial loans and $385 billion in real estate (Fed. Reserve Bull., November 1985, at A–16). On November 4, 1992, commercial banks had assets of $3.1 trillion of which $623 billion was invested in US government securities, $891 billion in real estate and $603 billion in commercial and industrial loans. Fed. Reserve Bull., March 1993, at A–18.

249. *See* Chapter 1, *supra* note 57, and accompanying text. *See also* this chapter, *supra* note 50 for the adoption of the US law by the FRB. This adoption is largely mirrored by other banking regulatory agencies.

250. Litan, *supra* note 15 at 15. *See also* James R. Forest, Dan Brumbaugh, Jr., and Robert E. Litan, THE FUTURE OF AMERICAN BANKING 102 (1992).

251. *See* Chapter 1, *supra* note 226, and accompanying text.

252. *See* Chapter 3, *infra* Part I for the argument for a lead regulator in the securities and derivative market area.

253. In *Board of Governors v. Dimension Finance Corporation*, 106 S. Ct. 681 (1986). The Court rebuffed the Federal Reserve's attempt to expand the definition of bank deposits to cover virtually all short-term money market assets and to include NOW accounts within its definition of "demand deposits."

254. One of the assessments of the costs of the S&L bailout by the Congressional Budget Office is that bad investments in commercial real estate diverted money away that could have been successfully invested, and that consumers saved less than they would have because they were unaware of the tax liability that they would be facing.

255. *See* Chapter 4, *infra* note 194.

256. Christopher Carroll, "The Buffer Stock Theory of Saving: Some Macroeconomic Evidence," Brookings Papers on Economic Activities 2: 1992, pp. 61 and 117, using data from Federal Reserve Statistical Release 619, various releases.

257. Glen B. Canner, and Charles A. Luckett, "Developments in the Pricing of Credit Card Services," 78 Fed. Reserve Bull., September 1992, pp. 662 to 666.

258. *See*, for example, "Buffer Stock Theory of Savings," *supra* note 256, at 116, citing "Statistical Abstract of the United States, 1987," Government Printing Office 1987, p. 716, Table 1293.

259. *Ibid.*, at 118 using data from Mortgage Bankers' Association, "National Delinquency Survey," various issues.

260. Marco Pagganano, and Julio Japelli, "Information Sharing and Credit Markets," Center for Economic Policy Research Discussion Paper No. 579 (London, October 1991).

261. Buffer Stocks, *supra* note 256, at 120.

262. Paul Volcker, and Toyoo Gyohten, CHANGING FORTUNES: THE WORLD MONEY AND THE THREAT TO AMERICAN LEADERSHIP, 171–173 (1992). "After all the trouble we had trying to stop the money supply from increasing, it suddenly dropped precipitously, we could only catch up with that, like the decline of the economy itself when we got the statistics a few weeks later. As soon as the magnitude of the drop became apparent, money was eased, but there was a lot of criticism from economists, monetarists, and Keynesians alike, that we hadn't moved fast enough. We were willing to put the country through the agony of high interest rates when inflation was raging, but we weren't doing enough to prevent the crash" (p. 173).

263. "Survey: International Banking," THE ECONOMIST, April 7, 1990.

264. *See generally* Jonathan Macey, *Interest Groups Legislation of the Judicial Function, The Dilemma of Glass-Steagall*, 33 EMORY L. J. 1, 5 (1984).

265. Monetary policy is also impeded by financial innovation, in general. *See* Bank for International Settlements, *Recent Innovations in International Finance* (1986).

266. *See supra* note 92.

3

Systemic Risk and Intermarket Regulations in US Securities and Derivative Markets

Financial innovations in the banking sector, such as securitization, have been accompanied by innovation in the securities markets and include stock options strategies and the phenomena of stock index futures. These securities market innovations, that usually involve simultaneous trading in principal and derivative markets, provide the focal points of this chapter.

Since the market break of 1987, efforts have been made to improve clearing and payment systems, to prohibit brokers from "front running" clients' orders and engaging in other forms of market manipulation, to provide for intermarket cross-margining arrangements that potentially reduce gridlock and to institute circuit breakers. At the same time, little has been done to change the basic regulatory apparatus or to consider the relationship of financial market structure to the underlying economy.

Part I discusses the idea of a single regulator for securities and derivative markets. Part II considers clearance and settlement systems, differentiating securities and index future clearing and discusses foreign exchange issues. Part III considers the impact of futures exchanges on market volatility; and Part IV examines net capital rules for stocks and futures. Part V discusses the use of circuit breakers; and Part VI considers the broader issue of futures trading practices and investment horizons. Part VII concludes that subtle long-term issues have not been addressed in spite of the technical proficiency employed in dealing with clearance, payment and settlement issues.

Part I: The Single Regulator

After the 1987 market break, a presidential task force (the Brady Commission) was charged with investigating the break. The Brady Commission concluded that the prospect of clearing house failures reduced the willing-

ness of lenders to finance market participation, leading to a "crisis of competence" that raised the specter of full-scale financial breakdown. To reduce the possibility of financial gridlock and attendant risk to the financial system, the task force recommended that clearing for stock options and stock index futures be unified through a single mechanism.[1] Similarly, the Brady Commission concluded in its study of the market break that all securities and derivative markets composed one market. While the implications of this "unified market theory" are not immediately clear, current administrative and legislative initiatives are intent on establishing effective intermarket regulation.[2] The principal regulatory changes since the 1987 market break have been instituted at the exchange level.

The SEC and the Commodities Futures Trading Corporation (CFTC) came to different conclusions regarding jurisdiction over derivative instruments. Pursuant to the Shad Johnson accord in 1982, the SEC has jurisdiction over all options, while CFTC has jurisdiction over all futures contracts.[3] After the October 1987 market collapse, an SEC report came to the conclusion that the futures market volatility was largely responsible for the abrupt drop in the underlying securities markets, and that the function of market makers was undermined by the workings of the futures market which left no time for the market maker mechanism to function.[4]

In 1987 the total daily dollar volume of trade in the Standard & Poors 500 stock index futures was 1.5 times that of Standard & Poors 500 stocks traded on the New York Stock Exchange (NYSE). The low transaction costs associated with futures and options make them more attractive vehicles than underlying securities and thereby facilitate the ability of money managers to alter portfolios.[5] For example, in 1984 the one way commission cost of selling 100 S&P 500 future contracts was approximately $1,250 while the cost of selling the same amount of underlying stock would have been $17,500.[6]

A growing sentiment exists that consolidation of the CFTC and the SEC is required to coordinate the actions being taken by stock exchanges, futures exchanges and options exchanges to reduce market volatility. In this regard the SEC would be the likely candidate.[7] The need for centralized regulation of financial markets prompted Congress to grant the FRB participation in the process of regulating margin requirements on financial and stock index futures,[8] but there appears to be very little feeling among regulators that the FRB has any interest or ability to regulate margin requirements on futures.[9] While it has held the power to regulate stock margin requirements since the Securities and Exchange Act, margins have remained the same since the early 1970s.

Part II: Clearance and Settlement

Following the 1987 market break, a plethora of reports were issued regarding clearance and settlement systems.[10] The reports are varied in

their specific recommendations. Nonetheless, they tend to concur in en-visioning a shorter period of delivery and an integration and harmonization of market mechanisms, such as circuit breakers and triggers. A great deal of progress has been made in the last few years regarding the administration of intermarket activities, including intermarket front-running (a firm trad-ing ahead of its client) and self front-running (a firm trading simultaneously in dual or triple activities and affecting price by virtue of its participation in different markets). Because clearance and settlements of futures already occur intraday rather than over a several day period, issues in securities clearance and payment systems differ from those in futures settlement systems.

The Bachmann Task Force on clearance and settlement reform in the US securities markets concentrated on the current clearance and settlement system with a view toward strengthening the safety and soundness of the clearing system.[11] The Task Force noted that shortening the settlement period will reduce risk where time equals risk. The view that time equals risk is one reason that margins on S&P 500 futures are so much lower than those on stock equities. For example, the Working Group on Financial Markets concluded, on the basis of historical volatility in the period June 1, 1984 to October 2, 1987, that the maintenance margin providing pro-tection against 99% of price movement is 2.32% for the S&P 500 Index and 7.88% for the typical stock, assuming protection is required for the one-day settlement period in futures and the five-day settlement period in stocks.[12]

The Bachmann Task Force concluded that equities markets can be sub-stantially improved by shortening the settlement cycle for corporate equity transactions from five to three days. According to the report, dual equities and futures market participants having losses in one market may be unable to meet obligations in other markets and both clearing organizations may cease to act for the participant in question. A recently signed agreement between the Options Clearing Corporation and the National Securities Clearing Corporation provides each clearing corporation with funds equal to any margins collected at the other clearing corporation, if the dual member becomes insolvent and the clearing corporation suffers a loss as a result of liquidating the member's transactions.[13] These arrangements, which involve member insolvency, are to be distinguished from cross-mar-gining agreements, discussed below, where the same margin account is used for separate positions.

There is an express exemption from the automatic stay contained in Section 362 of the Bankruptcy Code for margin and settlement payments.[14] Under FDICIA bilateral netting, pursuant to contractual provisions, of any obligations of financial institutions or members of any clearing orga-nization (including broker dealers and futures commission merchants) is exempt from "any other provision of law."[15] Notwithstanding Bankruptcy

Code provisions exempting gross obligations from any stay by a bankruptcy court, it was necessary to determine whether obligations such as margin or settlement obligations were contemporaneous with the transaction. FDICIA, by looking toward net obligations, should render the obligations of financial institutions to clearing corporations less ambiguous and should further establish bilateral netting between financial institutions (particularly in the foreign exchange domain).

Specific legal issues about revision of the Bankruptcy Code and the Uniform Commercial Code (UCC) were addressed in an interim report of the American Bar Association.[16] Principal among these recommendations was the recognition of the need for changing the UCC to outline a framework for perfecting a security interest in a securities account.[17]

Circumstances exist under which financial institutions may enforce contracts notwithstanding the automatic stay and other restrictions under the Bankruptcy Code, such as rights of set-off and security interests.[18] However, cross-margining agreements and solvency arrangements do not protect clearing corporations with risks posed by "off-exchange markets."[19]

The Options Clearing Corporation (OCC) and the Chicago Mercantile Exchange (CME) have jointly developed an inter-creditor agreement to share control over collateral positions held by common participants in special cross-margin accounts. Participants must agree to grant OCC liens on futures positions maintained at the CME and to grant the CME liens on options positions maintained at the OCC. This arrangement has significantly reduced overall margins requirements. For example, in the market break on October 13, 1989, one firm reduced its margin requirements by approximately 54.2% from what would have been required without cross-margining.[20]

In general, market participants rely on bank credit for liquidity. The Federal banks located in Chicago rely on New York money center banks to determine the creditworthiness of clearing organization participants, so that as a practical matter New York money center banks, which are few in number, will take the lead in initiating credit. Thus, it was fairly simple for Chairman Greenspan to arrange for the access of credit by informally contacting New York money center banks.[21]

One authority, the Group of 30, recommended that securities settlement systems achieve delivery versus payment by 1992.[22] However, this goal is far from being accomplished. A BIS report takes issue with the benefits to be derived from delivery versus payment.[23] The BIS report distinguishes between credit risk, which can be alleviated by delivery versus payment, and liquidity risk, which is likely to be increased despite the fact that credit risk would no longer exist. The report also draws an analogy between currency clearing systems and securities clearing systems, and determines that, because of their direct effect on national payment systems, liquidity and credit risks are inherently greater in currency clearing systems than in

security clearing systems.[24] The BIS report notes a distinction between foreign exchange netting systems, which may require limits to credit exposure, and maximum fund transfers.[25] However, the report concludes that such credit standards are not necessarily appropriate to securities markets. In this connection, it is valuable to note that the Fedwire system provides for gross payments and finality, while the National Securities Clearing Corporation and Depository Trust Corporation provide for netting and unwinding.[26]

Studies on the 1987 market break showed an extraordinary consistency for concerns about clearing and settlement systems without really delving into the causes of the abrupt market break.[27] The failure of the G–5 countries to give any clear signals about the direction of the dollar, taken together with the massive support of the dollar required throughout 1987 by Germany and Japan,[28] led to concerns about an international currency crisis and may have been an essential ingredient leading to the 1987 market break.

Recent attention to bank settlement systems has focused on currency risk, principally because it is by definition incapable of being addressed by a domestic clearing and settlement system.[29] "Herstaat Risk" has been at the forefront of concern over an international clearing and settlement system.[30]

The complex structure of settling currency transactions drastically reduces the ability of dealers to control the timing of the settlements of the different legs of their currency contracts. One potential incentive could be created if central banks encouraged the establishment of a market-based system for daylight credit.[31] Furthermore, the use of bilateral and multilateral netting would significantly reduce risks between specific institutions. The questions of multilateral netting arrangements have been addressed by the G–10 BIS forum.[32]

The FRB has given approval to a significant step dealing with payment system risks. Beginning in April 1994, fees will be charged for daylight overdrafts in accounts at the FRB thereby indirectly reducing Herstaat Risks.[33]

Both the US Working Group and the Bachmann Report recommend that payments by financial intermediaries and the institutional clients be made in same-day funds,[34] and the Bachmann Report also notes that disturbances in the forex market, particularly as they affect affiliates of regulated broker dealers, may have substantial impact on securities and derivative markets.

Part III: Stock Index Futures and Market Volatility

In spite of the failure of portfolio insurance in 1987, a continuous process of "indexation" by institutional investors is underway.[35] Transactions in

stock index futures are an ideal way to change the balance between debt and equity. A holder of a portfolio of common stocks may, by selling an index futures contract, achieve the functional equivalent of selling off the stock and investing the proceeds in Treasury Bills or some equivalent instrument. Buying futures contracts when stocks are already owned in a portfolio is equivalent to margining that portfolio and selling short-term debt instruments and investing the proceeds in stocks.[36]

In the view of Merton Miller and other leading finance theorists, the timing of portfolio insurance sales did not magnify the impact of the 1987 crash. The SEC report notes that portfolio insurance and index arbitrage, though accounting for no more than 20% of the S&P 500 volume for the entire day of October 19, 1987, and no more than 40% during the fateful 1–2 PM period EST, accounted for more than 60% of the S&P's 500 stock volume in three ten-minute intervals in that hour.[37] But, as Miller notes, there must have been shorter intervals in which portfolio insurance trades approached 100% of total trade.[38] The implication is that an artificial time period will produce skewed results.

Because percentage margins on futures are smaller than most margins required on purchases of stocks, the argument has been made that greater leverage can be achieved in the futures market, which has thus become subject to speculation and great volatility. Evidence of this hypothesis is wanting. It has also been argued that large movements in stock prices are not correlated to stock index features and that this kind of financial innovation has actually reduced volatility.[39] The importance of stock market margins on the eve of the crash of 1929 has been largely overstated. Stock brokers had actually begun to increase margin requirements and by the time of the crash of 1929, actual margins were 50% and total outstanding margins were equal to only about 10% of the value of outstanding stocks.[40]

Miller notes that the open positions in margin index futures in October 1987 was the share equivalent of only 2% of the value of shares listed on the NYSE. This open (uncovered) position actually expanded slightly during October 19, and futures traders whose margin accounts were classified as speculative were substantial buyers of futures on October 19.[41] But the role of margin cannot be argued away so simply. The percentage that margin requirements impose on a total value of shares is misleading, in that a small percentage of share volume can be an initiating factor in a market decline. The value of stock index futures compared to that of the underlying stocks is not necessarily the determinant of market movement. FRB Chairman Greenspan has stated that the margin levels are basically adequate, however he has indicated that low margins may make necessary abrupt augmentation of margins on stock index futures in the event of market volatility.[42] Therefore, even though it is unlikely that the FRB will be involved with the regulation of stock index futures margins on a day-to-day basis, FRB control over stock index futures regulation will result

in slightly higher margins generally; but the ambivalence of the FRB toward regulating stock margins suggests it will not fully utilize its authority.

Part IV: Circuit Breakers

Circuit breakers are temporary trading halts in various kinds of trading practices and include price limits for indexes, restrictions on program trading and index arbitrage. The current integration of circuit breakers between the NYSE and the CME has been staged with due consideration to the interrelationship between the two markets.[43] In addition to these integrated circuit breakers which first occur at 100 point movement in the Dow Jones Industrial Average (Dow), NYSE Rule 80A restricts institutional program trading and index arbitrage by providing for "collars," that restrict trading program orders on the electronic superdot order routing system whenever there is a movement of 50 Dow points. The paradox revolving around Rule 80A is that it actually acts to disconnect the futures market from the underlying market by severing the arbitrage link between them whenever the price level moves by 50 Dow points.[44]

The evidence on the efficacy of circuit breakers in practice is uneven at best. Studies of the use of circuit breakers in the market break of October 13, 1989, call into question the impact of circuit breakers in general. One study by the SEC's Office of Economic Analysis found more price dispersion, when circuit breakers were in place, on October 13, 1989, than on October 16, 1987, another Friday on which the market fell by about 60 points with no circuit breakers in place. Consequently, the study concludes that circuit breakers may have impaired, rather than aided, price discovery on October 13.[45]

In the period immediately after the crash of 1987, the main emphasis of those calling for better regulation was on the danger to the safety and integrity of the entire payment system imposed by the massive flows of cash margin funds. The force of this argument may have been undercut by the fact that the financial system managed to survive despite the biggest one-day move in US stock market price history. Several functional disabilities were apparent. The first was that the quotations for stock prices were running 60 to 90 minutes behind,[46] which led to the illusion of a discount on the futures market and purveyed misinformation to the stock market. With many halts on the NYSE on the morning of October 20, it was feared that all trading in New York might come to an end, leaving the CME to face the flood of sell orders alone. With no offsetting arbitrage buying demand, the CME floor traders would have had little hope of unwinding the long positions they had assumed on the way down, and no way of absorbing more of the selling wave from New York. Prices might have collapsed, thus threatening the solvency of the clearing firms. The CME closed that Exchange at 12:15, local time.

It follows that the best rationale for circuit breakers is not that they make markets more efficient but rather that they provide breathing spaces where markets have become technically incompetent to deal with the volume and direction of orders. Whether they accomplish the added feat of aiding price discovery in the short term is really inconsequential, compared to the damage that can occur in their absence when clearing systems are simply overwhelmed.

Part V: Net Capital Rules

The purpose of the net capital rule has been to promote liquidity and to require that broker dealers maintain specified amounts of net capital in relationship to aggregate indebtedness of customer related receivables under the customer protection rule and on proprietary positions.[47] The functional purpose of the rule is to ensure that a broker dealer can liquidate without the need for a formal proceeding if it falls below minimum net capital rules.[48] Under the "basic method" of the rule, the broker dealer must maintain net capital in excess of the greater of a specified minimum or 6–2/3% of its aggregate indebtedness.[49] Most major securities firms use the alternate method discussed below. A broker dealer must also maintain capital of 2% of its customer related receivables.[50]

The broker dealers are also required to deduct from their net worth certain percentages, known as "haircuts," of the market value of securities and commodities positions. The rule takes into account the holding of unrelated long and short positions in securities. Under the basic method a broker dealer is required to deduct 30% of the greater of the long or the short position (a "haircut"). The smaller position is deemed to be hedged by the larger position, but the dealer is required to apply an additional 15% haircut to the smaller of the short position to the extent that the smaller position exceeds 25% of the larger position.[51] In 1975 the SEC adopted a new alternative method, allowing firms electing the alternate method to take a 15% haircut on long positions. The haircut on a short position, to the extent that it exceeded in value 25% of the long position, was taken at 30% of the market value.[52] Under the proposed amendments, the calculation of haircuts under the alternative method and under the aggregate indebtedness method would be standardized and the haircuts for both long and short positions would be 15% of market value, and an additional 15% would be assessed on the market value of the lesser position to the extent it exceeded 25% of the greater position.[53]

Section 15(c)(3) of the Securities and Exchange Act of 1934 prescribes rules that safeguard the acceptance and use of customer securities and the carrying and use of customers' deposits or credit balances.[54] Pursuant to Section 15(c)(3), the Commission adopted the Customer Protection Rule 15(c)(3–3): broker dealers in computing net capital must make additional

adjustments to net worth relating to unrealized profits and losses,[55] subordinated liabilities,[56] contractual commitments,[57] collateralized liabilities,[58] options,[59] commodities, commodities futures[60] and stock index futures.[61]

Under the catchall provision, the rule treats unsecured receivables and securities for which there is no ready market as being subject to a 100% risk weighting. The SEC also applies 100% deduction to any proprietary position if a broker dealer cannot demonstrate that a ready market exists for the securities.[62] Obviously, these custom made financial instruments can be diverted to unregulated affiliates. Even proprietary positions that require broker dealer status can be traded in other markets, particularly London.[63]

The CFTC, which regulates futures commissions merchants (FCMs), relies solely on segregation of customers' accounts to determine FCM capital. Unlike the SEC's capital rules, which derive from the net debit of customers accounts,[64] the CFTC requires complete segregation of customers' accounts[65] and requires that FCMs hold 4% of customers' money as net capital.[66] The CFTC's jurisdiction over net capital rules extends to broker dealers to the extent that they hold "hedged" or "covered" positions.[67]

The haircuts required for broker dealers on equities are substantially higher than are those required under the CAD of the EEC.[68] However, an unhedged long or short position of the S&P 500 index under the CAD may attract a 10% weighting (8% + 2%). If a hedged position were held, the CAD would apply a weight of 2% maximum (together with possible additional capital requirements by member states to ensure that the index moves with the underlying securities), that, in sum, may be far lower than the 5% minimum that US net capital requirements would apply.[69]

Unlike US capital rules, the CAD deals only with proprietary positions of broker dealers. Rules regarding the segregation of customer funds are conduct of business rules and are consequently considered the prerogative of the individual member states, although there is a 2% specific risk capital requirement on gross positions. Another contrast between the United States and the EEC is that underwriting may be capitalized with 45-day subordinated debt in selected circumstances, and in all cases original maturity of one year debt as opposed to debt with an original maturity of two years minimum in the EEC,[70] but US regulators require haircuts on securities that are the subject of an underwriting unlike the CAD.

It is questionable whether US capital rules alone would have been sufficient to prevent a market meltdown had not the FRB urged banks to lend to securities firms and thus keep liquidity in the security system during 1987. Their ability to do so was augmented by the fact that at the time, securities activities were not conducted in bank affiliates as they currently are in "Section 20" subsidiaries of bank holding companies. Furthermore, several broker dealers might have failed had they not had sufficiently strong parents, including, Shearson Lehman, which is a subsidiary of American

Express, and Prudential Bache, which is a subsidiary of Prudential Insurance.[71] Securities houses are regulated only for those activities within the broker dealer's status. The holding companies of broker dealers are largely unregulated, although the Market Reform Act of 1990 enables the SEC to obtain information about the holding company and the upstreaming of funds.[72] One corporation which owns broker dealers has over 200 separate entities and three holding companies within its organizations, and another broker dealer has over 400 subsidiaries and 300 affiliates.[73] The Bachmann report notes that market disturbances in unregulated affiliates, particularly those engaged in forex, interest rate swaps, currency forward and futures transactions, are likely to have a spillover effect on regulated entities, broker dealers and futures commission merchants.[74] And consequently, as liquidity and solvency concerns increase for the conglomerate, trading activity in the securities and derivative markets may also be subject to a spillover effect. This absence of consolidation is a big advantage that US firms enjoy over EEC counterparts.

To bolster the capital required of firms with large dealer operations, the SEC adopted an amendment prohibiting the broker dealer from making withdrawals of net capital if after these withdrawals the broker dealer's net capital would be less than 25% of the firm's haircut on its securities position.[75] The SEC believes that if a firm were to reach this level, regulatory authorities would be able to increase surveillance and take appropriate action, including requiring the firm to liquidate securities positions.[76] Pursuant to this amendment, the SEC may also restrict, for a 20-day period, withdrawals of capital based on the insecure financial position of a broker dealer.

The risk assessment of holding companies[77] consisting primarily of report requirements for affiliates of broker dealers, is novel to the security regulatory system but is an exception to the concept of form supervision, as opposed to consolidated supervision. The SEC has adopted rules requiring reporting for holding companies which are "material associated persons" of broker-dealers.[78] Among the important activities conducted by securities houses that are not regulated by the SEC are all forms of futures and futures index trading, which are regulated by the CFTC, and interest rate swaps, currency swaps and bridge loans, which are frequently conducted in unregulated subsidiaries. The leverage ratio (which is the ratio of total liabilities to total equities) for all registered broker dealers has increased from 13 to 1 in 1980 to 18 to 1 in 1990. Among the 13 largest US broker dealers studied in a Government Accounting Office Report, the leverage ratio was 17 to 1.[79] According to this Government Accounting Report based on SEC sources, US securities firms had excess capital (i.e., that capital in excess of that required) averaging 6 to 12 times required capital. This statistic indicates that net capital rules do not account for the real risks of doing business; and that for securities firms capital rules, unlike

bank capital adequacy ratios, are far below the real level necessary in the course of business.

Part VI: Securities, Derivative Markets and Short-Term Horizons

Beginning with the fall of stock market prices in 1974, finance theory changed the way stock markets did business. Two theorems accounted for most of the change: the efficient market hypothesis[80] and the theory of portfolio diversification.[81] Regardless of whether these two theories might be empirically proved, they radically changed the way stock markets and institutional investors functioned. When the Employee Retirement Income Security Act (ERISA) required pension plan trustees to diversify their investments, the impact of finance theory was here to stay.[82]

Although portfolio diversification may be achieved with as few as 15 stocks,[83] institutional investors do not readily believe in their ability to beat the market. As stock markets continue to evolve, more and more funds will be indexed. Holding a significant stake of one large company will inevitably make unloading it more costly than selling the S&P index in any but the most extraordinary circumstances.

Two possible linkages exist between shareholder investment horizons and market trading practices: (1) excess volatility may lead to a higher cost of capital and thereby reduce investment; and (2) an information gap between management and shareholders may lead management to undertake short-term strategies which maximize short-term share price at the expense of long run investment. Measuring volatility is difficult. With the introduction of futures' contracts, all stocks tend to react with equal speed, and at an equal rate, to economy-wide news: whereas previously, only large capitalization stocks reacted quickly to such developments. Thus, volatility over short periods may rise while leaving long-term volatility unchanged.[84] No substantial evidence exists that volatility affects the cost of capital and, consequently, the time horizons of investors.

Three preconditions must be present for a stock-price effect on investment to exist: (1) managers must place some emphasis on current stock prices; (2) investment expenditure must suffer from an information gap; and (3) stock prices must be sensitive to current measures of profitability. For instance, many studies have shown that Japanese managers of industrial corporations are less concerned than their American counterparts with share prices,[85] partially as a result of the prevalence of short-term institutional investors and the threat of takeover.

Significantly, the investor-management information gap is consistent with the efficient market hypothesis, in that the gap issues from non-public information. More important, while all relevant public information may be widely disseminated, the information on which traders, whose horizons

are short-term, are apt to trade on is not necessarily all public information. An analyst who has a short-term time horizon will focus on different research agendas than one with a longer horizon.[86]

The efficient market hypothesis has been significantly eroded in recent years. Michael Jenson was able to write in 1978 that "the efficient market hypothesis is the best established fact in all social sciences."[87] However, the hypothesis lost ground rapidly following the finding that stock market volatility was far greater than could be accounted for by changed dividends.[88]

Alternatives to the efficient market hypothesis have rested on two assumptions: that not all investors are fully rational, and that their demand for risky assets is affected by beliefs or sentiments that are not fully justified by fundamental news (i.e., news about stock price fundamentals).[89]

Arbitragers trade to ensure that if a security has a perfect substitute (i.e., a portfolio of other securities that yield the same return with the same risk), and that the price of that security equals the price of the substitute portfolio, they sell and buy to equalize prices. When the substitute is actually perfect, this form of arbitrage is riskless.[90]

An arbitrager who sells short on overpriced stock and who is thinking of liquidating his position in the future bears the risk that stocks will be even more overpriced later on.[91] Thus, arbitrage can be performed most efficiently on short-term financial assets, because fundamental mispricing of these assets will exist only for a short period of time. Arbitragers will tend to arbitrage takeover targets rather than the long-term horizons of corporations.

Many kinds of non-fundamentals are reflected in stock price, such as a new stock's inclusion into the S&P 500 stock index. Being added to the S&P 500 index is not a plausible example of new information about a stock, since stocks are picked for their representativeness and not their performance potential. Nevertheless, announcements of inclusion into the index are accompanied by share price increases of 2% to 3%.[92]

Another example of pressure exerted on stock price in the absence of news is seen in the "January" effect, the fact that small cap stocks outperform market indices by a significant percentage each January, because investors, to realize capital losses, often sell small cap stocks and buy them back in January.[93] Additional empirical work has demonstrated that movements in the aggregate stock market are not largest on the days when the most important fundamental news is made public and vice versa.[94]

Many shifts in investor demands for securities appear not to be rational and are characterized by the term "noise trading." Examples of noise trading are myriad and are exemplified by investors who follow market gurus or forecasters and by those who follow "technical analysis" which calls for buying more stock when stocks have risen or broken through a barrier.[95] How "noise traders" can survive for a long-term period in the

market has been a question of concern to researchers since first posed by Milton Friedman in 1953.[96] Friedman's answer was that noise traders will not survive for a long period of time in a market, and that a market will return to fundamentals. However, it has recently been posited that noise traders unwittingly undertake excessive risks which, when leading to higher-than-average returns, allow them not only to survive but to flourish—albeit unsystematically, and to co-exist with arbitragers.

Another strategy of noise traders is their tendency to chase trends. Trend setters buy stocks after they rise and sell stocks after they fall. They follow positive feed-back strategies. Other stock strategies which are closely associated with positive feedback strategies suggest buying large stop orders, which require selling after a certain level of losses, regardless of future prospects; and, according to one author, program trading, which often involves buying more stocks to raise exposure to risk when prices rise and selling stock to cut exposure to risk when prices fall.[97]

The term noise trader obviously characterizes a goodly number of investors in today's market who employ both finance theory and noise trading on a daily basis. Whether government should do anything to protect noise traders from themselves depends on the social welfare externalities of the stock market. Modern research which finds noise traders to be prevalent continues to use the analogy of the casino first employed by Keynes in *The General Theory* to describe the workings of a stock market.[98] And, there is also a close resemblance between positive feedback noise traders and the stock market as a beauty contest as described by Keynes.

Even if the efficient market hypothesis were correct, pressure from concerns about stock market prices could cause corporate management to bolster short-term share prices at the expense of long-term investment. Such behavior could occur because of "signal jamming." Because the stock market uses earnings to make a rational forecast of firm value, higher earnings in the present may be correlated to higher earnings in the future, encouraging managers to manipulate shareholders' signals by pumping up earnings to raise forecasted values. In spite of being unable to fool the market, managers may be trapped into behaving myopically. The situation has been analogized to the "prisoner's dilemma."[99] The preferred cooperative equilibrium would involve no myopia on the part of managers and no conjecture of myopia by the stock market. Yet, no one manager will buck the trend under this myopic model of corporate behavior.[100]

The question of whether derivative markets (options and futures) divert funds from underlying markets is one that has been raised by regulators.[101] It could be said that to the extent that futures markets provide a vehicle for smoothing the timing of distribution of dividends and creating cash flow certainties, they are efficient; but, like any insurance scheme, if used for unintended purposes, it becomes inefficient. Futures markets have certainly drawn capital from the equities market, but their existence has also

enabled increased institutional investor participation in equities which has proceeded largely through indexing.[102]

One obvious advantage of the futures market is that it provides for regulatory competition between the SEC and the CFTC. The reporting systems of the CFTC seem almost instantaneous when compared with the gathering of data by the SEC.[103] Pursuant to the Market Reform Act, the SEC has proposed rules which would implement a large trader reporting system under the authority of § 13H of the Securities and Exchange Act of 1934, adopted as part of the Market Reform Act of 1990. Rule 13H–1 would establish an efficient, activity-based reporting system for gathering information about large traders and their trading activity.[104] The SEC was arguably spurred to do so by superior CFTC data.

Part VII: Conclusion

Encouraging long-term major stakeholding by institutional investors would require a major overhaul of the financial services industry. Even though a capital gains tax for long-term holdings may cause investors to hold stocks for a longer period of time, it will not convince institutional investors to hold a large percentage stake. A tax advantage for companies that hold over a certain percentage (5 or 10%) is an alternative. A securities or derivative market transaction tax would disrupt the essence of markets. The same result could be achieved by higher futures margins.

Current intermarket regulation is successful to the extent that it is con-cerned with the mechanics of securities clearance and settlement. In fact, securities markets performed remarkably well in the 1987 break. When it comes to the more substantive issues, such as promoting investment through long term shareholding, regulatory and legislative initiatives have been lacking. Appropriate intermarket regulation ought to be directed to stemming systemic risk. A priority is the consolidated regulation of secur-ities holding companies to the extent these companies engage in related unregulated securities, derivatives and forex business.

NOTES

1. *See generally Report of the Presidential Task Force on Market Mechanisms*, January 12, 1988 (hereinafter Brady Report).

2. *Hearing before the Subcommittee on Telecommunications and Finance of the Committee on Energy & Commerce*, House of Representatives, 101st Congress, 1st Sess. on HR 1609, *A Bill to Amend The Securities Exchange Act of 1934 To Provide Additional Authorities To Prevent Disruptions To The Nation's Securities Market*: Testimony of William J. Brodsky, President Chief Executive Officer, Chi-cago Mercantile Exchange, p. 1581. Arrangements have been instituted at the New York Stock Exchange and the Chicago Mercantile Exchange for cross-margining systems between the CME and the Options Clearing Corporation. (A system has

been developed through the Intermarket Surveillance Group to police frontrunning and self-frontrunning ["Testimony of Gerald Bearne," Ibid. at 59].) One of the means by which frontrunning or similar strategies may be achieved is by means of exchange of "physicals" where futures are sold and securities are purchased. This strategy is usually executed in London in order to avoid NYSE restrictions and to avoid disturbing the US market. This strategy demonstrates the need for greater international regulatory control (Memorandum to Chairman Ruder from Richard G. Ketchum, Director, Division of Market Regulation, *Ibid.*, at 239).

3. Alan Shick, *A Review and Analysis of the Changing Financial Environment and the Need for Regulatory Realignment*, 44 Bus. Law. 43, 45 (November 1988).

4. *See* Brady Report, *supra* note 1; *see also* Division of Market Regulation, SEC, role of index related trading in the market decline on September 11 and 12, 1986.

5. *See* Division of Market Regulation, SEC, The October 1987 Market Break (1988).

6. Shick, *supra* note 3, at 51, citing H. Stoll, and R. Whaley, "Expiration Day Effect of Index Options and Futures," p. 1, included in background material for Roundtable on Index Arbitrage, July 9, 1986 (SEC).

7. *Ibid.*, at 61–64.

8. *Future Trading Practices Act*, 106 Stat. 3590; Pub. Law 102–546; Title 5, § 501 amending 7 USC § 2a; any contract market in a stock index future shall file any change in the level of margin on the contract with the FRB. The FRB may request that levels be set to preserve the financial integrity of the contract market or its clearing system or to prevent systemic risk.

9. Board of Governors of the Federal Reserve System, *A Review and Evaluation of Federal Margin Regulations, A Study by the Staff* (1989); *see also* Paul Kupiec, "Initial Margin Requirement and Stock Returns Volatility; Another Look," Federal Reserve Board, Finance and Economic Discussion, Series No. 53 (1989), and Mark Warshawsky, "The Adequacy and Consistency of Margin Requirements in the Markets for Stocks and Derivative Products," Federal Reserve Board; Staff Study No. 158 (1989).

10. In addition to the studies cited in *supra* notes 1 and 3, *Interim Report of the Working Group on Financial Markets* submitted to the President of the United States, May 1988; J. R. Kessler, "Study on Improvements in the Settlement of Cross-Border Securities Transactions in the European Economic Community," "Study for the Commission of the European Community," Directorate Generale XV, Financial Institutions and Company Law, July 1988; *Clearance and Settlement Systems in the World Securities Market*—Report of the Group of 30, New York and London, March 1989.

11. *Report of the Bachmann Task Force on Clearance and Settlement Reform in the US Securities Markets*, Securities and Exchange Commission, Release No. 34–30802, 57 Fed. Reg. 17,812 (June 22, 1992).

12. *See* Working Group on Financial Markets, *supra* note 10. *See also* Hans Stohl, "Margins on Stock Index Future Contracts," Risk Management Tapes 34 (Spring 1990), and Board of Governors of the Federal Reserve System, "A Review and Evaluation of Federal Margin Regulations," Staff Study, 1984, Washington, D.C.

13. Bachmann, *supra* note 11, at 27812.

14. Section 362 also provides protection for margin and settlement payments and provides protection from Title 11. (§ 201 of Title 11 US Code [as amended by § 101]). Separate legislation enacted in 1989 extends similar protections to counterparties dealing with most US bank and thrift institutions. See § 11 of the Federal Deposit Insurance Act, 12 USC § 1821, as amended by § 212 of the Financial Institutions Reform, Recovery and Enforcement Act of 1989.

Section 362 also allows non-bankrupt parties to terminate swap agreements following the filing of a bankruptcy petition and to use collateral held. (101st Congress, 2nd Sess., HR 4612, An Act To Amend Title 11 of the United States Code Regarding Swap Agreements and Forward Contracts [1990]. Sections 102, 105 and 106.) Additional provisions allow counterparties to enforce netting agreements for a broad range of forward rate agreements, allow parties to net out or offset termination values and provides for express protection against transfers. The Act further provides that a broad range of forward contracts are exempt from the automatic stay and anti-termination and preference provisions and applies to a broad range of forward contracts referred to in the Commodities Exchange Act (Sections 201, 202, 203 and 204).

15. FDICIA (cited in Chapter 2, *supra* note 133) § 402 Definitions, 403 Bilateral Netting, § 404 Clearing Organization Netting, § 405 Pre-Emption.

16. American Bar Association, Section of Business Law, *Interim Report of the Advisory Committee on Settlement of Market Transaction, Exposure Draft for Comment* (February 15, 1991).

17. *Ibid.*, Recommendations A–1 through A–5.

18. The Bankruptcy Code currently excepts from the automatic stay of § 362A the right of certain financial institutions and intermediaries to set-off claims, mutual debts and property for margin and settlement payments subject to the rights of the Securities Investor Protection Corporation. *See* Bankruptcy Code, § 352B(6), *et seq.* Currently the only authority that a broker dealer may rely upon for margin calls made after the petition is filed are statements from the House Report of the 1984 Amendments to the Bankruptcy Code. Section 555 could permit a liquidation of the securities account, subject to certain questions, that is, whether a securities contract exists after the securities are settled in the account, and whether the broker dealer has a right to liquidate positions as a result of the bankruptcy. (ABA Report, *supra* note 14, at 23). The rights to make settlement payments and margin payments are covered under § 546E of the Bankruptcy Code and are defined in § 741(5) and § 761(15). Uncertainty about what constitutes a settlement payment may signal the need to clarify existing law (*see* for example *Bevill Bresler and Schulman, Asset Management Corp. v. Spencer Savings and Loan Assoc.*, 878 F.2d 742 (3d Cir. 1989).

19. The Bachmann Task Force also considered a daily mark-to-market for securities in the NSCC System, but felt that it would require constant bookkeeping and a complex payment system. Twenty-one percent of retail purchase trades are settled by check delivered through the mail, and only 20% of these trades as measured in dollar value arrive on or before T plus 3, thus without requiring cash management accounts, it is necessary to implement an electronic payment system as a payment option for securities customers (Bachmann, *supra* note 9). Negotiations are already underway to use the Automated Clearing House, an electronic

payment system used by over 22,000 banks, thrifts and other financial institutions on behalf of corporations and individuals for securities transactions. For institutional trades, it may be necessary to create an interactive system for affirmation of trades (*Ibid.*, at 19).

It is also very helpful in shortening the settlement cycle to reduce the use of physical certificates. The number of certificates provided to investors and participants through the Depository Trust Corporation dropped from 16 million certificates annually in 1980 to 6 million certificates in 1990 (*Ibid.*, at 20). However, the US Working Committee of the Group of 30 clearance and settlement project and the Bachmann Committee recommend that settlement among financial intermediaries and their institutional clients occur in a book entry form and has made a series of proposed rule changes that would enable the implementation of this recommendation (*Ibid.*, at 21).

20. Commodities Futures Trading Corporation, Division of Economic Analysis, *Report on Stock Index Futures and Cash Market Activity during October 1989*, May 1990.

21. *Ibid.*, at 17.

22. Group of 30 *Report on World Clearance and Settlement Systems* (1990), *supra* note 10.

23. Bank for International Settlements, *Delivery Versus Payment in Security Settlement Systems: Report prepared by the Committee on Payment and Settlement Systems of the Central Banks of the Group of Ten Countries* (Basle, September 1992).

24. The report also speaks to the advantages of same day payments by showing the association of next day payments with the creditworthiness of the guarantor (either the settlement bank or the clearing system).

25. *Delivery Versus Payment, supra* note 23, p. 33, citing G–10 and Bank for International Settlements, *Report on Multi-Lateral Netting* (1990).

26. *Cf.* BIS *Delivery Versus Payment, supra* note 23, at A20 and A22–24.

27. *See Report of the Presidential Task Force on Market Mechanisms, supra* note 1, and *Interim Report of the Working Group on Financial Markets, supra* note 10; Group of 30, *Report on World Clearance and Settlement Systems, supra* note 10; *Bachmann Report, supra* note 11.

28. I. M. Destler, and C. Randall Henning, Dollar Politics: Exchange Rate Policymaking in the U.S. 62–65 (1989).

29. "Herstaat Risks" refer to the 1974 failure of the Herstaat Bank because of currency speculation. This failure disrupted the Eurodollar interbank market for several months.

30. *See* "Large Value Payment Systems: What Have We Learned?" Remarks of Wayne Angel, Board of Governors, Federal Reserve System at the 12th Payment System International Conference, October 7, 1992, London, England.

31. *Ibid.*, at 15.

32. *Delivery Versus Payment, supra* note 23, citing *Report on Multi-Lateral Netting, supra* note 25.

33. "Large Payment Systems," *supra* note 30.

34. *Ibid.*, at 23.

35. Carolyn Brancato, Institutional Investor Project, Columbia. "Institutional

Investors and Capital Markets: 1991 Update," Columbia University School of Law, Center for Law and Economic Studies (September 1991).

36. Merton Miller, FINANCIAL INNOVATIONS AND MARKET VOLATILITY 38 (1991).

37. SEC Report, *supra* note 4, at xiii.

38. Miller, *supra* note 36, at 58.

39. Franklin Edwards, *Futures Trading and Cash Market Volatility: Stock Index and Interest Rate Futures*, 8 J. FUTURES MARKET 421 (1988).

40. The Brady Report, *supra* note 1, Appendix, Analytic Study VIII, VIII–2.

41. Miller, *Financial Innovations, supra* note 36, at 63.

42. *Report to the Congress on Intermarket Coordination* submitted by Alan Greenspan, Chairman, Board of Governors of the Federal Reserve System, May 19, 1992, in fulfillment of Section 8a of The Market Reform Act of 1990.

43. *Market Volatility and Investor Confidence: Report of the Board of Directors of the New York Exchange* (June 7, 1990), p. 4.

Stage 1	*Stage 2*	*Stage 3*	*Stage 4*
12 S&P pts.	24 S&P pts.	36 S&P pts.	48 S&P pts.
100 Dow pts.	200 Dow pts.	300 Dow pts.	400 Dow pts.
Duration			
60 mins.	90 min.	120 mins.	150 mins. (Ibid.)

44. Miller, *supra* note 36, at 253.

45. *Ibid.*, at 245.

46. *Ibid.*

47. Steven Molinari, and Nelson S. Kibler, *Broker Dealers' Financial Responsibility Under the Uniform Net Capital Rule—A Case for Liquidity*, 72 GEORGE. L. J. 1 (1983); and Michael Jamroz, *The Net Capital Rule*, 47 BUS. LAW 863 (May 1992).

48. The net capital rule promotes orderly self-liquidation of broker dealers and reduces the likelihood that the failed broker dealer would have to be liquidated pursuant to the Securities Investor Protection Act of 1988 (15 USC §§ 78aaa–78lll). Recently the SEC has proposed rules for raising the minimum capital to $250,000 because of the $250 million in customer property self-liquidations in 1987 and 1988. One firm held $70 million of customer securities although it only had $61,000 of net capital. Proposed Rule Securities and Exchange Commission 17 CFR Part 240 Release No. 34–272249, 54 Fed. Reg. 40395, October 1989.

49. Or $25,000, 17 CFR § 240.15c3–1(a).

50. 17 CFR § 240.15(c)(3)–1(f) (1991) defining the computation of customer receivables is at *Ibid.* 15c3–3(a).

51. 17 CFR § 15(c)(3)–1(c)(2)(vi)(J) (1991).

52. 17 CFR § 240.15(c)(3)–1(f) (1991).

53. SEC Release, *supra* note 48, at 40,403.

54. 15 USC § 780(c)(3) (1976), 17 CFR § 240.15(c)(3). The first part of the rule deals with customer securities and requires broker dealers to have physical possession or control of all fully paid and excess margin securities carried for the accounts of customers. The broker dealer must make a daily account to show that it is complying with this section of the rule. *Ibid.*, 15c–3c.

The second part of the rule deals with customer's funds and requires broker dealers to make a weekly computation of the form for debt of reserve requirements (15c3–3a). If the credit exceeds the debits, the broker dealer must deposit the excess by the morning of the second business day following computation in a special bank account for the exclusive benefit of customers. *Ibid.*, 15(c)(3–3el).

55. *Ibid.*, 15(c)(3)–1(c)(2)(i).

56. *Ibid.*, 15(c)(3)–1(d).

57. *Ibid.*, 15(c)(3)–1(c)(2)(viii).

58. *Ibid.*, 15(c)(3)–1(c)(2)(xiii).

59. *Ibid.*, 15(c)(3)–1a). In 1985 the SEC issued a no-action letter that allowed broker dealers who were not options market makers to compute deductions based on the market value of the option rather than on the underlying security, with a maximum deduction of 50% of the market value of the option. Deductions depend upon whether the broker dealer is a market maker.

60. *Ibid.*, 15(c)(3)–1(b).

61. The CFTC net-capital rule can be found at 17 CFR § 1.17 (1991). If the broker dealer is a clearing member, the broker dealer must deduct the margin requirement of the applicable clearing organization. If the broker dealer is a member of a self-regulatory organization, the broker dealer must deduct 150% of the maintenance marginal requirement.

62. 17 CFR § 240.15(c)(3)–1(c)(2)(vii) (1991).

63. Securities commissions represented about 34% of broker dealer revenues in 1980, but this figure dropped to about 17% by 1990. Meanwhile, the proportion of broker dealer revenues derived from other sources such as interest income or fees from handling mergers increased from about 31% to 47%. (Government Accounting Office, *Securities Firms: Assessing the Need to Regulate Additional Financial Activities* [April 1992]) at 839.

64. Rule 15(c)(3), *supra* note 54.

65. This segregation broke down in the market break of 1989 according to the CFTC Report.

66. 17 CFR § 1.17(a)(i)(B).

67. 17 CFR § 1.17(c)(5)(x). The word "cover" is used in a manner fundamentally equivalent to "hedge" as defined at 17 CFR § 1.17.J(1). The definition of "covered" or "hedged" is unclear because positions shift rapidly. The SEC issued a no-action letter to the NYSE stating that in the event a position is determined not to be covered in the future by the CFTC, the net capital requirement for a basket or an index will be no less than 5%. Letter from Michael A. Macchiaroli, Assistant Director, Division of Market Regulation, SEC, to David Marcus, Executive Vice-President, Regulatory Services Group, New York Stock Exchange, Inc., February 17, 1986.

68. *See* Chapter 1, *supra* note 226 and accompanying text.

69. *See* Chapter 1, *supra* note 258 and accompanying text. For example, the S&P futures contract of 6/22/92 was $210,000 and the margin requirement was 5.87% (interview with staff of CFTC), which equaled $12,320. Under the CAD this would attract a weighting of $21,000 for an unhedged position, but a hedged position would only require $4,200 capital.

70. 17 CFR § 240.15c3–1(d)(11)(5). Temporary and Revolving Subordination Agreements. The 45 day term is available three times a year for firms that maintain

120% more of the minimum requirement. The exemption on which broker dealers rely more is allowing them to enter into subordination agreements for less than one year, but net capital must be 200% of the minimum requirement. See also, Chapter I Part IV B and accompanying text.

71. For example, American Express provided an additional $750 million in capital to Shearson Lehman Brothers Holdings Inc. and its broker-dealer to offset the $966 million loss incurred by these entities in 1990, following major restructuring expenses and decreased operating revenues. Following similar difficulties in 1990, the Prudential Insurance Company of America provided $200 million in capital to the holding company of its broker-dealer, now called Prudential Securities Inc., and purchased $600 million in bridge loans from an affiliate of the broker-dealer. Finally, General Electric purchased $750 million of high yield bonds and bridge loans from Kidder, Peabody & Co. Inc., and Credit Suisse contributed $300 million in capital to, and purchased a $250 million bridge loan from, The First Boston Corporation's immediate holding company. Kidder, Peabody & Co. Inc. experienced a net loss during 1990. Information about the First Boston Corporation's 1990 earnings was not publicly available (Government Accounting Office, *supra* note 63, at 43).

72. *See infra* notes 76 and 77, and accompanying text.

73. Government Accounting Office, *supra* note 63, at 31.

74. *Bachmann Report, supra* note 11.

75. 17 CFR § 240.15(c)(3)–1(e)(2) (1991).

76. Net Capital Rule Exchange Act Release No. 28,347, Fed. Sec. L. Rep. (CCH) 84,618, at 81,014 (August 15, 1990). *See also* Jamroz, *supra* note 47 at 895–896, for an account of the Drexel case.

77. 17(h)(1) Risk Assessment for Holding Companies, added by Act of October 16, 1990 (Market Reform Act), § 4(a) Pub. Law. 101–432, 104 Stat. at 963; 17(h)(2) Additional Information; 17(h)(3) Associated Person Subject to Banking Regulation; 17(h)(4) Exemption; 17(h)(5) Authority to Limit Disclosure.

78. The rules require the following disclosure:

1. organizational chart;
2. risk management policies;
3. pending legal proceedings;
4. off-balance sheet items;
5. aggregate securities and commodities positions;
6. financial instruments;
7. bridge loans;
8. funding sources;
9. real estate holdings;

(Regulation 240.17(h)–1T Requirement to Maintain and Preserve Information [57 Fed. Reg. 32,159]; Regulation 240.17(h)–2T Reporting Requirement of Risk Assessment Information Required to be Maintained by § 240.17(h)–1J [57 Fed. Reg. 32,159]).

79. *Ibid.*, at 41.

80. Paul Samuelson, *Proof that Properly Anticipated Prices Fluctuate Randomly,* 6 INDUST. MANAGE. REV. 41–50 (Spring 1965); and Michael Jensen, *The Performance of Mutual Funds in the Period 1945–64,* 23 J. FIN. 587–616 (December 1965).

81. Harry M. Markowitz, *Portfolio Selection* VII J. Fin. 77–91 (March 1952).

82. *See* Chapter 4, *infra* note 120, and accompanying text.

83. *See* Chapter 4, *infra* note 121, and accompanying text. The issues discussed in this chapter in terms of market regulation are revisited in Chapter 4, in the context of corporate law, stakeholders and relational financing.

84. Kenneth Froot, Andre Perold, and Jeremy Stein, "Shareholder Trading Practices and Corporate Investment Horizons," Council on Competitiveness and Harvard Business School p. 11 (December 1991). Also appearing in another version as NBER Research Paper No. 3498.

85. James Abegglen, and George Stalk, Jr., KAISHA, THE JAPANESE CORPORATION (1985); and Jay Lorsch, and Elizabeth McGuiver, TIME HORIZONS IN THE US AND JAPAN (1992). *See generally*, Chapter 4, *infra*.

86. *See generally*, Froot, Perold, and Stein, *supra* note 84.

87. Cited in Andre Schleifer, and Lawrence H. Summers, *The Noise Trader Approach to Finance*, 4 J. ECON. PROSPECTIVES 19 (Spring 1990).

88. Robert J. Schiller, *Do Stock Prices Move Too Much to Be Justified by Subsequent Changes in Dividends?* AMER. ECON. REV. 421 (1981).

89. Schleifer and Summers, *supra* note 87.

90. *Ibid*.

91. Andrew Schleifer, and Robert W. Vichney, "Equilibrium Short Horizons of Investors and Firms," American Economic Review Papers and Proceedings 1990.

92. Andrew Schleifer, *Is Demand Curves for Stocks Slope Down?* 41 J. FIN. 579–590 (July 1986).

93. Schleifer and Summer, *supra* note 87.

94. *Ibid*.

95. *Ibid*.

96. Milton Friedman, *The Case for Flexible Exchange Rates, in* ESSAYS IN POSITIVE ECONOMICS (1953).

97. Schleifer, *supra* note 92.

98. *See* Chapter 4, *infra* epigraph to conclusion.

99. The "prisoner's dilemma" is the often used paradigm of the co-conspirator who finds it in his interest to betray his companion because in the absence of communication he does not know what the other prisoner will do.

100. Jeremy Stein, *Efficient Capital Market, Inefficient Firms: A Model of Myopic Corporate Behavior*, QUART. J. ECON. 655 (1989).

101. This paragraph is drawn from interviews with regulators from the Securities Investment Board, members of the US Government Accounting Office and former economists at the Securities and Exchange Commission.

102. Of the total assets under management in 1990, 11.6% were in indexed equity funds, up from 9.3% in 1986. As of September 30, 1990, the largest 15 pension funds with investments in indexed equities had invested a total of $143.6 billion in all types of equities, or 41.3% of their total assets. Of this, $89 billion was explicitly invested in indexed equities. Indexed equities, therefore, accounted for a dollar weighted average of 62.0% of all equities in these funds and 25.6 percent of their total assets. *Ibid.*, at 13.

103. Interview with staff member of the CFTC.

104. Securities and Exchange Act Release No. 29593 56 Fed. Reg. 42,550 (August 14, 1991).

4

A Comparative Analysis of the Legal Structure of Corporate Finance in the United States and Japan

No issue in international relations is more in evidence than the trade friction and economic competitiveness of the United States and Japan. Too frequently, this subject has been argued in terms of trade law, fair trade, the General Agreement on Tariffs and Trade, and other matters relating to the trade of goods and services. Far less frequently has a comparative examination of the structure of corporate governance and finance in the United States and Japan been undertaken. When this approach is used, it has generally centered on the unfair oligopolistic structure of the Japanese Keiretsu, leading the observant student of international finance to conclude that the United States had better take protectionist measures. It is the thesis of this chapter that the corporate financial structure of Japanese and US firms are indeed very different, but that these differences point toward the need for harmonization of laws governing financial reporting, public disclosure and financial affiliation.

This chapter is divided into five parts: Part I surveys the interplay of monetary policy, financial regulation, and the cost of capital, and sets the stage for the assertion that inequities in the world capital market produce different costs of capital and may in the long run create disequilibrium. Part II considers the capital market structure, the comparative capital markets of Japan and the United States in terms of size and investors, discusses the role of institutional investors in the United States and Japan, and considers the degree of institutional monitoring that occurs in Japan, and the argument for institutional monitoring in the United States. While the costs of financial distress in each system cannot be adequately weighed, the inevitable consequences of the organization of Japanese capital markets is to provide maximum capital formation enabling the increase of market share at the expense of financial market stability. Part III examines the impact of Japanese capital markets on US capital markets, and the precautions which can and cannot be taken to protect the US domestic capital

markets. Part IV examines the inadequate regulatory structure of Japan's banking system in light of asset deflation, with special emphasis on real estate assets. Part V concludes that the structure of Japanese corporate markets has led to a speculative bubble which does, in all likelihood, contribute to international financial market volatility; but that such volatility has also been created by a US strategy of portfolio investment that creates an illusion of liquidity and provides no means for effective monitoring or for long-term capital formation to the degree necessary in today's global market place. This chapter concludes that there is a need for harmonization of laws governing finance, banking and securities in order to enable the continued internationalization of world financial markets.

Part I: Causes of the Balance of Payment Disequilibrium: Exchange Rates, Cost of Capital, Leverage and Investment

A. EXCHANGE RATES

The first and most obvious cause of trade disequilibrium has been an undervalued Yen. Despite momentous fluctuations in the Japanese stock market and short-term interest rates, the Yen–dollar rate has fluctuated in the narrow range of 123–142 since 1988, when the dollar was at its low, until the end of 1992.[1] Japanese external adjustments in the years 1985 through 1991 reflect only a slow and modest adjustment to the devaluation of the dollar, notwithstanding the view that nominal exchange rates can reduce current account surpluses.[2] One reason for the failure of Japan to adjust is the lower prices of US and oil imports, which are priced in dollars, lowering the "pass through ratio" of the Yen–dollar exchange rate. Furthermore, there is a tendency in Japan to price by export destination.[3] One author observes that in 1991, Japan's current account surplus continued to increase (or began to increase again), largely because of Japanese exports to Germany, where unification has led to a trade deficit.[4] The author concludes that the world savings shortage is a direct result of Japan's external surplus, but as we shall see in Part III of this chapter, Japan's capital market structure and its emphasis on market share rather than profitability may be the decisive factor behind the trade surplus and the world capital market shortage.

B. THE COST OF CAPITAL

New fields of research have evolved which give considerable attention to the role of the cost of capital.[5] Higher cost of capital in the United States would explain a higher "hurdle rate" for investment, leading to comparatively less investment in the United States than in Japan and thereby diminishing competitiveness. Differing interest rates would be the most

obvious cause of a cost of capital differential. Professor Frankel concludes that lower real interest rates played a major role in the lower cost of capital in Japan in the 1970s and 1980s. These low interest rates, taken together with the high expected growth rate, explain the high level of equity and land prices (relative to earnings and rent), but do not explain the meteoric rises of the late 1980s.[6] Other studies have shown that the real interest rates throughout the eighties were not equal but nevertheless favored one country as much as the other.[7]

Generally, there are two components to the cost of capital: the cost of debt and the cost of equity. Because it is impossible to calculate the national cost of debt and equity, indices of leading corporate bonds and equities are substituted. The measure of the cost of capital most commonly employed is the Weighted Average Cost of Capital (WACC). The average cost of capital may differ from the marginal cost of capital, and it is the latter that affects real investment decisions.[8] Some studies have concluded that the marginal cost of capital has not been substantially different in Japan and the United States.[9] A different approach is to consider the "hurdle rate," the rate of return corporations demand on their capital investment, but this will inevitably involve subjective definitions of investment.

Return on net operating assets is considerably higher in the United States than in Japan; and, on the whole, the real average rate of return on traded US firms was 10.4% for the period 1975–1991, while the average for Japan was 5.9% for traded companies over the same period.[10]

Because no consistent differential can be found in real interest rates or in the cost of debt which is derivative of it, cost of capital studies have focused their attention on the cost of equity. Fundamentally, three different approaches have been used to measure the cost of equity: (1) capital appreciation as measured over a time period by market value;[11] (2) earnings per share; and (3) dividends as measured by current dividends and expected future yields,[12] after tax. The latter two formulations will yield a higher cost of equity in the United States, while the former will yield higher cost of equity in Japan. Until the recent Tokyo stock market slump, determining the cost of equity by earnings per share would have yielded a higher cost of capital in the United States.

Any attempt to measure the cost of equity will result in conceptual as well as technical measurement problems. In bull markets, the cost of issuing equity is low, and in bear markets it is high. A company will try to issue equity more frequently in a bull market, thereby lowering its overall equity costs.

Another study concludes that Japan's actual cost of debt advantage is modest in spite of a large nominal difference in interest rates,[13] but, in the late 1980s Japan enjoyed a lower cost of equity. This study considered three approaches for measuring the cost of equity funds: (1) historical,

using stock market returns as a proxy; (2) current market based numbers, usually the price earnings ratio, on the grounds that these numbers incorporate market expectations of future developments; and (3) a prospective method that uses either a dividend discount model or a discounted cash flow model to calculate a return.

The paradigm the study's author proposes must also avoid the tendency to interpret a decrease in the market discount rate as an increase in the cost of capital, while incorporating the many unique features of Japanese markets, such as consolidation, stock cross-holdings and high land values. This paradigm, according to the author, works well in conjunction with either a price-earnings ratio or a discount method. Each company is divided into core operations and financial activities consisting of two main types—cross-holdings and land. One can then identify the "true earnings" values that should be attributed to each of the three sectors.[14] In order to determine core operations, gross earnings will be reduced to the extent the companies receive dividends as the result of its holdings of securities and also to the extent that the firm would have to rent back its land holdings at current market values. Adjustments are also made for depreciation and consolidation with affiliated companies. According to Richard Mattione, with the many adjustments, Japanese firms enjoyed a real cost of equity 388 basis points lower than that of US firms from 1987 to 1989.[15] However, since 1991, the gap has swung in favor of US firms. The same method implies that during 1991, the real cost of equity was an average 79 basis points higher in Japan than in the United States and that at the end of March 1992, the real cost of equity was 9.19% in Japan, 225 basis points higher than the cost of equity in the United States. But, some of this shift may be due to differences in economic cycles in the two countries. The recession left US corporate earnings below trend, which led to a lower cost of capital,[16] and this cyclicality has since reversed, with Japan suffering an economic downturn.

The cost of borrowing by non-financial companies was affected by the availability of new bank funds created by Japan's adaptation of the G–10 capital adequacy framework. This allowed banks to include up to 45% of the appreciation in market value of marketable securities as "reevaluation reserves."[17] This in turn caused a surge in bank capital and consequently a surge in lending (which was largely invested by corporate borrowers).

Implications abound from the decline of share prices: first, leverage is likely to be higher (on a debt-to-market value basis) than has been traditional, and investment cannot be efficiently curtailed fast enough to comport with the fall in share prices.

According to one analyst, the G–10 Capital Adequacy levels can be met in Japan so long as the stock market does not dip lower than the 17,000 level for the Nikkei 225 index. At any level above 17,000, banks' short-term requirements for new capital are modest: 1.54 trillion Yen for the 21

city long-term credit and trust banks, and Japanese banks will be able to increase loans at a pace consistent with moderate economic growth. If the stock market were to fall again to the 15,000 level, banks could sustain their current level of risk assets but might have trouble raising capital sufficient to support any economic recovery.[18]

Six banks would have total capital ratios below 7.6% when the Nikkei index is at 17,000. Even before the recent stock market turbulence, Japanese banks were aware that the hidden gains might not be sufficient to cover their tier-two capital needs; thus, during the fiscal year ending March 1991, the major banks raised approximately 4 trillion Yen of subordinated loans. With the poor stock market performance, banks rushed to raise additional subordinated debt with less encouraging results. If the Nikkei index were to fall to 15,000—exactly 1 of 21 major banks (Nippon Trust) would meet the capital adequacy standards.[19] At a Nikkei level of 15,000, the 21 banks would have to raise approximately 3.6 trillion Yen in capital, including over 400 billion Yen of tier-one capital.

Since the mid–1980s, Japan has issued net new equity,[20] while between 1984 and 1989, the US corporate sector retired, on net, $676 billion in equity and issued $1,070 billion in new debt.[21] The relevance of this fact, however, must not be overstated and is very likely a result of particular circumstances present in the 1980s, in particular an overheated stock market in Japan and mergers and acquisitions in the United States, as discussed here and in sub-section C, below.

A potentially useful indicator of real leverage is the ratio of corporate debt to cash flow, which has been higher than historical levels in the United States, and did not decline between 1982 and 1987 despite national economic expansion.[22] Because of problems in consolidating Japanese corporate returns, no similar studies exist for Japan, but it is likely Japanese companies would show an increase in debt to cash flow in the 1990s.

Only a small percentage of increased leveraging in the United States can be accounted for by leveraged buyouts. For instance, the industries that recorded the largest increase in leverage in the eighties were coal and petroleum-related products, which recorded no leveraged buyouts (LBOs), and other low-tech manufacturing, such as stone and glass.[23] In general, those industries that underwent significant increases in leverage tended to be those with the lowest return to capital in 1980. This is in sharp contrast to Japan, where the equity-linked market provided considerable new sources of funding for similar low-tech, high-resource industries.

Although the Japanese economy overall will not be seriously affected by equity-linked bonds, according to Richard Mattione, several sectors of the Japanese economy will be severely affected. In a representative survey of 240 firms, the stock market would have to advance above the

34,000 level on the Nikkei index for even half the issues now outstanding to convert.[24] Over 10% of the sample firms would find profits diminished by more than 30% if they were forced to replace equity linked bonds with straight debt. For these firms, equity linked bonds alone pose a significant risk. Another 25% of the sample firms, would see profits fall between 10% and 30%.[25] There are four "problem industries": transportation, non-bank credit, brewing and trading companies.[26] Steelmakers and miscellaneous heavy industries, mining, oil, cement, paper and glass, also have a high average exposure with a fair number of exposures in excess of 20% of profits.[27] Although these firms do not match exactly the industries most highly leveraged in the United States in the 1980s, they are distinctly low-tech sectors and the average exposure is low for high-tech sectors. These firms also tend to be domestically, rather than internationally, oriented[28] having less "comparative advantage" in the international marketplace.

The low savings rate may be one of the principal causes of the low investment rate that has predominated in the United States since the 1970s. In the United States, a substantial share of overall dissaving, particularly in the 1980s, can be attributed to the US budget deficit; but it is also true that private savings declined more than three percentage points.[29] This decline in private savings is open to epiphenomenal explanations; but the explosion in consumer financing credit, as discussed in Chapter 2, however, is certainly a factor. The consumer credit revolution may in part have been enhanced by the increase in corporate leverage in the 1980s. Payouts to shareholders tended to be consumed rather than reinvested.[30]

If the degree of capital mobility were sufficiently high, the going interest rate would be tied to the world interest rate by international capital flows.[31] However, it is very probable that international capital mobility does not imply the existence of the same real rate of interest in every country. An important cause of the interest rate differential affecting the cost of capital in the United States and Japan is the past interest rate ceiling in Japan (which still exists for post office accounts), and the fact that time deposits and demand deposits of less than one year remain regulated.[32] However this situation appears to be in the process of amendment and, in the future, only demand deposits will remain regulated, and overall free market interest rates on deposits are quickly coming into existence. The existence of interest rate ceilings reflects a tradition of financial regulation which existed in an earlier period of credit allocations and was intended to ensure the diversion of funds away from consumption and toward investment. However, financial innovations have been rapid in Japan, particularly since the mid-seventies. The market for unsecured debentures began in earnest around 1979. Money market interest rates are free market, as are call

money interest rates, which are price flexible, and further, in 1988, the commercial paper market came into existence.[33]

The question of the ceilings on interest rates is closely related to the availability of savings for consumption and the degree to which household consumers benefit from Japanese corporate wealth. It has been noted that the US savings rate does not reflect the actual wealth of the US household because the savings rate does not take into account the accretion of wealth due to the market value of assets owned by households.[34] US and Japanese householders differ substantially in the kind of wealth into which they invest their savings. The evidence suggests that Japanese householders invest a large proportion of their savings in fixed assets that do not appreciate as much as equities. US individual equity investment is much more substantial because of the role played by pension and money market funds.[35] The high rate of Japanese fixed asset investment, together with Japan's high savings rates, is largely accountable for the lower-than-market rate of interest on Japanese cost of capital.[36] Arguably, the low interest rate that prevailed in Japan in the 1980s resulted in a run-up of asset prices and consequently a low cost of equity capital. Excess liquidity (not specifically mentioned in cost of capital studies) could explain both high land and equity prices.[37]

Excess liquidity also enabled the Japanese to tap the low real interest rates of the Eurobond markets by issuing Eurodollar equity warrants (i.e., convertible bonds). The vast majority of these issues were bought by Japanese institutions probably on behalf of institutional investors such as Investment Trusts. Among the questions posed by the issue of Japanese equity warrants are how such issues could have been made, considering the vast amount of the Japanese trade surplus that was invested abroad, and why it was so necessary that these issues be made in international markets, with the dollar as the standard currency unit? Furthermore, why, when these dollars were changed into Yen, did the Yen rate not rise?

The value of an investment opportunity will vary according to the person investing so that a Japanese investor who might be able to make only 2% on a Yen investment might prefer this return to a higher yielding dollar investment. Therefore, the low rates of return on convertible equity warrants in Japan may be explained as a desire by Japanese investors to take up Japanese issues rather than to invest in foreign currencies.

If international capital mobility posited by theorists existed, it would imply an equal real rate of interest to an international investor; however, this does not take into account the fact that the portfolio investor from Japan, for example, may have an aversion to international investment in favor of Japanese investment. Consequently, there are limits to quantifying international capital mobility. An international investor, when deciding

which country's assets to buy, will not compare the different countries in terms of their expected purchasing power. That investor will evaluate assets in terms of the same basket of goods as the one that is consumed by that particular investor.

Although an investor may have a preference for borrowing in his own country, a truly multinational corporation will prefer to borrow in the country with the lowest rate of interest, depending on that multinational enterprise's investment in that country. The dearth of domestic savings in the United States has been two-thirds offset by net inflows of foreign capital in the form of direct and portfolio investment.[38] Less investment may result from fewer investment opportunities. Declining returns to capital are said to result from a productivity frontier[39] that is the result of unusually high productivity in the postwar era. This hypothesis is borne out, to a certain extent, by the distinction between gross investment which rose in the early 1980s, and has stabilized at traditional levels, and net investment, which plummeted in the same period. While net investment would intuitively appear to be the right measure of the adequacy of investment, the increasingly short life of capital assets requires a consistently higher share of Gross Domestic Product (GDP) to maintain a fixed rate of net investment. Those who believe that the United States is adequately invested can take comfort in its stock of capital per capita which exceeds that of Japan, and per capita productivity, which is also higher than in Japan.[40] However, it is worth noting in this regard that: (1) certain expenditures in which Japan exceeds the United States, such as job training, are considered ordinary and necessary business expenses and are not included in investment; and (2) if current patterns persist, Japan will, at some point, overtake the United States (in stock of capital per capita). The fact that considerable savings exist in the form of capital gains appreciation is irrelevant in the investment debate because these price reevaluations are clearly reflected in the national capital stock.

Writing in 1980, Martin Feldstein found, to his surprise, a strong correlation between national savings and investments, despite international capital mobility.[41] In 1991, Feldstein continued to find a high correlation between savings and investments, despite the unprecedented increase in international flow of capital to the United States.[42] His findings are disputed by Dornbusch, among others.[43] The existence of a high correlation between national savings rates and rates of investment upsets the premise of international capital mobility.

The rise in the Japanese stock market and asset inflation are significant causes of Japanese high investment rates in the 1980s. Low US savings resulted from the explosion of consumer credit which was only partially offset by capital inflows. Of the "cost of capital" differential arguments, only the view that low dividend rates in Japan created a cost of capital advantage has credence; however, asset inflation did result in a temporary

capital allocation advantage which may lead to a long-term overinvestment disadvantage.

Part II: Capital Markets in the United States and Japan

A. THE ROLE OF PORTFOLIO ARBITRAGE AND INVESTMENT IN THE EVOLUTION OF JAPAN'S SECURITIES MARKETS

The Japanese capital market is characterized by the existence of the Keiretsu, loosely organized groups of companies descended from the earlier "Zaibatsus," which dominate listed companies on the Japanese stock markets. The Keiretsu (cross-holdings) increases the price of Japanese equity stock and reduces the cost of capital. Because nearly two-thirds of the corporate equity in Japan is held by other corporations, a considerable adjustment of about 15% of Japanese stock market capitalization may be accounted for by intercorporate share ownership.[44] However, even when discounting for cross-holding ownership, 1989 estimates of the range of world capitalization accounted for by the United States and Japan were at 36% for the United States, and ranged from 33% to 39% for Japan.[45] With the Japanese stock market at its current level (17,500 at this writing), the price/earnings level of Japanese shares is only slightly greater than that of US shares—around 30 to 1,[46] making capitalization of the US and Japanese markets roughly proportional per capita and to GDP.

Index arbitrage in Japan is widely held to be responsible for the stock market collapse, although monetary policy seems to provide more direct causation.[47] Professor Merton Miller believes that some foreign firms that were heavily involved in arbitrage were also involved in the Japanese futures market, enabling them to arbitrage the basically fixed commissions on common stock which, according to Professor Miller, were in some cases 30–50% higher than commissions for futures transactions (although this spread was not the same for foreign firms that had membership on the Tokyo Stock Exchange). According to Miller, foreign firms dominated the arbitrage market because Japanese firms preferred to allocate their capital to their own highly profitable retail networks, that are effectively closed to foreign competition.[48] Not long ago, in a move to counter this foreign domination, the Ministry of Finance imposed strict quotas on index arbitrage activities by foreign firms, required disclosure of arbitrage positions, and increased the cost of trading futures by raising margin requirements.[49]

Recently, the high cost of trading futures in Tokyo has led to a substantial volume of futures being transferred to the SIMEX (Singapore International Monetary Exchange). This development is consistent with Professor Miller's view that the attempt to raise margin requirements leads to loss of

business to foreign exchanges. It is this loss of revenue that limits the creation of a regulatory environment more stringent than that of other international markets.[50]

Japan is attempting to retain its current retail commission structure, but in an era of internationalization of financial markets, its success is in doubt. The recent deflation of the Tokyo stock market brings its price/earnings ratio in line with that of the United States, the international economy with which it is most integrated. Professor Miller believes the Ministry of Finance (MOF) should put an end to its unreasonable expectations about its power to control profits and stock prices. He asks, "what better way for MOF to do that than to join the rest of the world in deregulating its financial market?"[51] Thus, the issues of regulating commissions and margin requirements for stock margin futures are seen by Miller as part of the outmoded regulatory structure prevalent in Japan until recently; and, for him, the need to move toward deregulation is overwhelming. At the same time, it must be noted that the relative solvency of The Big Four Japanese Securities Firms results from the regulated commission rates; and, if such rates had not been regulated, these firms, would by now have become insolvent, which may have led to a systemic crisis in Japan. It seems that the issue of deregulation in the context of futures markets is analogous to that of interest rate deposit ceilings in the banking arena. Markets that were regulated seemed to allow for less systemic risks, but to provide less efficiency. The measure of public good provided by deregulation remains to be seen. Nonetheless, the internationalization of financial markets has increasingly made deregulation the norm. What this bodes for the dominant form of relational financing in Japan is not readily apparent. In the future, two markets will exist in Japan: market-based financing and relational financing.

Japanese shareholders through both direct and indirect investment such as pension funds and investment trusts, own far less of the securities market capitalization than do their US counterparts. As discussed above, the assets of most Japanese households are in the form of land, houses and other fixed assets: 63.4% in 1982, as compared to 33.4% in the United States.[52] Yet, the degree of Japanese assets that are held as financial assets should not be underestimated. The Japanese investment trusts and pension funds have substantial amounts under management. In Japan, pension assets totaled 123 trillion Yen in 1989,[53] although subject to a limitation allowing only 30% of the total portfolio to be invested in equity.[54] Japanese investment trusts which manage pension funds and other portfolio assets had 57 trillion Yen under management as of 1989 and account for a disproportionate percentage of stock market transactions.[55] They have underperformed the market, suggesting that they do not make use of portfolio insurance to the same degree as do US institutional investors.

But Japanese portfolio investment is not an insubstantial factor in the Japanese economy and, like the recent upsurge in bond issues, suggests a

movement away from the preexisting structure of cross-holdings and bank monitoring. Still, the extent of the transformation of the Japanese economy to an arm's-length capital market should not be exaggerated. Although a considerable body of knowledge suggests that the role of the Keiretsu, and consequently of relational financing, is overstated,[56] recent research suggests otherwise.[57]

B. THE ROLE OF INSTITUTIONAL INVESTORS AS MONITORS

The principal question formulated by a comparative study of US and Japanese capital markets is whether the organization of Japanese capital markets enables a more efficient and/or a more successful organization of financial and corporate structure so as to enable Japanese firms to out-compete their US counterparts. Beyond consideration of the cost of capital to the extent that it derives from savings rates and interest rate differentials, the roles played by institutional investors in the United States and Japan result in incomparable capital market structures. Japanese institutional investors are able to monitor the behavior of financial firms in which they invest, principally through the role of the long-term or city bank, under what is called the main banking system[58]; whereas the US system is considered to be a true capital market because investors have historically operated at arm's length from corporate managers, and express their displeasure with corporate decisions by selling shares rather than by participation in corporate governance. US institutional investors typically have a large portfolio of investments with little concentration of investment. Bank holding companies are limited to a 5% investment in non-financial companies, and insurance companies are limited by various state laws to small percentage ownership. Neither play active roles in corporate governance,[59] because of this limitation and SEC thresholds such as the Williams Act filing at 5% ownership and the definition of insiders at 10% ownership.[60]

The degree of monitoring for publicly listed corporations in the United States has historically been low, and until recently there have been few examples of institutional investors waging a successful proxy fight for the control of a board of directors. The view that US corporations are categorized by separation of ownership and control was firmly established by Berle & Means in 1932.[61] Whether the separation of control is a consequence of the economic and technical forces which shaped US capitalism or an adaptation to political forces that limit the scales and powers of financial institutions is still being debated.[62]

The recent developments which caused a turnover of chief executive officers at General Motors, Westinghouse, IBM and American Express are thought by some to presage a new era in which pension funds will be

required to take a more active interest in the progress of corporations in which they have substantial positions. According to this view, because of the size of the pension fund holdings, there is no longer true liquidity for pension fund holdings, and therefore more active monitoring of investments is required.

Nonetheless, it is perfectly correct for legal scholars to be wary of applying the Japanese institutional investor model to the US scenario.[63] Participants in an organization may either "voice" their views or "exit" from the organization. In the corporate governance arena, shareholders may voice their views through participation, either through proxy solicitation or through election to the Board of Directors; or, they may simply "exit" by selling their shares.[64] Voice is predominant in Japan, exit in the United States.

Professor Coffee has phrased the debate about US institutional investor participation in corporate governance as "Liquidity versus Control." It is his contention that shareholders in such countries as Japan and Germany forego liquidity for control, that it is difficult, if not impossible, to unite the two, and that the choice between liquidity and control is simply a specific application of the choice between "exit and voice."[65]

Japanese financial institutions are allowed to take large positions in both the debt and equity of the same firm. Some commentators suggest that the differing interests of shareholders and debtholders in the Japanese corporation are in this way minimized, thereby reducing the difference between the going concern value of a firm and its liquidation value.[66] US commercial banks have less than 1% of outstanding corporate equity while Japanese commercial banks have 20.5%. US life insurance companies have 3% of US corporate equity, while Japanese life insurance companies have 13.3%.[67] Consequently, it may be that overlapping debt and equity claims by Japanese financial institutions reduce agency costs. The inference is that Japanese firms because of lower agency costs enjoy greater leverage; thus, the same amount of equity can contribute to greater corporate opportunity.

A series of articles have shown that Japanese firms with main bank ties perform better after the onset of distress than those without such ties.[68] Anecdotal evidence suggests that Japanese banks will lend money to such companies at favorable interest rates and will encourage them to sell their shares in the main bank so as to raise capital (the market for such share prices will not be reduced because other corporations within the same Keiretsu will maintain the share price). Studies also suggest that corporations with main bank ties are less influenced in their investment patterns by liquidity than are similar firms without such main bank ties.[69]

However, Japanese capital markets are becoming distinctly more open, as arm's-length transactions between borrowers and lenders replace close-knit Keiretsu relations.[70] Bank monitoring appears to be on the wane, as well-capitalized companies are capable of issuing their own highly rated

bonds.[71] It may also be that "implicit agreements" by banks to reduce financial expenses such as interest do not exist. Banks have evolved elaborate security collateral and pledge agreements to ensure their control over collateral.[72] The rate at which Japanese firms have changed their main banks is disputed,[73] yet the rate of defection is inconsequential when compared with that of United States firms. Bank-firm ties are representative of Keiretsu ties in general and specifics of bail-outs of distressed companies will be considered in this context in the next section.

Commercial bank cooperation and affiliation may produce financial market ineffectiveness. The existence of stable shareholding enables large portions of new issues to be placed within the Keiretsu and the bulk of shares listed on Japanese exchanges are never traded.[74] Financial groupings can be viewed as entrenchment mechanisms defending incumbent management against hostile takeovers. And bank monitoring in Japan may be viewed as a lax form of monitoring.[75]

The separation of banking and commerce and the separation of banking from investment and securities is entrenched in Japanese law under Section 65 of Japan's Securities and Exchange Act of 1948, and Bank ownership of commercial firms is limited by the anti-monopoly law of 1947.[76] However, these restrictions failed to take hold in Japan because prohibitions that are explicit in US law about attribution of ownership to affiliates and subsidiaries are not present in the restrictions on bank ownership in Japan. Affiliates of major banks operate under no restriction with regard to investments in security firms.[77] For example, Mitsubishi Bank, together with its affiliates, owns more than 78% of the outstanding shares of Ryoko Securities, through its parent and 29 affiliates.[78] These informal linkages create a structure that is similar to the traditional Keiretsu, enabling companies that are cross-owned to carry out strategies based on cross-ownership and informal close relationships between companies. The importance of cross-holding by commercial firms of each other's shares within the Keiretsu will be explained in subsection C.

Japan's formal separation between banking and securities activities is currently in the process of amendment. Beginning in 1993, reciprocal entry for banks into securities activities, and for security firms into banking will be allowed.[79] Banks will be required to form separate subsidiaries to engage in security activities, and transactions between the securities affiliate and the bank will have to be at arm's length, while large credit exposure will be subject to consolidated supervision. Interlocking directorates between banking and securities firms will be forbidden. The securities part of the law redefines a public offering to include what were previously considered to be private placements, and private placements will be subject to limited resale. Additionally, there will be a streamlined process for small public offerings. Significantly, bank entry into securities firms will not allow banks to perform brokerage activities. This prohibition resulted from the impor-

tant role played by small brokerage firms (not the Big Four) in the brokerage business.

It is far too early to spell out the consequences of Japan's new reciprocal
entry laws. Limitations on bank brokerage activities will stymie any large
economic impact. If banks are able to underwrite corporate equities, the
main banking system will tend to decline and competition in underwriting
will reduce securities' commissions, currently high because of the Big Four
oligopoly. Although banks already own equity, the value of which is part
of their capital, underwriting poses additional risks. Gross underwriting of
equities in the 1980s in Japan was only one-sixth the amount of US gross
underwritings in dollar terms;[80] and bank entry into underwriting will probably increase gross equity issues. Whatever the consequences of Japan's
new securities laws, the prevalent system of relational financing is under
siege because Japanese bank capital is impaired and will be insufficient to
meet future demands of the commercial and industrial sector.[81]

The Japanese MOF is currently considering the proposal to create a US–
style Securities and Exchange Commission that will be directly responsible
for the orderly operation of securities and derivative markets. This change
is overdue and when accomplished will help to place Japan on an equal
footing with the EEC and the United States in terms of creating transparent
legal rules for its securities markets.

The main banking system may enable Japanese firms to engage in an
inefficient empire building policy of hording free cash flow that could otherwise be more effectively used by shareholders.[82] Nevertheless, certain aspects of Japanese financial monitoring may do more than serve as a
mechanism for managerial control if, as has been surmised, banks supplement their legal rights under security agreements with an informal monitoring process.[83] The conflict between the legal and the relations
orientations of Japanese finance may be expressed in terms of the dichot-
omy between implicit and explicit contracts that has been utilized to explain
corporate contractual relations in the United States.[84] If complete or comprehensive contracts were to specify the payoffs and actions for every
conceivable state of events, there would be no conflicts. However, when
contracts are incomplete, contracting parties may attempt to mitigate conflicts by certain ex-ante contractual arrangements. The alternative to un-
constrained bargaining is to delegate to one of the parties the right to make
decisions not specified in the contract. The residual control rights are residual property rights.[85]

The application of this theory to Japan might rationalize the elaborate
structure of cross-holding as a dispute resolution mechanism. Aside from
the many intermediate and high-level meetings among firms with the presidents' clubs coordinating action,[86] and the implicit undertaking not to
compete within the firm and to prefer intra-Keiretsu trading to trading
outside of the Keiretsu,[87] the relationships among Keiretsu members may

effectively form an organization that acts as a social norm to facilitate better creditor relations. Although banks may be tempted to act only from a profit motive when distress looms,[88] this tendency may be lessened by the fact that other members of the President's Group, who together will own a controlling interest in the bank, will be able to provide commercial rather than pure banking expertise, and thus inform decisions of banks in various situations.

By contrast, US institutional investors until recently were loathe to involve themselves in management issues. They are portfolio investors and are subject to loss of business if they deviate from this norm.[89] While the dominant mode remains exit rather than voice in the United States, institutional investor activism through participation in the corporate governance process has been buoyed by a rule adopted by the SEC that alter the process of proxy solicitation.[90]

The gains from shareholder voice under the rule are somewhat limited.[91] To enumerate a partial list: shareholders may monitor compensation to officers, limit expansion of the business, decide on a dividend payment policy to the extent of earnings, and determine in general which part of the business should be wound up. Even this agenda might be considered excessive to incumbent management.[92] According to Professor Black, shareholders are most able to affect process and present structural proposals: rescinding or weakening poison pills, opting out of any takeover statutes, changing the state of incorporation and the related law, and determining the level of management compensation.[93] In the language of contract theory, shareholders can help resolve conflicts between management and shareholders by resuming or exercising residual power. Such exercise in the current economy can be particularly economically efficient because of limitation on sources of funding for corporate takeovers and the evolution of anti-takeover statutes throughout the United States.[94]

It has become almost conventional wisdom that an effective device for minimizing agency costs is according to independent directors the primary monitoring role and the support staff necessary to fulfill this function, a method endorsed by such forums as The Business Roundtable.[95] Yet, independent directors typically serve at the behest of management.[96] It remains to be seen if the recent activism of the pension funds will continue and how they will exercise a monitoring role.

Legal restraints limit the active role or stance which institutional investors can take in the running of a company, and current law militates against large stakeholding by institutional investors. Under Section 13(d) and related SEC rules pursuant to the Williams Act, a 5% stake triggers disclosure requirements that can be onerous.[97] Furthermore, owning a 10% stake can trigger short swing profit forfeitures under Section 16(b) of the Securities and Exchange Act of 1934 and related rules.[98] Section 16(b) currently requires that any gain by any officer, director, or 10% beneficial holder of

any class of equity securities of a reporting company, resulting from a purchase of securities that occur within six months of any earlier purchase or sale must be disgorged to the corporation.[99] The SEC has indicated that if investors form a "voting" group that requires disclosure under the Williams Act, such group will be deemed to be subject to Section 16(b) if it collectively controls 10% or more of a class of equity securities.[100] One obstacle to institutional investor participation in corporate management is liability under insider trading rules. Aside from Section 16(b) liability for short-swing profits, any institutional investor which has its nominee serving as a corporate director will have access to inside information, which could create liability under the SEC rule.[101] A controlling shareholder is liable for securities law violations committed by "controlled corporations" unless an affirmative defense can be established.[102] Obviously, any entity attempting to exercise control would lose some of its ability to trade securities. Consequently, there is an inherent trade-off between control and liquidity. Minor clarifications for a Section 16(b) indexed investor who buys for the long term but recurrently needs to adjust his portfolio would not solve the problem posed to an institutional investor who would actually seek a measure of control.

Professor Coffee believes that restricted diversification resulting in greater stakeholding in individual corporations is necessary for institutional investors to enable them to act as corporate monitors to contain legal liabilities. This may be consistent with finance theory that suggests that 20 securities are adequate for portfolio diversification.[103]

What are the real benefits to be derived by institutional investors' active participation in corporate affairs? Unless a new field of expertise were to evolve, in which investment advisors, who are certainly responsible for the bulk of investment, became knowledgeable about business strategy, Keynes' view that the good investor is the one who determines the strategy of the average investor will stand.[104] The creation of a US system that mirrors the Japanese system would require far more than the active participation of institutional investors. It would probably require bank and other institutional ownership of securities on a non-diversified basis and involvement in investment banking on a larger scale than is currently permitted.[105] The repercussions of such deregulation could be phenomenal. The effect of commercial bank ownership of securities would make banks subject to the vagaries of the stock market, as they have been in Japan,[106] and would render the US financial system less stable than it currently is.

In Germany and Great Britain, where substantial limitations on bank ownership of equity securities have not existed, financial institutions still have not exceeded the 5% level of ownership.[107] However, in Japan, banks own considerably more.[108] Although bank holding companies in the United States are entitled to hold up to 5% of their assets in equity securities, banks have made little use of these powers. For example, Citicorp, the

largest US banking institution, with total assets of over $200 billion, holds only about $1 billion in equities.[109] Banks and open-end mutual funds, which must stand ready to redeem securities on a daily basis, have very thin equity and are thus unwilling to actively invest in equities for long-term holding.[110] Banks and insurance companies are the institutions least willing to oppose corporate management.[111] Private pension funds are subject to a related form of pressure in that corporate management can and does instruct the professional investment management firms on matters usually including voting in a proxy contest.[112] Money managers are also reluctant to be labelled "activist shareholders," lest institutional activism trigger political repercussions. The 1989 report of the New York State Task Force on Pension Fund Investment, which recommended restrictive legislation barring pension fund involvement in takeovers, was one ominous sign.[113] Furthermore, California Governor Peter Wilson attempted to oust the CalPERS Board and take direct control over a particularly active pension fund.[114] The clearest example of legislative pressure aimed at institutional investors is the recent Pennsylvania Anti-Green Mail statute, but this statute contemplates only the institutional investors of today who take a large stake in a corporation for the purpose of realizing speculative short-term gains.[115]

Today, nearly one-third of all equity investments held by institutional funds are indexed to a standard index such as Standard & Poor's.[116] The New York Stock Exchange has reported that analysts estimate between $200 and $300 billion, or 30% of institutional assets, are held in portfolios that replicate a market index.[117]

While large stakeholding by an institutional investor would reduce liquidity, the indexed investor does not achieve real liquidity by trading control for liquidity. The trade-off between liquidity and control is not complete because the indexed investment guarantees liquidity only as long as the market functions properly. In 1987, the market ceased to function properly and futures markets did not offer appropriate safety for institutional investors.

In the mid–1980s, the US Department of Labor warned ERISA fiduciaries that participation in corporate governance was not optional,[118] and Department of Labor rulings required pension plan trustees to monitor "the activities of the investment manager" to whom voting discretion is delegated.[119] As discussed above, the best way to make institutional investors active is to restrict portfolio diversification, and a diversified portfolio may be achieved with as few as 15 or 20 stocks.[120] An obstacle is created by ERISA which mandates diversification under Section 1104A "so as to minimize the risk of large losses" unless it is clearly prudent not to do so.[121] Furthermore, incentive compensation contracts are strictly forbidden for investment advisors registered under the Investment Advisors Act of 1940.[122] Under the existing scenario where institutional investors enjoy

illusory liquidity, Professor Coffee's characterization of institutional investors as "resembl[ing] spectators at the Roman Coliseum content with bread and circuses, unwilling to organize for political reform as long as the gain continues,"[123] is quite appropriate.

C. THE KEIRETSU

Although representing only about 10% of the industrial firms listed on the Tokyo Stock Exchange as of the late seventies, firms formally affiliated with one of the six Keiretsu groups controlled between 43% and 56% of total sales in natural resources, primary metal, chemical and industrial machinery sectors. Financial institutions affiliated with these groups represented 40% of total bank capital companies, 53% to 57% of total insurance companies and 55% of real estate business. In distribution, 67% of sales were accounted for by formal Keiretsu companies, primarily through general trading companies (Sogo Shoshas).[124] The more flexible definition indicates an increase in affiliations over the past two decades.[125] Under the looser definition (Keiretsu Kenayu), 577 firms in the first section of the Tokyo Stock Exchange had Keiretsu affiliations, an increase of over 200 companies from those quoted in the 1970 volume. Total assets and total sales accounted for by these companies as a share of first section firms increased from 66% to 69% and from 71% to 76%, respectively. Under the more formal criterion, defined as membership in the President's Council of the Big Six Keiretsu, membership expanded rapidly, gaining 56 new participants, an increase of 41% over a 23-year period ending in 1980. Perhaps the most telling characteristic of Keiretsu is the established and still increasing stability of their top ten shareholders. 73% of all Japanese companies' top ten shareholders remained stable during two-year intervals in the early seventies. This number had increased to about 87% in the mid-eighties.[126] Other figures about stable shareholding for a two-year period show an 81% stability among the top ten shareholders in the Keiretsu firms and 83% for non-Keiretsu firms, while the comparable statistic for the United States was 23% (results are from a survey of 250 large corporations in each country).[127]

There has been a tendency for the reliance on bank financing in Japan to decrease, and this would seem to suggest that reliance on the Keiretsu structure has decreased. Furthermore, such extremely strong companies such as Toyota and Matsushita Electric have no external debt and are therefore able to avail themselves of capital market financing at extremely advantageous rates.[128] But securities and other capital markets are largely mediated by institutions through a complex set of strategic relationships with corporate users of capital. The relationship between banks and securities houses is quite significant, despite the limitations imposed by the Securities Act of 1948.[129] Among Sumitomo Group's top 20 companies,

for example, all but four relied on Daiwa securities as their lead underwriter as of 1989, and all but one of these companies had been doing so for the past two decades. Daiwa, in turn, is linked to Sumitomo's Group by virtue of the fact that its two leading shareholders and reference banks are Sumitomo Bank and Sumitomo Trust.[130] Banks and insurance companies continue to be net purchasers of securities and together control nearly one-half of publicly traded shares in Japan.[131] The interlinking between banks and securities firms has been particularly close because the capital adequacy requirements of the G–10 Agreement necessitated a short-term boost in bank capital.[132] During the six years from 1984 to 1990, Japan's 23 largest banks raised 13.5 trillion Yen in equity capital, a substantial portion of all equity capital raised, and non-financial firms, in order to maintain their stable shareholdings in banks, also utilized 30% to 40% of their own new capital to acquire bank equity issues.[133] By contrast, US banks, which have required capital, have relied on the free market for securitization of assets and international capital markets where, until 1986, they successfully raised perpetual and long-term debt through floating rate notes on the Eurobond market.

The Keiretsu is characterized by the internalization of transactions. Outside directors are 21 times more likely to come from affiliated firms than from outside the Keiretsu.[134] Internalization to own-group firms, defined as top ten shareholders, is over 25% for all six Keiretsus and over 50% in the three former Zaibatsu groups.[135]

Preferential trading within groups is not as high as might be expected, aside from the Sogo Shoshas' (trading companys') domination of distribution.[136] In general, firms are about three times as likely to trade within groups (defined as 9 to 20 companies). This figure, while not pronounced, excludes Sogo Shoshas and vertical suppliers.[137] Connected with the loosely linked definition of the Keiretsu are the tight connections between suppliers and customers (i.e., vertical integration). Core firms in Nissan Suppliers Association provide over 90% of its input, and, out of 150 suppliers in Toyota's Suppliers Association, only three departed over a 12-year-period.[138] Preferential trading has specific implications in the international arena. It has been argued that distribution by Sogo Shoshas make penetration of Japanese markets difficult for foreign companies. Preferential trading carries over in foreign direct investment.[139]

Groupwide information technology associations have proliferated in the 1980s. For example, a Mitsubishi group consisting of 38 companies was established to provide high-level data transmission that will link firms via electronic banking.[140] Private as opposed to governmental research and development (R&D) expenditure in Japan accounts for a far higher proportion of overall R&D than in the United States, and the government provides a very small source for private sector funding, so these information technology groups have particular importance in Japan.[141]

Thus, in Japan, stakeholders in a corporation have several overlapping claims. They are simultaneously shareholders, debtholders and suppliers. Consequently, the residual claimant—the shareholder—will have information not usually available to the US shareholder. Agency problems in Japan are therefore less frequent than in the United States. In assessing the comparative ownership patterns of Japanese firms, it is possible to go beyond the distinction made by Williamson between arm's-length and relational contracting[142] and to consider whether the efficiency of Japanese corporate financing is enhanced because of overlapping legal claims owned by each stakeholder.[143] Certainly, transactional costs in restructuring are reduced. The going concern value of the firm, rather than its liquidation value, is more likely to be retained.[144] This approach to corporate governance is not without costs and may result in wasteful allocation of capital to declining firms.[145] But circumstantial evidence suggests that withdrawal of capital has been orderly and systematic in Japan.[146] In any event, multiple claims (as supplier, shareholder, debtholder) by shareholders would tend to reduce investment in declining industries and may be as effective in shifting capital out of declining industries as leveraged buyouts are in the United States.

The importance accorded balance sheets in the US financial markets where claimants have single arm's length claims (i.e., shares or bonds) may have created a process of capital budgeting that diminishes investment intangibles.[147] Intangible productivity-enhancing investments include specialized information, education and training, and systems for coordination and integration necessary to achieve superior performance in terms of speed, quality, flexibility and innovation.[148] Profitability is also demonstrated when a company cannibalizes its resources; that is, replaces an existing product or process with another that is currently worth less, but may in the end be worth more. Examples include replacing old equipment when cost savings do not justify capital expenditures and introducing a new product that decreases sales of existing products.[149] The reorganization of most large corporations into a set of stand-alone business units makes profit and cash flow statements for each business unit available to top managers and their advisors.[150] Thus, each individual profit center would have to report to the central management structure. This tends to increase the importance of profit because ultimate management is uninvolved in the decision-making process of each individual unit and may be unimpressed by anything other than the bottom line.

The economic organization of the Japanese firm may be more conducive to innovation than its US counterpart. In those patent areas recognized by the US patent office in which the United States still maintains a strong position, a majority (over 80% in one study) are marked by deterioration vis-à-vis Japan.[151] Japanese firms tend to concentrate basic R&D in parent companies but allocate marketing responsibility to satellite firms. Japan's

six major computer and communication equipment firms had 129 majority-owned subsidiaries and 48 affiliated companies, and total investment in these subsidiaries and affiliates averaged 194.8 billion Yen.[152]

Criticism of high-tech exploitation in the United States has focused on the difficulty of such ventures—spinoffs or venture capital—in gaining access to downstream capabilities and capital necessary to exploit commercial ventures.[153] It is not that Japanese firms are more far-ranging—much the opposite. Japanese firms are far less diversified than US companies, and diversification into unrelated areas is also rarer in Japan (7% versus 20%); but in 1984 Japanese companies invested 44% of their own paid-in capital in satellite firms, and the figure was higher still in Japan's automobile industry.[154] In Japan there is no counterpart to the $33 billion a year (1989) US venture capital market, and the market for initial public offerings is a fraction of the US market. Consequently, users were involved in the origination of 26% of R&D projects versus 1% in the United States.[155] Suppliers in Japan are also more heavily involved in basic component engineering (70% of outside purchases in Japan are of supplier-proprietary parts, versus 19% in the United States and 46% in Europe).[156]

Thus informational networks of suppliers, customers, parents, subsidiaries, affiliates and captive-affiliated companies within the Keiretsu, may provide Japan with an international advantage in innovation. How much of this comparative edge in the economic organization of innovation can be attributed to the legal and financial structures? Can the US economy be reorganized to capture these benefits? Relational financing or subsidiaries, affiliates and suppliers (whose ownership structure is not yet studied) is clearly involved; yet, greater R&D spending by Japanese firms may also account for greater innovation. Also, the existence of the venture capital and IPO markets in the United States may deter major companies from certain investment in R&D and downstream commercialization. Large firms in the United States may simply acquire innovative high-tech firms. The economist Joseph Schumpeter believed that acquisition of small innovative firms by large firms would sound the death knell of capitalism. The Japanese keiretsu have managed to sidestep this problem.

The funding of technological innovation and the growth of R&D in Japan, in general, supports the view that financing for Japanese companies is based on long-range considerations. In general, it may be that long-term transactions between banks and corporate borrowers help to improve information (particularly on such questions as R&D) and to signal other banks on a company's soundness.[157]

This is the central question in assessing the ultimate efficacy and efficiency of the Japanese firms in the international economy and, consequently, in determining what changes are necessitated in the structure of US capital formation and finance. Is relation-oriented financing more efficient than capital market financing? While Japan has an underdeveloped

portfolio investment sector,[158] it is not clear that a capital market structure will continue to serve advanced industrial countries in the twenty-first century. The analysis of this issue ought to be at the forefront of the fair trade issue.[159]

The evidence that the Keiretsu structure facilitates adjustment in declining industries is weak.[160] What we can ascertain in a loss-sharing situation is the pattern of risk management utilized by the Japanese Keiretsu structure. The continued infusion of capital into declining industries may represent one economic function of the Keiretsu,[161] but the efficiency of the Keiretsu as an ex ante risk-sharing insurance contract has little factual support,[162] and the ability of the Japanese financial system to make adjustments in depressed and declining industries is questionable. The example of the aluminum industry provides some indication of the pattern of adjustment.[163] Although loans were made by 11 major parent firms for a total of 275 billion Yen, these loans were made in many cases to finance existing deficits, and capital injections were usually made in conjunction with a writing off by the parent company of equity claim.[164] There are also numerous instances of loss sharing mechanisms that do not show up directly in corporate accounts.[165] General trading companies also perform essential functions in facilitating risk-sharing in corporate groups.[166] Confidential documents unearthed by one researcher suggest that a complex formula exists for risk-sharing among group members, allocating nearly all the loss to banks and insurance companies.[167]

Artificially high share prices of distressed companies suggest that commercial firms commit significant capital to failing firms. In 1974, NEC reported net income of 10 billion Yen on sales of 343 billion Yen. It earned 13 Yen per share, a book value net worth of 106 Yen per share and a share price of around 200 Yen. The company was described in the Japanese Company Handbook as a "top" manufacturer of telecommunications and electronic equipment within the Sumitomo Group, positively advancing overseas in the telecommunications equipment field. Meanwhile, Sumitomo Coal earned 1 Yen per share, had not paid a dividend in years and had a negative net worth close to 70 Yen per share. Its share was priced around 100 Yen against 16 Yen in 1971. The Japanese Company Handbook described it as follows: "Belongs to the Sumitomo Group, mining coal, diversifying business on basis of civil engineering and supermarket management and plans to separate the coal division." By 1990, Sumitomo Coal had escaped bankruptcy by diversifying out of coal mining. Sumitomo Coal Mining (the subsidiary), at the same time, accomplished its long-term recovery and reported substantial net earnings.[168]

The unrealistically high share price of Sumitomo Coal has two effects: (1) banks gain substantial net capital based on the inflated share price, and (2) other commercial firms in the group lose liquidity because of the very low real worth of these shares. Thus, commercial firms appear to share

some of the down side of unrealistic share prices. How different is this result from what would have been obtained in the United States, where companies have portfolio investments and lose the value of shares on a mark-to-market basis, is difficult to say. Ultimately, the question reduces itself to one of the comparative cost of restructuring under the US and Japanese systems. Once again, this is a question that can be addressed only anecdotally and theoretically.[169]

It is not clear that the Japanese process of economic adjustment is superior to the comparative US process on empirical grounds alone. The supposition that Japanese firms enjoy implicit contractual insurance and follow a corresponding investment policy rests on theory.[170] Although it may be true that Japanese firms are less constrained than are US firms by considerations of liquidity,[171] the absence of such constraints does not imply more effective monitoring than that provided by US capital markets. This topic would be a fruitful area for future study. The Japanese structure facilitates the development of a mutual assistance society in which companies, by buying the shares of other companies, bid up the market value of their own shares, thereby enabling greater amounts of capital formation.

Unlike the US stock market, in which significant price rises are the result of significant trading, Japanese markets may be bid up significantly by very thin trading.[172] The evidence suggests that Japanese brokerage houses will, in many instances, lose significant amounts of money on trading, and that their trading is in large measure intended, or necessary, to ensure the liquidity of the market. Some major companies' stocks may not even be traded for a several-day period. Although there is a considerable turnover, only about a quarter of the shares are traded on the Tokyo Stock Exchange (TSE), and the rest remain in stable holdings. Consequently, a very large share price rise can occur on very slim trading. For example, the Industrial Bank of Japan saw a share price rise of 8% of August 7, 1989, creating $7 billion in shareholder wealth on a mere $25 million worth of trading. Only 3.7% of its 2.3 billion shares outstanding are considered floating shares.[173] The fact that shares are so slimly traded on the TSE may make the Japanese financial system more susceptible to economic shocks than the true capital market system. There are many sources of financial news in Japan.[174] However, the information they supply could never equal that accessible to insiders within the Keiretsu group. Investment trusts have consequently underperformed the Nikkei average.[175]

Operating profits for TSE-listed manufacturers have grown by 2.8% since 1981 and for non-manufacturers (other than financial organizations), the rate has been even lower (0.6%).[176] Consequently, falling interest rates and reduced debt were the biggest contributors to the 5% annual increase in net income for all non-financial companies, but the number of shares increased so rapidly that earnings per share grew by only 2.8% per year.[177] By contrast, listed companies on the NYSE saw their profits grow by 4.1%

annually in 1981 through 1989, and earnings per share rose even more rapidly due to share repurchases by corporations.[178]

The growth of investments in token and trust funds, together with the off-shore dollar equity warrant market based in London, contributed substantially to the capitalization of Japanese companies. However, investment by such companies tends to be largely in financial assets because of what can be considered a negative cost of capital.[179]

Among listed companies, Toyota had the largest net, non-operating income of 169 billion Yen in 1989, of which 114 billion Yen were derived from interest on bank deposits and notes receivable and the rest from equity dividends and sales of stocks and bonds.[180] This dividend income is termed the "zaiteku" profit. Net operating profits are far lower than net profits. Net operating profits in the automobile industry, for instance, fell 48% from 1985 to 1987. Nissan's net income went from a profit of 237 billion Yen to a loss of 31 billion Yen, and Honda's profits fell 43%. However, their share prices did not change. The operating profits of Nissan's parent company fell from 71 billion Yen to a loss of 8 billion Yen.[181] But recurring profits, which include earnings from Zaiteku, fell only from 148 billion Yen to 118 billion Yen.[182] The overall impact of Japanese financial market practices, when compared with similar US practices, is that during the years 1985 through 1989, non-financial corporations in the United States retired a net $500 billion in equity while their Japanese counterparts issued 11.4 trillion Yen on $80 billion net.[183]

The importation of the Keiretsu to the United States would be difficult, and its benefits are not quite clear; but, allowing commercial-bank affiliation as suggested in the Treasury proposal for modernizing US financial services[184] would gradually result in main bank groups, although not in commercial firm ownership of banks absent a complete restructuring of US financial markets. The Keiretsu is a uniquely Japanese conglomeration; but the creation of long-term stable shareholding by US institutional investors, as distinct from commercial firms, may result in a more efficacious financial system in the United States without the championing of market share to the exclusion of profitability considerations, or the thin liquidity characterizing the TSE.

It is clear that the way Japanese stock markets functioned in the 1980s led to overinvestment. In Keynesian economics, overinvestment will eventually lead to cyclical slumps; and only when overcapitalization is used up will new capital investment take place.[185] But Keynes' *General Theory* was applicable mostly to a closed economy. Japanese overinvestment may be sustained for long periods if it is responsive to overconsumption and underinvestment in the United States.

Even considering Japan's, rather than the world's, welfare, the loss of goodwill leading to increased protectionism, instability in internal capital markets and a halt toward the internationalization of the Yen are heavy

prices to pay for a corporate finance structure rivalling that of the United States in inefficiency and instability.

Part III: The Role of Japanese Institutions in the US Economy: Preserving the Integrity of US Capital Markets in an International Marketplace

In an international marketplace, the expansionary forces of the Japanese economy can have a substantial impact on US capital markets, and Japanese monetary and credit policies may undermine US policy concerns. This section examines the impact of Japanese financial institutions on the US economy. The growth of Japanese banks is correlated with the growth of trade. However, it has also been determined that the role of Japanese financial institutions in the United States goes well beyond the financing of Japanese subsidiaries.[186] While Japan's foreign direct investment in the United States is believed to be less than that of Holland and the United Kingdom, the data on which such belief is founded are not that reliable. Foreign portfolio investment in the United States is of more immediate concern. While it has never been clearly demonstrated that the extension and withdrawal of credit by Japanese financial institutions contributed to the rise and slow-down in the United States economy in and through the real estate sector, much anecdotal evidence exists to this effect. According to one study, direct and indirect Japanese investment in US real estate reached $76 billion at one point in 1990.[187] Retrenchment by Japanese financial institutions in the US real estate market and in the US Treasury market[188] may have been a factor in the US credit crunch.

Secondary dependency on Japan for financing the increasing US federal government debt was clearly reduced in 1991,[189] as was total Japanese investment abroad.[190] Instead of an outflow of $120 billion or more a year from Japan in 1986 to 1988, $30 to $40 billion a year is now flowing into Japan.[191] Japanese international banking assets were reduced by $190 billion in 1991, in contrast with 30% to 40% growth since 1985, although much of this reduction can be accounted for by financial liberalization within Japan.[192] All of the differential in Japanese investment, amounting to well over $160 billion a year, is most likely to be accounted for by shifts in portfolio investment.[193] Foreign direct investment is likely to have remained in place.

Foreign government entities have investments in US Treasuries which exceed those of the Federal Reserve's bills and notes, enabling foreign governments to conduct open-market operations on a scale comparable to that of the FRB.[194] This is both a dilemma and a benefit resulting from the US dollar's role in the world economy.[195] While budget deficits can be monetized from abroad and have been since the early seventies, the use of the dollar as the world reserve currency requires other governments to

invest in dollars. Sometimes, such investments are made to support the dollar, but these treasury bill purchases, equal to the size of the US M–1 or M–2, resulted in excessive credit expansion in the 1980s. This explanation may be conjectural to a monetary economist, but it accounts for the inability of the FRB to make a market in long-term treasuries and limits the efficacy of monetary policy.[196]

In 1989, Japanese banks had $1.75 trillion in international assets compared with $675 billion in US international banking assets.[197] The process of Japanese domination of the international finance system is an obvious result of the US trade deficit (which is in part a consequence of the US budget deficit). The US net disinvestment position (and external debt) is somewhere in the neighborhood of $650 billion.[198] In testimony before Congress regarding the impact of the rapid Japanese stock market decline of US capital markets and the international financial market, SEC Chairman Breeden noted that net capital rules should be kept strong in spite of the minimal direct risk of developments in Japan to the US market, but he noted that nevertheless, the US system should be designed to withstand shocks from foreign as well as domestic sources.[199]

The Report of the American Banker's Association[200] notes that Japanese banking has followed a path similar to that of other Japanese industries in the United States: just as Japanese auto manufacturers first produced and sold standard low cost cars, Japanese firms' transactions have been in the "plain vanilla" category.[201] Japanese banks have been known to offer Letters of Credit for one-fourth of the fees charged by US banks. As a result, Japanese banks were the leading providers of Letters of Credit for US municipal bonds, accounting for 69% of the market, and as of March 1989, Japan accounted for 33.8% of the industrial and commercial loans in California. Japan's institutions provided 30% of the Kraft and RJR Nabisco financing and 25% of Time Warner financing.[202] While, in 1993, no one is complaining about credit supplied by Japanese banks, Japanese banks clearly contributed to the overheating of the California economy and the mergers and acquisitions phenomena in the 1980s.

Part IV: Capital Adequacy in Japan

The role of stock market fluctuation and long-term investment is inherently different in the United States than it is in Japan. In the United States, disconnected stock market and investment behavior make for separate trajectories. In Japan, a downward stock market spiral automatically reduces bank capital and requires a restriction of bank credit, which may have international repercussions. In the United States, bank capital is at least not yet directly affected by stock market fluctuation.

The crisis in Japanese banking is hardly less dramatic than that in the United States. Disclosure rules make it impossible to know how bad Japan's

bank crisis is, but, private analysts' estimates range from in excess of 22 trillion Yen ($164 billion)—nearly triple the government's estimate—to nearly 60 trillion Yen (about $500 billion) in non-performing loans.[203] Kleinworth Benson International, Inc., believes that the total cost of bailing out all of Japan's financial institutions, including insurance companies, may prove far larger than the US cost of resolving the thrift institution crisis.[204] Nonetheless, investments in bad real estate in the United States were also inflicted on insurance companies and pension funds, and such a comparison may be incongruous. At any rate, the problems posed by undercollater- alized real estate loans are extremely significant in Japan, as well as in the United States. While the Japanese regulatory division in special purpose banks is different from that in the United States, Japan's eight home loan finance companies (JUSEN) established by banks and other major lenders in the 1970s now have non-performing loans of about 5.7 trillion Yen, about 40% of their total lending.[205] In general, it is the long-term credit banks rather than the city banks that are particularly exposed to the real estate industry. The US/Japan overinvestment in commercial and residen- tial real estate becomes increasingly difficult to differentiate.

Japan has proposed a plan to bail out its undercapitalized banks that involves fostering consolidation by allowing a substantial write-off for real estate related assets. The Collateralized Real Estate Credit Buying Com- pany has been formed to pool the less-than-credit-worthy real estate loans of small and large banks.[206] The structure of this company is not fully clear, but it will be privately owned and will be given tax concessions by the National Tax Authority.[207] This plan is still nascent and how far it will go toward preventing moral hazard is not evident. Since Japan has no expe- rience with bank failure in its postwar history, considerable uncertainty exists as to how to resolve the current crisis. Explicit regulation comparable to FDICIA will not evolve quickly as long as administrative guidance rather than law is the rule of the day.

Although both Japan and the United States are signatories to the G–10 Agreement,[208] and both include loan loss reserves in tier-two capital up to 1.25% of capital, what accounts for loan loss reserve in each of the countries differs. Although the specific language of the G–10 Agreement requires that only general loan loss reserves be included in tier-two capital, Japanese banks tend to include specific loan loss reserves. More important, however, is the general disparity between the strict US standards for writing down loans (particularly real estate loans with impaired collateral), and the more lax Japanese standards allowing loans to be carried at book value. How- ever, the formation of the Collateralized Real Estate Company may alter this disparity in the long term. Ultimately, the best measure of comparative supervision may be the government budget amount allocated for the closing of inadequately capitalized institutions. Meanwhile, circumstantial evi- dence suggests that, in Japan, real estate is not being written down. This

means that Japanese banks are not comporting with the spirit of the G–10 Agreement, and that bank lending has not contracted to reflect the deflation of bank real estate assets.

Although Japanese banks are subject to administrative guidance, nothing like the "prompt corrective action" provisions of FDICIA[209] exists in Japan. In fact, there has never been a failure of a Japanese bank. Thus, moral hazard, that is, the absence of a restraining market consideration,[210] is considerably more pervasive there than it is in the United States, given the bank failures that have occurred in the United States since 1988. The import of the G–10 Agreement may be called into question by the wide range of differing prudential supervision standard existing in Japan and the United States.

FDICIA also calls for closer supervision of foreign bank operations in the United States.[211] Most important, the act requires the Secretary of the Treasury to develop and publish criteria to be used in evaluating the operation of any foreign bank in the United States that the FRB has determined is not subject to comprehensive supervision or regulation on a consolidated basis.[212] This provision may prove to be the financial law analogue to Super 301 in the trade field and may come to supplement the G–10 Agreement on capital adequacy.

Unlike the United States, where anti-trust concerns span only the periphery of banking issues, particularly in relation to the question of tie-ins,[213] anti-trust issues are at the center of the banking reform debate in Japan. The Fair Trade Commission (Japan Anti-Monopoly Commission) has criticized the monopolistic tendencies of Japanese financial institutions, including the "follow the leader" approach on setting deposit rates and lending rates. Furthermore, the Fair Trade Commission has criticized both the heritage of administrative guidance with which the MOF has influenced the banking and securities sector, and the anti-competitive nature of trade associations such as the Japanese Bankers Association and the Japanese Securities Association.[214] The severe problems posed by deteriorating real estate loans held by banks, and the falling price of shares that constitute bank equity, taken together with the losses suffered by Japan's security houses, leave observers to believe that the use of "cartelization" is likely to be employed in the financial services sector, as Japan has successfully employed this approach in the past to deal with changing economic climates (particularly through the middle 1970s to deal with industries that were uncompetitive, e.g., steel as a result of the oil shock).

Part V: Conclusion

The spectacle of modern investment markets has sometimes moved me towards the conclusion that to make the purchase of an investment permanent and indissoluble, like marriage, except by reason of death or other grave cause might be a

useful remedy for our contemporary evils where this would force the investor to direct his mind to the long-term prospects and to those only, but a little consideration of this expedient brings us up against a dilemma and shows us how liquidity of investment markets often facilitates though it sometimes impedes the course of new investment for the fact that each individual investor flatters himself that his commitment is "liquid" though this cannot be true for all investors collectively and calms his nerves and makes him more willing to run a risk. . . .

When the capital development of a country becomes a byproduct of the activities of a casino, the job is likely to be ill done. The measure of success attained by Wall Street regarded as an institution of which the proper social purpose is to direct new investment into the most profitable channels in terms of future yield cannot be claimed as one of the outstanding triumphs of laissez-faire capitalism which is not surprising if I am right in thinking that the best brains of Wall Street have been in fact directed towards different objectives. . . .

These tendencies are a scarcely avoidable outcome of the successful organization of "liquid investment markets." It is usually agreed that casinos should, in the public interest, be inaccessible and expensive and perhaps the same is true of stock exchanges. (John Maynard Keynes, *The General Theory of Employment, Interest, and Money*, 1935.)

Chapter 3 discussed the short-term bias of the efficient market hypothesis that is the basis of portfolio investment in US–style capital markets. This chapter has focused on the issue by contrasting US capital markets with the relational financing system existing in Japan and found the US system wanting; but it also may be that there is nothing inherently efficient about the Japanese firm and financial structure. Rather, the diversion of funds away from consumers and toward producers and the emphasis on the firm within the structure of Japanese society, taken together with the unrealistic amounts of investment used to obtain market share, explain the better performance of Japanese firms.

It has been argued that Japanese workers are the residual owners of Japanese firms and presumably forego consumption for investment.[215] Much literature has focused on the closure of the Japanese market system.[216] Additional and more interesting literature has focused on the structure within the Japanese firm.[217] Only a very inconsequential amount of literature has focused on actual international consequences of Japanese corporate organization and financial markets.[218]

Recently, we have seen that asset deflation isn't likely to have the same effect in Japan as it does in the United States and hasn't caused an international financial crisis, although it may generate international financial lethargy. Relational finance will inhibit mass defaults, lifetime employment contracts will buffer a fall in gross income and fiscal stimulus (virtually unlimited because of Japan's small deficit) will pick up the slack. On the other hand, it will be a long time before Japanese consumers reach purchasing power parity with their US counterparts.

The indicated long-term strategy for US initiatives is therefore to remove structural impediments in trade with Japan, by liberalization of consumer credit in Japan over a period of time and continued financial liberalization (by the enforcement of anti-trust laws) and movement toward an arm's-length financial market which will limit overinvestment. The goal is to make financial ratio covenants, rather than self-fulfilling future market share, the criterion for lending by banks and securities firms.

The financial structure of the Japanese firm impacts on trade policy and on discussions about non-tariff barriers. However, it is shortsighted to view questions of import barriers as distinct from questions of finance. For example, the Structural Impediments Initiative identified many areas where prices were higher for Japanese consumers, but where, for various reasons (perhaps because these were not export-oriented industries), the full force and effect of US anti-dumping duties countervailing tariffs and even unilateral action under Section 301 of the Omnibus Trade Act of 1988 did not come to bear.

The Japanese financial system may be severely stressed because of the low capital adequacy ratios of banks. The fall in the Nikkei Index, now at 60% of its high, has been explained by some observers as inconsequential because of the already existing high price/earnings ratio; and such observers have noted that such ratios are still in excess of US ratios. A better view is that the fall in the market simply shows how the Japanese financial system is inefficient in spite of, or perhaps because of, the high degree of emphasis placed on investment. The coming due of a substantial amount of convertible bonds may pose a dramatic crisis for Japan. Furthermore, reorientation toward a consumer-oriented society will require a great deal of adjustment on the part of Japan.

Clearly, US corporations must reorganize in order to compete in world markets. Shareholder participation may be helpful to limit executive compensation and to direct investment toward the field of the subject corporation's expertise. However, an entirely new theory of corporate governance is necessary to enable American corporations to retake the lead in international competition. As Professor Coffee suggests, providing a safe harbor under Section 16(b) of the Securities and Exchange Act can be helpful in achieving this end by promoting large stakeholding and corporate monitoring, as can performance contracts by money managers. However, these measures are in themselves inadequate. For example, performance contracts by money managers would need to take place over a period of years rather than weeks as is currently expected by the short-term gains oriented marketplace. The US financial system needs to rethink its objectives in terms of long-range goals. So long as pension fund managers are interested in providing an unsustainable return on their investments, the United States will find it difficult to compete with Japanese companies, which are not constrained by the need to issue comparable dividends.

A problematic situation is posed to the extent that the future of US corporate governance must rely on pension funds managers, as suggested by Coffee, rather than on banks and insurance companies. A higher duty of fiduciary care must be exercised by banks and insurance companies in order that they, who are better positioned to be monitors than are pension funds, can become responsible, stable, long-term shareholders like banks and insurance companies in Japan. This may require amendment to the banking laws as discussed in Chapter 2 and to state restrictions on insurance company ownership of large stakes. The 1980s debate over the efficacy of mergers and acquisitions is inapposite today, given the degree of state takeover legislation which has been upheld by the US Supreme Court, but the geometric rise in indexed investors tends to bode ill for investor monitoring despite advances made by individual pension funds such as Cal-PERS.

An entirely different arena is entered into when considering the macroeconomics and distribution of international investment. Issues of monetary policy and, more recently, the primacy of capital adequacy come into play. Japanese overinvestment withdraws from world markets capital required by the emerging Eastern European republics and will surely contribute to a worldwide capital shortage in the 1990s. Equally important, unless the Japanese are successful in hurdling local content requirements and tariff barriers, investment in Japan will fail to yield the significant return needed to enable the Japanese corporate financial system to weather the inherent weaknesses in its capital structure. Internationalists must contend with the growing parochialism of international trade economists who have structured a new strategic trade theory which rationalizes protectionism based upon increasing returns from production.[219] This strategic trade theory emanates from new mathematical models which are, in part, justified by the United States' seeming inability to compete in world markets despite the growth of exports, which simply do not match the rising level of imports.

As FRB Chairman Greenspan has noted, the decline of the Japanese stock market is likely to render Japan less important as a US export market. Statistics cited by Greenspan and Breeden as to the impact of Japanese portfolio investment on US markets, however, seriously underestimate the impact of such investment. A more reliable indicator than the outstanding shares supposed to be owned by Japanese private investors is the total foreign investment in the United States, including official investment in US Treasury securities, and this measure indicates a substantial role played by foreign investors as a whole. The US external debt of over $700 billion (albeit an exaggerated figure because it measures US foreign direct investment at book value) represents, if not a threat to our financial system, than at least an indication of the international nature of financial marketplaces in the late twentieth century. Ignoring the realities of the international marketplace is a recipe for the breakdown of the international trading

system, which is itself predicated and determined by the international financial system.

NOTES

1. By late 1990, nominal short-term interest rates had risen 350 basis points in Japan, and the growth rate of the Japanese money supply had plummeted in response. Real long-term interest rates rose by more than 200 basis points from late 1989 until late 1990. The latest decline of the Japanese stock market, which occurred between October 1991 and April 1992, saw a fall of 30% and placed the Tokyo Stock Exchange (TSE) price/earnings ratio in the neighborhood of 30, just above that for the Standard and Poor's 500 in the US market. Despite the stock market bubble and the change in short-term Yen interest rates, *see* notes 11 and 12 *infra*, the Yen–dollar exchange rate has been fairly stable, moving in a range of 123-142 until late 1992 (Alan Greenspan, Chairman, Board of Governors of the Federal Reserve System before the Committee on Banking, Housing and Urban Affairs, US Senate, April 19, 1992, p. 3), a far narrower percentage range than, for example, the DM–dollar range. (Testimony of Greenspan, p. 4)

2. Allen J. Lenz, *A Sectoral Assessment of U.S. Current Accounts of Deficit: Performance in Prospects*, in INTERNATIONAL ADJUSTMENT AND FINANCING: THE LESSONS OF 1985 TO 1991 (C. Fred Burgston, ed., 1991), which tells us that the key to US external adjustment lies in the manufacturing sector. This concludes that additional devaluation is required to achieve balance.

3. Masaru Yoshitomi, *Japan: Surprises and Lessons From Japanese External Adjustment in 1985 to 1991*, in INTERNATIONAL ADJUSTMENT AND FINANCING, *supra* note 2, at 123.

4. *Ibid.*, at 142.

5. David Meerschwam, *The Japanese Financial System and the Cost of Capital*, in TRADE WITH JAPAN: HAS THE DOOR OPENED WIDER? (Paul Krugman, ed., 1991); Jeffrey Frankel, Japanese Finance in the 1980's: A Survey, *in* TRADE WITH JAPAN, at 225.

6. Frankel, *supra* note 5.

7. Carl Kester, and Timothy Luehrman, *Real Interest Rates and the Cost of Capital: A Comparison of the United States and Japan*, 1 JAPAN AND THE WORLD ECONOMY, 279–301 (1989).

8. Carl Kester, and Timothy Luehrman, "Cross-Country Differences in the Cost of Capital: A Survey and Evaluation of Recent Empirical Studies," Time Horizons of American Management and the Harvard Business School and The Council on Competitiveness, p. 9, 1992.

9. Firms with identical assets but different capital structures have the same cost of capital, according to the Miller-Modigliani theorem, M. Miller, and F. Modigliani, *The Cost of Capital, Corporate Finance and the Theory of Investment*, 48 AM. REV., 261–297 (June 1958). Two firms with identical assets and different capital structures will have different costs of debt and equity, but their overall cost of capital will be the same. Failure to abide by the Miller-Modigliani theorem has been a flaw in all the studies that have found cost of capital differences between the United States and Japan, according to Kester and Luehrman, *supra* note 7.

10. George Haptsoupolos, and James Porterba, "America's Investment Shortfall: Probable Causes and Possible Fixes." Paper Presented at the National Science Academy Conference on Capital Allocation, September 8, 1992.

11. *See, e.g.*, K. French, and J. Porterba, "Are Japanese Stock Prices Too High?" CRSP Seminar on the Analysis of Securities Prices (April 1989).

12. Hatsoupolos and Porterba, *supra* note 10.

13. Richard Mattione, "The Cost of Capital Disadvantage for Japan?" J. P. Morgan, Tokyo, April 6, 1992.

14. *Ibid.*

15. *Ibid.*, at 7.

16. *Ibid.*

17. Japan will include as capital 55% of the difference between book and market value of its banks' securities, *Outline of Official Notification, Japanese Ministry of Finance Concerning Implementation of the Basle Accord Committee's Capital Adequacy Framework*, December 22, 1988. *See also* Chapter 1, *supra* note 71 for the provision in the G–10 Agreement allowing this reevaluation.

18. Richard Mattione, "Can Japan's Banks Meet the BIS Rules?" J. P. Morgan, Tokyo, April 27, 1992.

19. *Ibid.*, at 3.

20. *See infra* note 183.

21. Margaret Blair, and Robert Litan, *Corporate Leverage and Leverage Buyouts in the Eighties, in* DEBT, TAXES AND CORPORATE RESTRUCTURING (John Shoven, and Joel Wadfogel, eds., 1990).

22. *Ibid.*

23. *Ibid.*

24. Richard Mattione, "A Dangerous Dependency: Equity Linked Bond Issues, Corporate Profitability and Economic Activity in Japan." Prepared for the 67th Annual Western Economic Association, International Conference, San Francisco, July 1992, p. 5.

25. *Ibid.*, at 6.

26. *Ibid.*, at 14.

27. *Ibid.*

28. *Ibid.*, at 2.

29. Douglas B. Bernheim, THE VANISHING NEST EGG: REFLECTIONS ON SAVING IN AMERICA 10 (1991).

30. *Ibid.*, at 77.

31. Jeffrey Frankel, *Quantifying International Capital Mobility in the 1980s, in* NATIONAL SAVINGS AND ECONOMIC PERFORMANCE 227 (B. D. Bernheim, and J. Shoven, eds., 1991).

32. Interim Interest Adjustment Law of 1947.

33. Meerschwam, *supra* note 5 at 212; Jeffrey Frankel, "The Yen–Dollar Agreement: Liberalizing Japanese Capital Markets," *Policy Analysis International Economics* No. 9 (Institute for International Economics, Washington, D.C.).

34. David Bradford, *Market Value Versus Financial Accounting Measures of National Savings in* NATIONAL SAVINGS AND ECONOMIC PERFORMANCE, supra note 31, at 15.

35. *See infra*, notes 110 and 111 and accompanying text.

36. Reasons for the Japanese high savings rate include: (1) a high growth rate—

currently, there is a larger young population in Japan, which tends to increase savings; (2) an underdeveloped social security system (however, savings data includes social security data as well as pension payments); (3) the bonus system of compensation; and (4) the high price of land and housing, which requires greater savings.

37. A. Decker, *Comment on Frankel in* TRADE WITH JAPAN, *supra* note 5, at 268.

38. Bernheim, *supra* note 29, at 45.

39. For a discussion of this issue *see* Martin Bailey, R. Burtless, and R. Litan, GROWTH AND EQUITY: ECONOMIC POLICYMAKING FOR THE NEXT CENTURY, Chapter 2 (1993).

40. W. E. Farb, "An International Comparison of Investment Behavior as a Key to the Time Horizons of American Industry." Harvard Business School and the Council on Competitiveness (1992).

41. Martin Feldstein, and Charles Horioka, *Domestic Savings and International Capital Flows*, 90 ECON. J., 314–329 (1980).

42. Martin Feldstein, and Philippe Bachetta, *National Savings and International Investment, in* NATIONAL SAVINGS AND ECONOMIC PERFORMANCE, *supra* note 31, at 201.

43. Rudiger Dornbusch, *Comment on Feldstein and Bachetta in* NATIONAL SAVINGS AND ECONOMIC PERFORMANCE, *supra* note 31, at 220.

44. French and Porterba, *supra* note 11; J. McDonald, *The Mochai Affect: Japanese Corporate Cross-Holding Ownership*, 16 J. PORTFOLIO MANAGE., 90–95 (Fall 1989).

45. French and Porterba, *supra* note 11.

46. Testimony of Richard C. Breeden, Chairman, US Securities and Exchange Commission, concerning recent market developments in Japan, before the Committee on Banking, Housing and Urban Affairs, US Senate, April 17, 1992.

47. Merton Miller, "Relationship Between Cash and Derivative Markets— What Are They and What Are the Implications for Regulations and Exchange in International Environment?" Paper presented before the International Organization of Securities Commissions, p. 17, XVIIth Annual Conference, London (October 27, 1992).

48. *Ibid.*, at 6.

49. *Ibid.*

50. *See generally* Merton Miller, FINANCIAL INNOVATIONS AND MARKET VOLATILITY 38 (1991).

51. *Ibid.*, at 7.

52. Masahiko Aoki, INFORMATION, INCENTIVES AND BARGAINING IN THE JAPANESE ECONOMY 123 (1988), citing *Bank of Japan Monthly Report* (February 1984).

53. Robert Zielinski, and Nigel Holloway, UNEQUAL EQUITIES: POWER AND THE STOCK MARKET IN JAPAN'S STOCK MARKET, 107–110 (1990).

54. *Ibid.*, at 51.

55. *Ibid.*, at 52.

56. *See e.g.,* R. Komiya, JAPANESE ECONOMY, TRADE INDUSTRY AND GOVERNMENT (1990); Aoki, *supra* note 52, at 138; Meerschwam, *supra* note 5.

57. Michael Gerlach, *Twilight of the Keiretsu: A Critical Assessment*, 18 J. JAPAN. STUD. 79 (1991).

58. Takeo Hoshi, A. Kashyap, and D. Scharfstein, *The Role of Banks in Reducing the Costs of Financial Distress in Japan*, 27 J. FINAN. ECON. 67 (1990).

59. Mark Roe, *The Political and Legal Restraints on Ownership and Control of Public Companies*, 27 J. FINAN. ECON. 7 (1990).

60. *See infra* notes 97, 115–117.

61. Adolph Berle and Gardiner Means, *The Modern Corporation and Private Property* (Business Enterprise Reprint series 1982, reprint of 1933 edition).

62. Mark Roe, *A Political Theory of American Corporate Finance*, 91 COLUM. L. REV. 10; Mark Roe, *Political and Legal Restraints on Ownership and Control of Public Companies, supra* note 59.

63. John Coffee, *Liquidity Versus Control: The Institutional Investor as Corporate Monitor*, 91 COLUM. L. REV. 1277, 1300–1302 (1991).

64. *Ibid.*, and Bernard Black, *Agents Watching Agents: The Promise and Limits of Shareholder Voice*, 39 UCLA L. REV. 811 (1992).

65. Albert Hirschman, EXIT VOICE AND LOYALTY: RESPONSES TO DECLINE IN FIRMS' ORGANIZATIONS AND STATES (1970).

66. Stephen Prowse, *Institutional Investment Patterns and Corporate Financial Behavior in the United States and Japan*, 27 J. FIN. ECON. 43 (1990). *See also* M. Jenson, and W. Meckling, *Theory of the Firm: Managerial Behavior, Agency Costs and Ownership Structure*, 3 J. FIN. ECON. 30 (1976).

67. Federal Reserve Board Flow of Funds Account (September 1987), Japanese Securities Research Institute, "Securities Markets in Japan" (1988) cited in Prowse, *supra* note 66, at 45.

68. Hoshi, Kashyap, and D. Scharfstein, *supra* note 58, at 70.

69. Takeo Hoshi, A. Kashyap, and D. Scharfstein, *Corporate Structure, Liquidity and Investment: Evidence from Japanese Industrial Groups*, 106 Q. J. ECON. 33 (1991). *But see also*, Paul Sheard, *Main Banks and Internal Capital Markets in Japan.* 157 SHOKEN KEIZAI 255 (1986).

70. Takeo Hoshi, A. Kashyap, and D. Scharfstein, *Bank Monitoring and Investment: Evidence from the Changing Structure of Japanese Corporate Banking Relationships, in* ASYMMETRIC INFORMATION CORPORATE FINANCE AND INVESTMENTS 105 (R. Glenn Hubbard, ed., 1990).

71. *Ibid.*, at 113.

72. Mark Ramseyer, *Legal Rules in Repeated Deals: Banking in the Shadow of Defection in Japan*, 20 J. LEGAL STUD. 91, 103 (1991).

73. *Ibid.*, at 98, footnote 18, citing the fact that every five years, 15% of the firms listed on Section 1 of the Tokyo Stock Exchange switch main banks citing Akiyoshi Horiuchi, "The Function of Financial Institutions" (1987); and 33.2% change such connections over ten years, citing Yoshiro Miwa, "Main Banks and their Functions." But the evidence regarding bank ties also suggests an increase in stability as the rates of defection from main banks have declined from 17% from 1962–1967, to 15% during a five-year period in the late sixties and early seventies, and has decreased still further to 11% from 1978 to 1983. Recent data suggests that publicly traded Japanese companies increased their borrowing by 29 trillion Yen between 1980 and 1989. The issuance of stocks and bonds accounted for 43 trillion Yen for these companies, while new capital produced or retained earnings increased 24 trillion Yen during this period. (Gerlach, *Twilight of the Keiretsu, supra* note 57, at 99 citing *Nikkei Business* [January 15, 1990].) However, US firms

also increased their borrowings substantially in the eighties, and it was only because of the growth of the market value of equity that the debt/equity ratio did not alter significantly.

74. Eric Berglof, and Enrico Perotti, "The Japanese Financial Keiretsu as a Collective Enforcement Mechanism," Massachusetts Institute of Technology Japan Program 91–09 (1991).

75. Coffee, *supra* note 63, at 1294.

76. Securities Exchange Act §65, Law No. 25 of 1948—provides that a Japanese bank may not engage in investment banking under Section 11 of Japan's Anti-Monopoly Act regarding the prohibition of private monopolies and the maintenance of fair trade (§ 11a, Law No. 54 of 1947). Banks may not own more than 5% of a non-banking firm. Originally the Anti-Monopoly Act placed a maximum level at 10%, but this was reduced to 5% by Law No. 63 of 1977. Banks were given until December 1987 to divest excess holdings. Ramseyer, *supra* note 72, at 99, footnote 21, and Coffee, *supra* note 63, at 1294.

77. Coffee, *supra* note 63; Ramseyer, *supra* note 72.

78. *Ibid*.

79. Law Amending Laws in Relation to Financial and Exchange System Reform (June 19, 1992), promulgated June 26, 1992.

80. Kenneth Froot, Andrew Perrold, and Jeremy Stein, "Shareholders Trading Practices and Corporate Investment Horizons." Council on Competitiveness and Harvard Business School (December 1991). This is despite the fact that Japan issued new net equity of $80 billion in the late 1980s while the United States added $500 billion in leverage (*see infra* note 183).

81. *See* Part IV.

82. Coffee, *supra* note 63, at 1299, and Michael Jenson, *Agency Cost of Free Cash Flow, Corporate Finance and Takeovers*, 76 Am. Econ. Rev., 323 (1986).

83. Ramseyer, *supra* note 72.

84. Oliver Hart, *An Economist's Perspective of the Theory of the Firm*, 89 Colum. L. Rev. 1757 (1989).

85. S. J. Grossman and O. Hart, *The Cost and Benefits of Ownership: A Theory of Vertical and Lateral Integration*, 94 J. Pol. Econ. 691 (1986).

86. Michael Gerlach, Alliance Capitalism: The Social Organization of Japanese Business 137–150 (1992).

87. *See infra* notes 134–139, and accompanying text.

88. Ramseyer, *supra* note 72.

89. *See infra* notes 111–115.

90. The rule: (1). Permits the proxy statement to be used as solicitation material as long as it is not accompanied by a proxy card, and provided disinterested persons don't actually solicit proxies (broadly defined to include third party advisors and shareholders who have no material economic interest in a voting proposal, except as shareholders) from the need to file and preclear proxy statements.

(2). Permits a shareholder to obtain a full shareholder list including non-objecting beneficial owners. Securities Exchange Act Release no. 34–31,326 57 Fed. Reg. 48, 276 17 CRR 240 14a–1–103 (Oct. 22, 1992). For discussion *see* Black, *supra* note 64, at 829.

91. Robert Monks, and Nel Minnow, *Power and Accountability* (1991) at 256.

92. *See, e.g., Business Round Table Corporate Governance and American Competitiveness*, 26 Bus. Law. 241 (1990).

93. Black, *supra* note 64, at 831–834.

94. *See* J. Grundfest, *The Subordination of American Capital*, 27 J. Finan. Econ. 89 (1990).

95. The Business Roundtable on Corporate Governance and American Competitiveness, 46 *Bus. Law.* 241 (1990); the American Bar Association Committee on Corporate Law's Section of Corporations, Banking and Business Law, American Bar Association, Corporate Directors Guidebook, 33 *Bus. Law.* 1595 (1978); the American Law Institute Principles of Corporate Governance: Analysis and Recommendations § 3A.01 (proposed final draft, March 31, 1992) and the Delaware courts. *See* William Allen *Independent Directors in MBO Transactions: "Are They Fact or Fantasy?"* 45 Bus. Law. 2055 (1990).

96. Jay Lorsch, Pawns or Potentates: Reality of America's Corporate Boards (1989). *See also* Ronald Gilson, and Mark Roe, *Understanding the Japanese Keiretsu: Overlaps Between Corporate Governance and Industrial Organization* 102 Yale L. J. 871 (1993).

97. 15 USC § 78M(d) (1988), Rule 13(d)1 to 13(d)7, 17 CFR §§ 240.13(d)1 to 13(d)7.

98. 17 USC § 78P–D (1988), Rule 16A1 to 16B11, 17 CFR §§ 240.16A, 1–16E.11.

99. Securities and Exchange Act of 1934, § 16B, 15 USC § 78 P(B) (1988).

100. *See* SEC Rule 16A(1) 17 CFR § 240, Rule 16A–1A (1991).

101. As pension funds and mutual funds switch to the index strategy, a question arises as to what the purpose of monitoring would be for an index investor. Both Coffee, *supra* note 63, at 1340 and Monks and Minnow, *Power and Accountability*, *supra* note 91, believe that an indexed fund is a permanent shareholder and is consequently well positioned to behave as a corporate monitor. However, the great degree of diversification which indexation involves means that the benefits to be derived from corporate monitoring are small in such an instance.

102. Securities Act of 1933, § 15, 15 USC § 770 (1988); Securities and Exchange Act of 1934, § 20, 15 USC § 78T (1988). This rule is partly mitigated by Rule 144, which permits an affiliate to sell up to the greater of 1% of a class or the average weekly trade by a security every three months. Securities Act Rule 144(e) 17 CFR § 230.144(e) (1991).

103. Coffee, *supra* note 63, at 1355. *See also* note 120, *infra*.

104. J. Keynes, General Theory on Employment Interest and Money (1935).

105. *See* Chapter 2, *supra* note 138, and accompanying text.

106. *See supra* notes 15–28.

107. Coffee, *supra* note 63, at 1314.

108. Prowse, *supra* note 66.

109. Coffee, *supra* note 63, at 1315.

110. *Ibid.*, at 1319. (The proportion of equity capital to total assets has steadily fallen from 60% in the early nineteenth century, to 20% at the turn of this century, to below 10% since the early 1950s, to under 5% since the mid–1970s.)

111. James Brickley, Ronald Lees, and Clifford Smith, *Ownership Structure and Voting on Anti-Takeover Amendments*, 20 J. Fin. Econ. 267, 276 (1988).

112. "Pension Forum: Taking the Offensive," INSTIT. INVEST. 101 (December 1987); *see also*, Black, *supra* note 64, at 882–885.

113. Coffee, *supra* note 63, at 1323, citing New York State Task Force on Pension Fund Investments, "Our Money's Worth," *The Report of the Governor's Task Force on Pension Fund Investment* (1989).

114. *Ibid.*, citing Robert McCartney, and Kathleen Day, "California Governor Seeks to Control Pension Fund: Plan Would Cut Benefits of State Retirees," WASHINGTON POST, June 18, 1991, C1, C3.

115. 15 PA Cons. Stat. Annotated §§ 2573–2575 (1991).

116. Coffee, *supra* note 36, at 1339, citing David Walker, *The Increasing Role of Pension Plans in the Capital Markets or in Corporate Governance Matters*, *in* INSTITUTIONAL INVESTING: THE CHALLENGES AND RESPONSIBILITIES OF THE 21ST CENTURY, 34, 36 (Arnold W. Sametz, ed., 1991).

117. New York Stock Exchange Press Release (June 12, 1990), cited in Coffee, *supra* note 63, at 1339.

118. *Ibid.*, at 1353.

119. "Labor Department Opinion Letter on Proxy Voting," 17 *Pens. Rep.* (BNA No. 5, 244–246, January 23, 1990), cited in Coffee, *supra* note 63, at 1353–1354, footnotes 299, 302.

120. James Loreie, Peter Dodd, and Mary Hamilton Kempton, THE STOCK MARKET: THEORIES IN EVIDENCE 85 (2d ed. 1985); Richard Brealey, and Stuart C. Meyers, PRINCIPLES OF CORPORATE FINANCE 156 (3d ed. 1988), cited in Coffee, *supra* note 63, at 1355.

121. 29 USC § 1104A(1)C (1988).

122. Coffee, *supra* note 63, at 1363, citing Investment Advisor Act of 1940, § 205(a)(1), 15 USC § 80-b-5(a)(1) (1988); also, citing Tamar Frankel, 2 THE REGULATION OF MONEY MANAGERS 285–300 (1978); Harvey Bines, THE LAW OF INVESTMENT MANAGEMENT, § 503 (1978).

123. Coffee, *supra* note 63, at 1317–1318. Compare Keynes, *supra* note 104, cited in quote on pp. 166–167.

124. Gerlach, *supra* note 57, at 88. These percentages exclude financial and industrial firms in smaller city groups such as Daiwa as well as many companies affiliated with the industrial banks of Japan, the largest bank in Japan, which is government owned. Toshiba alone has 200 subsidiary companies and another 600 grandchild companies. A looser classification system based on stable capital affiliation finds that 577 of 986 stocks listed in the first section of the Tokyo Stock Exchange had identifiable affiliations with one of the Big Six Groups. These companies accounted for 69% of total assets of all first section firms and 76% of the total sales.

125. *Ibid.*, at 95.

126. *Ibid.*, at 96.

127. *Ibid.*, at 92–93.

128. Recent data suggest that publicly traded Japanese companies increased their borrowing by 29 trillion Yen between 1980 and 1989. The issuance of stocks and bonds accounted for 43 trillion Yen for these companies, while new capital produced or retained earnings increased 24 trillion Yen during this period. Gerlach, *supra* note 57, at 99 citing *Nikkei Business* (January 15, 1990). However, US firms also increased their borrowings substantially in the 1980s, and it was only because of

the growth of the market value of equity that the debt/equity ratio did not alter significantly.

129. *See supra* note 76.

130. Gerlach, *supra* note 57, at 103.

131. *Ibid.*, citing *Nikkei Business* (January 15, 1990) and SECURITIES MARKET IN JAPAN 10 (1990). The degree of direct financing, including funds raised for investment trust, is nearly 90% as of 1987. However, it is not clear that this figure would be significantly different for the United States.

132. *See* Chapter 1, *supra* Part III-B.

133. WALL STREET JOURNAL (March 18, 1991).

134. Gerlach, *supra* note 86, at 166 and 179.

135. *Ibid.*, at 168.

136. The Sogo Shoshas tend toward reinforcing Keiretsu ties, particularly for industries in decline. For example, in the Mitsubishi Group, as of 1983, the Group trading company handles 55% of sales for Mitsubishi Heavy Industries, and 75% for Mitsubishi Aluminum and Mitsui Shipbuilding (*Ibid.*, at 184, citing a 1983 study of Okumura Hiroshi).

137. Gerlach, *supra* note 86, at 187–188.

138. Banri Asanuma, *Manufacturing-Supplier Relationships in Japan as a Concept of Relation—Specific Skill*, 3 J. JAPAN. INT'L ECON. 130 (1989).

139. The tendency of Japanese firms to trade within the Keiretsu has been transplanted overseas. It is probably augmented by the role of Sogo Shoshas in foreign trade. Evidence suggests that a much higher proportion of Japanese firms trade within their corporate group than do similar American firms. (Robert Lawrence, *How Open Is Japan? in* TRADE WITH JAPAN: HAS THE DOOR OPENED WIDER?, *supra* note 5, at 9–40.) In 1986, intrafirm trade accounted for 48.5% of US exports to Europe and 32.0% of US imports from Europe; but intrafirm shipments accounted for 75% of US imports from Japan and 72% of US exports to Japan. Intrafirm shipments from US exporters accounted for 36.9% of US exports to Europe while Japanese exports to the United States were dominated by intrafirm shipments of Japanese exporting firms—66.1% of all US imports from Japan. This pattern suggests the international vertical integration process moving downstream internationally from producers to their markets, according to Professor Robert Lawrence (*Ibid.*). In 1986, Japanese affiliates in the United States shipped 58.4% of all US exports to Japan back to their Japanese parents. By contrast, US affiliates in Japan imported from their parent companies only 13.6% of all Japanese imports from the United States (*Ibid.*, at 9, 15–17). On President Bush's 1992 trip to Japan, Japanese promises to buy $20 billion per year in auto parts from the United States in order to reduce the merchandise surplus with the United States were criticized because most of these purchases would come from Japanese firms. The merchandise surplus of Japan and the corresponding US deficit with Japan would also be reduced. While an unfair trade issue may exist, the point to be underscored here is that intracorporate finance is bound up with intragroup trade, leading inexorably to unfair trade issues.

140. Gerlach, *supra* note 57, at 106.

141. 80% of National R&D was financed by private firms in Japan compared with 48% in the United States, and only 2% of private sector funding came from

the government in comparison with 35% in the United States. Gerlach, *supra* note 57, at 107.

142. Oliver Williamson, THE ECONOMIC INSTITUTIONS OF CAPITALISM (1985).

143. *See* Carl Kester, "Banks in the Board Room: The American Versus Japanese and German Experiences." Harvard Business School Research Colloquium, May 27–28, 1992.

144. Jensen, *supra* note 82.

145. Carl Kester, JAPANESE TAKEOVERS 169–235 (1991), and *infra* notes 160–169.

146. *Ibid.*, *see also infra* notes 160–169, and accompanying text.

147. Carliss Baldwin, and Kim B. Clarke, "Capabilities and Capital Investment: New Perspectives on Capital Budgeting." Prepared for the Counsel on Competitiveness and Harvard Business School, 1992.

148. *Ibid.*, at 5.

149. This study cites several other studies that show that cannibalism can make companies more competitive, including R. N. Foster, INNOVATION: THE ATTACKER'S ADVANTAGE (1986); C. H. Ferguson, "American Microelectronics in Decline: Evidence Analysis and Alternatives," Ph.D. dissertation, Massachusetts Institute of Technology, 1987; and C. Y. Baldwin, "How Capital Budgeting Deters Innovation, and What Companies Can Do About It," Research-Technology Management, 1991.

150. Baldwin and Clarke, *supra* note 147.

151. J. Davidson Frame, and Francis Narain, *The United States, Japan and the Changing Technological Balance* 19 RES. POL. 447–455 (1990).

152. Michael Gerlach, "Economic Innovation and Corporate Finance in Japan," 13 (1992) (unpublished).

153. Richard Florida, and Martin Kenney, THE BREAKTHROUGH ILLUSION: CORPORATE AMERICA'S FAILURE TO MOVE FROM INNOVATION TO MASS PRODUCTION (1990).

154. Gerlach, *supra* note 152, at 10.

155. Edwin Mansfield, *Industrial R&D in Japan and the United States: A Comparative Study*, 78 AM. ECON. REV.: PAPERS AND PROC. 223–228 (May 1988).

156. Gerlach, *supra* note 152, at 26; M. Aoki, *The Japanese Firm in Transition*, *in* THE POLITICAL ECONOMY OF JAPAN, (KOZO Yanamura, and L. Yasuba, eds., Vol. 1, 1987).

157. Gerlach, *supra* note 57, at 107; Horiuchi Akiyoshi, Frank Packer, and S. Fucuda, *What Role Has the Main Bank Played in Japan?* J. JAPAN. AND INT'L ECON. 159–180 (1988); Aoki, *supra* note 52.

158. *See supra* notes 52–55, and accompanying text.

159. The Structural Impediment Initiatives I and II began to address questions of financial structure, but only superficially.

160. *See infra* notes 168–169.

161. Zielinski and Holloway, *supra* note 53, at 123.

162. *See* Williamson, *supra* note 142, and Grossman and Hart, *supra* note 85. The application of the implicit contract theory as a risk sharing by the Japanese Keiretsu is attributable to I. Nakatani, *The Economic Role of the Financial Corporate Grouping*, *in* THE ECONOMIC ANALYSIS OF THE JAPANESE FIRM 227–258 (M. Aoki, ed., 1984).

163. Paul Sheard, *The Role of Firm Organizations in the Adjustment of a De-*

clining Industry in Japan: The Case of Aluminum, J. JAPAN. AND INT'L ECON. (1991).

164. *Ibid*. In the case of Sumitomo Aluminum Smelting, this company underwent share reduction each year between 1982 and 1985 and was dissolved in 1986. Between 1982 and 1986, Sumitomo Chemical injected 57 billion Yen in share capital into SAS, and in the same period wrote off 61 billion Yen in losses as a result of SAS's share capital write-down. (Zielinski and Holloway, *supra* note 53, at 123.)

165. Zielinski and Holloway, *supra* note 53. Banks played a major role in adjustment of the industry by providing interest rate reduction to the aluminum smelting firm. It was reported that in 1978, Nippon Light Metal's three main banks implemented interest rate reductions representing an annual interest subsidy of some 900 million Yen.

166. *Ibid*., at 124. In the case of one smelting company, it was found that three closely associated trading companies provided a total of 32 billion Yen in low interest off-balance sheet financing in 1981.

167. *Ibid*., at 128.

168. *Ibid*., at 107–110.

169. Jensen and Meckling, *supra* note 66.

170. Williamson, *supra* note 142; Grossman and Hart, *supra* note 85.

171. Hoshi, Kashyap, and Scharfstein, *supra* note 69. *See also* Hoshi, Kashyap, and Scharfstein, *supra* note 68.

172. Zielinski and Holloway, *supra* note 53, at 120.

173. *Ibid*.

174. *Ibid*.

175. *See supra* note 55, and accompanying text.

176. *Ibid*., at 138.

177. *Ibid*.

178. *Ibid*.

179. *Compare* Meerschwan, and Frankel, *supra* note 5, and the accompanying text.

180. Zielinski and Holloway, *supra* note 53, at 172–173.

181. *Ibid*., at 196.

182. *Ibid*.

183. *Ibid*., at 184–186.

184. *See* Chapter 2, *supra* note 1.

185. *See example*, Keynes, *supra* note 104, at 102–106.

186. Seth Rama, and Alicia Quijano, "Growth in Japanese Lending and Direct Investment: Are They Related?" New York Federal Reserve Bank Research Paper No. 9101 (1991).

187. Laventhal and Howarth, Inc., JAPANESE REAL ESTATE INVESTMENT IN THE U.S. (1992).

188. A credit crunch is the informal allocation of credit by banks.

189. Fed. Reserve Bull. April 1992 at A–5.

190. According to Greenspan, long-term portfolio investment by Japanese residents, including purchases of US and corporate bonds, averaged nearly $90 billion per year during 1986 to 1988, net of investments by foreign nationals in Japanese securities. (Testimony by Greenspan, *supra* note 1, at 4.)

Japanese investors hold only a small percentage of US Treasuries—2% to 3%

of outstanding marketable US Treasuries—and their holdings of equities are of even smaller magnitude. US data indicates that Japanese investors sold some net $20 billion worth of US Treasuries in 1990. (Testimony by Greenspan, *supra* note 1, at 6.) But interest rates on these instruments declined as other investors were willing to buy them. The big change was in net purchases by foreigners of Japanese securities in 1991. (Testimony by Greenspan, *supra* note 1, at 7.) *But see* Seth Rama, *The Credit Crunch in the U.S.: A Japanese Contribution* (unpublished).

In 1989 Japanese purchases and sales of US Treasury securities totalled $1.95 trillion, but that number had fallen to $1.3 trillion by 1991. As of the year end, 1991, Japanese investors actually held only approximately $78 billion, or less than 2%, of government and government-related debt. Japanese holdings of corporate debt was approximately $18 billion, or 1.1% of more than $1.6 trillion in outstanding corporate bonds. (Testimony of Breeden, *supra* note 46.) In US corporate equity markets, Japanese investors are the second largest group. Japanese purchases and sales of US equity securities totaled more than $106 billion in 1988. In 1991 the total value of Japanese trading in US equities was only $47.4 billion. In 1991 US investors purchased and sold a record $939 billion of foreign securities. Japanese securities were the second most actively traded foreign securities by Americans. In 1991 Japanese stocks comprised 20% of US foreign equity transactions and Japanese bonds accounted for 13% of US trading in foreign debt securities. (*Ibid.*, at 4.)

Most of the reduction of Japanese portfolio investment in the United States is accounted for in the Appendix to the Federal Reserve Bulletin entitled "Net Sales or Purchases of Securities by Foreign Investors." *Fed. Reserve Bull.* (April 1992), at A–65. Overall net purchases (sales) of US securities was minus $15 billion in 1990 and $12 billion in 1991.

191. James Sterngold, "Japanese Shifting Investment Flow Back Toward Home: Pressure on Rates in U.S.," NEW YORK TIMES, March 22, 1992, citing new data from the Bank of Japan.

192. BIS, *62nd Annual Report*, Basle, June 15, 1992, at 164. 45% of the contraction took place on local foreign currency markets in Tokyo, while 38% was due to reduction in assets of European banking affiliates. Over two-thirds of the contraction was accounted for by a scaling back of claims on non-related banks and on non-bank customers. Net borrowing by Japanese banks from non-related banks dropped from $226 billion at the end of 1990 to a low of $166 billion.

193. Japan is listed as having a positive purchase of about $50 million (an insignificant sum) of bonds that represents a significant decline from the $60 billion a year Japan purchased in the late 1980s. (Fed. Reserve Bull., April 1992, at A–65.)

194. This item is listed as item #34—Memo: Marketable U.S. Treasury Securities Held in Custody for Foreign and International Accounts and $251 billion as of January 1, 1992, as reported in the April 1992 *Fed. Reserve Bull.* at A–11, while total loans and securities held by the Federal Reserve were approximately $288 billion. (*Ibid.*, line 15). There appears to be a gradual increase in foreign government holdings of US securities. Compare *Fed. Reserve Bull.* (January 1992), at A–11. The formidable holdings of US Treasury by foreign government entities has acted as an ancillary reserve which has enabled the expansion of credit (broadly equivalent to M10 (total money and credit) to grow from approximately $5 trillion

in 1983 to $10 trillion in 1991). *Ibid.* "Total Credit" at A–42. Japanese banks, however, do not appear to have contributed to the credit crunch as they expanded credit to US entities in 1991. *See* Ronald Johnson, "The Bank Credit 'Crumble,' " *The New York Federal Reserve Bank Quarterly* (Summer 1991), pp. 40, 42, showing that while US–owned banks retrenched their business lending, foreign-owned banks continued to increase their lending at a 6% rate in 1990, although down from 10% grossed the year earlier. *See also*, Seth Rama, "Japanese Banks and the Credit 'Crunch,' " *New York Federal Reserve Bank*, 1992 (unpublished).

195. *See* Chapter 1, *supra* note 56, and accompanying text.

196. The desirability of making such a market was suggested by Keynes in *Treatise on Money* and is receiving increased attention from the Federal Reserve Board of Governors.

197. Bank for International Settlements, *59th Annual Report*, June 16, 1989, at 118.

198. Lois Steckler, "Position Data on U.S. Net Investment Position." Federal Reserve Board of Governors, International Financial Discussion Paper No. 339 (1988).

199. *Ibid.*, at 21.

200. *International Banking Competitiveness—Why It Matters*, A Report of the Economic Advisory Committee of the American Banker's Association (March 1990). *See also* Chapter 2, *supra* notes 9–13.

201. *Ibid.*

202. Thomas Hanley, John D. Lenard, and Diane B. Glossman, THE JAPANESE BANKS: EMERGING INTO GLOBAL MARKETS (1989).

203. Clay Chandler, "Japan's Bid to Bail Out Shaky Banks Threatens to be Slow and Costly," THE WALL STREET JOURNAL, October 16, 1992, p. 1.

204. *Ibid.*

205. *Ibid.*, at A–11.

206. JAPAN ECONOMIC JOURNAL, December 8, 1992, p. 29.

207. *Ibid.*

208. *See* Chapter 1, *supra* notes 57 and 72, and accompanying text.

209. *See* Chapter 2, *supra* note 209, *et seq.*, and accompanying text regarding U.S. Treasury Capital Equivalency Study.

210. *See* Chapter 1, *supra* note 46 for a discussion of moral hazard. *See* Chapter 2 Part VIA for a discussion of the collapse of the S&L industry and the threat to the safety and soundness of commercial banks.

211. *See* Chapter 2, *supra* note 133. FDICIA Title II, Regulatory Improvement, Subtitle A, Regulation of Foreign Banks, § 202, Regulation of Foreign Bank Operations.

212. *Ibid.* § 202(E)(7) amending § 7 of the International Banking Act of 1978 (12 USC § 3105).

213. *See* Chapter 2, *supra* notes 122–124.

214. Fair Trade Commission Report, November 1990.

215. Aoki, *supra* note 52; James Abegglen, and George Stalk, KAISHA, THE JAPANESE CORPORATION (1985).

216. Chalmers Johnson, *Trade Revisionism and the Future of Japanese-American Relations in* JAPAN'S ECONOMIC STRUCTURE: SHOULD IT CHANGE? 105–136 (KOZO Yamamura, ed., 1990); Edward Lincoln, JAPAN'S UNEQUAL TRADE (1988).

217. Gerlach, *supra* note 57; Sheard, *supra* note 163, and Gerlach, *supra* note 86.

218. *But see* Zielinski and Holloway, *supra* note 53.

219. NEW STRATEGIC TRADE THEORY (Paul Krugman, ed., 1986).

5

Conclusion

The most momentous agreement of recent times in international financial circles has been the G–10 Agreement on Capital Adequacy. This agreement has corollaries in US regulation, Japanese regulation and in the EEC directives on banking, but capital adequacy for banks' investment activity is different than its trading activity or the trading activity conducted by securitized firms. In general, financial assets that can be pooled are more fungible, and obligations undertaken in the securities business are far more short-term, requiring less long-term capital. The worldwide tendency toward securities markets and away from traditional lending, and the securitization of asset pools, has become possible because of the growth of institutional investors such as money market and pension funds. The G–10 Agreement on capital adequacy, because it achieved agreement only on bank capital, inevitably lags today's international capital markets.

The debate of the 1970s and 1980s over monetary policy has been replaced by one in which capital adequacy is at the fore. The impending failure of European Monetary Union may impact on the single market program for financial services. Certainly, it will slow down the pace, but the principal changes which must proceed in banking and securities regulation and consolidated supervision are unrelated to monetary union.

Capital adequacy definitions and their impact depends on the treatment of reserves and other local accounting standards, the distinction between securities and banking activities, and the facility of national markets to create hybrid instruments which qualify as capital. In the United States, FDICIA has created rigorous definitions of capital for US banks. By contrast, the Japanese are less fervid in their regulation of bank capital; and bank supervision is inherently different in "capital market" countries, such as the United States and the United Kingdom, from such supervision in production exporting countries, such as Japan and Germany. Japan and

Germany do not apply GAAP principles; and in both countries there are substantial intercorporate holdings. To the extent that banks own equity shares, their capital is subject to the fluctuations in securities markets.

Consolidated supervision of financial conglomerates is far more prudent in the United States than in the EEC, to the extent that these conglomerates include banks. Although capital requirements for securities firms in the EEC are more lax than for their US counterparts, the EEC, unlike the United States, has adopted a consolidated supervision approach for securities firms.

The growing importance of securities markets in Germany and Japan calls for concerted regulator initiatives. Internationalization resulted in the activation of Japan's futures markets and may have been responsible for the precipitous fall of stock markets. As Germany and Japan move toward arm's length securities markets, a regime of investor protection and market regulation becomes essential. Such a regime is nascent in the EEC single market program for financial services, particularly the Consolidated Supervision Directives, the Investment Services Directive, the Unit Trust Market Directive, the Listing Particulars Directives and the Mutual Recognition of Prospectus Requirements Directive.

At the same time, the United States has allowed, through judicial and regulatory expansion of the Glass-Steagall Act, bank participation in the securities market through Glass-Steagall Section 20 Subsidiaries. As a result, the financial system will inevitably become less resilient to securities market fluctuations. Banks will be less able to create confidence by arm's-length lending to the securities markets as they did under Chairman Greenspan's direction in 1987, because these banks with Section 20 subsidiaries may now tend to lend to their own subsidiaries, thereby reducing confidence in the overall financial market structure. Rather than further expanding securities activities of banks, their profitability can continue to be enhanced by allowing bank underwriting of the securitization of their own consumer and mortgage-backed loans; and, in fact, the tendency of the 1980s has been toward such securitization.

Finance companies that are extremely well capitalized, including GM, Sears and Ford, have higher capitalization than banks but are subject to few of the same rules. Such finance companies are in the business of banking and they ought to be regulated as banks, particularly since they form a very important part of the financial structure of the US economy. If they are regulated as banks, their affiliation with commercial companies would be prohibited by the Bank Holding Company Act of 1956. Perhaps financing of parent company equipment (i.e., appliances or automobiles) should be specifically exempted from such a prohibited affiliation.

The Chairman of the SEC has said that US capital rules enabled the liquidation of Drexel Burnham without recourse to the securities investor protection fund. However, other firms, such as Prudential Bache or Shear-

Prudential Bache or Shearson Lehman, would have failed under the same stresses to which Drexel Burnham was subject had they not been tied to financial conglomerates. While there are new disclosure rules governing the parents of subsidiaries which are registered broker dealers, these rules do not enable the parent companies to be seen in their true light; and the hidden risks posed by these parent companies may pose potential threats to the financial system. The United States must follow the worldwide trend toward consolidated supervision of securities firms. The function of the US capital markets has not enabled US investment to occur at a sufficient pace. While the low savings rate in the United States may be blamed, the stock market has been a critical force in leveraging the US economy. According to one source, $500 billion of equity has been removed from the financial system in the 1980s, while Japan has added $80 billion in investment, not counting convertible bond issues. While the Japanese financial structure is extremely fragile because of illiquidity, the cross-holding has enabled investment to occur at a far faster pace than in the United States. Japan appears to invest far more than the United States, but overinvestment can be extremely damaging to a financial structure. In order for investment to yield a return, a marketplace for consumers must exist, and Japan has a limited internal marketplace. To the extent it can jump trade and tariff and non-tariff barriers, Japan may remain a pivotal force in the world economy; but, it lags behind the EEC and the United States to the extent it is forced to rely on its own undeveloped consumer market. Greenspan, in his testimony before the Senate Banking Committee, has said that Japan will become a less important trade partner because of its recent stock market and capital adequacy problems. A boom and bust cycle in Japanese financial markets impacts directly and indirectly on US financial markets through increasing the US trade deficit and contributing to a US credit crunch.

The failure of financial structures in the United States, the EEC and Japan to converge will bode ill for all participants in the international trading system. If Japan faces downscaling in its low-tech, internationally uncompetitive industries because of overleverage through convertible bonds, will it react by opening these industries to competition or by traditional protection? Will Japan withdraw capital from the United States to meet bank capital requirements? Underlying these questions is the question of whether Japan's economy is built on a structural surplus. Unlike Mr. Greenspan, this author believes that financial disruptions in Japan have a potentially devastating effect on the United States. A bear raid on the dollar is a possibility, and many commentators have remarked upon the instability that would be created by a collapse in clearing and settlement resulting from a rapid dollar decline.

World financial markets will require convergence in saving and investment. Japan must liberalize its financial structure via anti-trust enforcement

and liberalization (i.e., the end of administrative guidance), that will reduce the savings rate through the provision of consumer credit and end the allocative process that has led to overinvestment. Similarly, in the United States it may be necessary to restrict the endless flow of consumer credit by regulating money market funds and finance companies as banks, thereby tending to raise the savings and investment rate.

Nonetheless, the vehicle for US financial success and international competitiveness is the development of a long-term strategy by US corporations. Whether or not a long-term strategy can be achieved by institutional investor monitoring of corporate actions, the current regulatory framework makes a long-term strategy impossible because short-termism is built into US securities regulation and practice.

Restrictions which preclude large shareholdings by institutional investors must be removed. These include SEC Section 16 limitations on 10% shareholders, relevant parts of the Investment Advisors Act of 1940, and definitions of fiduciary standards under ERISA. Furthermore, banks, pension and mutual funds must be protected from conflicts of interest which arise between them and corporate managers allowing them to vote shares in the best long-term interest of the corporation.

Financial regulation must proceed across boundaries. The coordination of capital treatment of real estate assets and securities firms, the derivative instruments in which they trade and the consolidated supervision of all financial firms are requisite aspects of regulation. Ultimate reliance ought not be placed on self-regulatory organizations of securities and derivative markets which promulgate idiosyncratic rules, incomprehensible to national, let alone foreign, regulators. The safety and soundness of the international financial system is best ensured, and perhaps only ensured, by the harmonization of financial regulation.

Afterword

In April 1993, the Basle Committee on Banking and Supervisory practices issued three papers: the Supervisory Recognition of Netting for Capital Adequacy Purposes;[1] the Supervisory Treatment of Market Risks;[2] and, the Measurement of Banks' Exposure to Interest Rate Risk.[3]

Following up on the 1990 report on interbank netting schemes,[4] it was agreed that credit and liquidity risks could be reduced by some form of bilateral and multilateral netting. The bilateral netting would employ the current exposure method, meaning the mark-to-market value of interest rate or currency instrument, plus add-on. Since the replacement cost can often amount from 50% to 80% of the total capital charge—replacement cost plus add-on—bilateral netting (of replacement cost) can reduce replacement cost by up to 50%, which would represent a 25% to 40% alleviation in capital charge (depending upon the counterparty).[5] Naturally, netting must be by novation—the fictional creation of a new contract.

Multilateral netting inevitably involves the use of a clearing house that would have to replace the losses that defaulting members' portfolios of forex or interest-rate swap contracts would have produced. Consequently, losses would have to be calculated by requiring each member to post collateral equal to its own net debit with the clearing house.

Pursuant to the EEC Capital Adequacy Directive (CAD),[6] which became final in 1993 subject to future international agreements, the Basle Committee issued a statement or a proposal on the supervisory treatment of market risks. The proposal applied to position taking in debt and equity securities in the trading portfolio (as opposed to the investment portfolio in the 1988 G–10 Agreement).[7] The 1988 G–10 Agreement was mainly directed toward the assessment of capital in relation to credit risk (the risk of counterparty failure). However, deregulation of interest rate risk, capital controls and financial innovation permitted a range of activities that have

increased the opportunity for banks to incur market risks, particularly banks trading in derivative products.[8]

Fundamentally, these market risks, because they derive through a bank's trading book, are on a somewhat shorter time horizon than traditional banking activities. The G–10 Committee favors capital requirements as opposed to limits for international convergence in the treatment of market risks,[9] principally because this form of regulation allows complex hedging activities. Trading positions are understood to mean the bank's proprietary position in financial instruments, which are taken with the intention of benefiting in the short term from actual or expected market movements,[10] and does not include positions specifically required to hedge a bank book.[11] The G-10 proposal is identical to the EEC Capital Adequacy Directive in employing the building block approach which differentiates between specific risks and general market risks. Specific risk is the risk of loss caused by an adverse movement of a security or derivative principally due to factors relating to the issuer (which has some parallels with credit risks); general market risk is the risk of loss caused by an adverse movement unrelated to a specific security. The extent to which the proposal would lead to higher or lower capital charges depends on whether a bank has well-hedged positions or significant holdings of high grade corporate securities.

The definition of tier-three capital under the proposal mirrors the CAD: capital (1) must be unsecured, subordinate and fully paid up; (2) must have an original maturity of at least two years; (3) must not be repayable before the agreed repayment date unless the supervisors agree; (4) must be subject to a lock-in clause that stipulates that neither interest nor principal may be paid even if mature if such payment would mean that the capital allocated to the trading book for debt securities and equities would fall below a threshold of 20% above minimum required capital. Tier-three capital would be limited to 250% of tier-one capital, which is allocated exclusively to the trading book. This means that a minimum of 28.5% of trading book risks would need to be supported by tier-one capital not required to support other risks.[12] Tier-two capital could be substituted for tier-three insofar as the overall limits in the 1988 G–10 Agreement were not breached—that is, that tier-two capital could not exceed total tier-one capital and long-term debt could not exceed 50% of tier-one capital.

As in the CAD, certain qualifying debt securities would require a lower position weighting, such as 1/4 of a percent for residual maturities from 3 to 6 months; 1% for residual maturities between 6 and 24 months and 1.6% for residual maturities exceeding 24 months.[13] Futures and forward contracts and swaps are treated as the combination of a long and a short position and as two notional amounts with relevant maturities. No offsetting would be allowed for positions in different currencies. Thus, the separate legs of cross-currency swaps or forward exchange deals would be

treated as notional positions in the relevant currencies. Closely matched swap positions would be treated as off-setting one another, provided they related to the same underlying instruments and were of the same nominal value and denominated in the same currency. For swaps and forward-rate agreements, the reference rate would need to be identical and/or the coupon for fixed rate positions closely matched within 10 to 15 basis points. The residual maturity would have to correspond within the following limits: less than one month, the same day; between 1 month and 1 year, within 7 days; over 1 year, within 30 days.[14] As far as equities are concerned, the general risk weight requirement is 8%—consistent with the CAD, and the specific risk requirement will be not lower than 5% and a minimum of 8% will be applied to portfolios of stocks that fail to meet liquidity and diversification tests. This differs from the CAD in that the minimum for a highly diversified portfolio, specific risk component is 2%. Because equity derivative products are converted into positions in the relevant underlying portfolio, there is no general risk requirement where a correspondingly diversified portfolio is held. However, a standard specific risk of 2% is applied to the net position in indexes comprising a diversified portfolio (this is regardless of the fact that an index is matched with an underlying position).

Unlike the CAD, the Basle Agreement has a special category for index arbitrage which will include taking baskets of stocks that do not equal an entire index, provided that a basket of stocks represents at least 90% of the market value of the index; and a 4% capital requirement reflecting 2% on each side of the position is required. This is somewhat in line with the US position that enabled major market indexes as well as complete indexes to be subject to a 5% total requirement.[15]

The Banking Supervisory Committee also issued a paper on interest rate risk. Each currency in which the bank has significant positions should be measured separately for each maturity ladder, and banks should present a comprehensive reporting return for all major branches and subsidiaries. The Committee has left it open as to whether principal (and the amortization thereof) and interest should be calculated separately or together. Where the precise reset date is uncertain for any instrument, it could be placed in either of the first two bands according to the estimated average range between the change in their interest rates and the change in market rates. Long and short positions with the same reference rate could be netted. Actual maturity may be very different from contractual maturity. For example, deposit liabilities may remain available to the bank long beyond their contractual repayment date. Consequently, empirical evidence as to behavioral activity will be considered and non-interest bearing deposits will be treated differently. In situations such as fixed rate mortgages where the holder can prepay without penalty, estimated cash flow

should be based upon expected prepayment behavior. Interest rate risk in derivative products would be the same as those set out in the paper on market risk.[16]

The Committee proposes that the same methodology as that set out in the market risk paper be employed for interest rate risk in the banking book, in spite of the fact that different volatility factors might justifiably be used because the time horizon over which the banking book should be judged is longer than the trading book. The duration of a fixed rate security is influenced by its coupon; and the lower the coupon, the more volatile the price. Thus, bonds with coupons of less than 3% should be reported separately and subject to higher weighting. Floating rate instruments with caps and floors can in theory be treated as a combination of floating rate securities with a series of options. However, this complicated approach may be unnecessary and the Committee has proposed that options whose caps are more than 1% above the current interest rates should be treated as floating rates and those whose caps are within 1% of the current interest rate levels should be treated as fixed rate instruments sliding in accordance with their final maturities.

This is in marked contrast to the US methodology in FDICIA Section 305, which is very rudimentary and seeks to identify outliers exposed to interest rate fluctuations of more than 1%.[17] Currently, there is no discussion of implementing this proposal into US law.

There is also little chance that the paper on the supervisory treatment of market risks as written is likely to be implemented. However, an agreement on debt instruments is being considered for implementation in the United States at the SEC state level, pending decisions by the SEC as to how to treat mortgage-backed securities. Presumably, exceptions will be made for interest only and principal only strips.

As noted above, that part of the market-risk proposal that concerns indexation requires a minimum of 2% on each side of the hedge of an index position. This is in contrast to the US requirement for a minimum of 5% total on both sides of the transaction for a hedged index fund;[18] and, it expands upon the EEC Capital Adequacy Directive[19] to allow for this favorable treatment for baskets that do not represent the full index.

The treatment of equities under the proposal approximates the EEC Capital Adequacy position in requiring 4% of the sum of long and short positions and 8% of the net. However, it falls far short of US capital requirements.[20] The SEC has never accepted the EEC's view on open equity positions, and no agreement has been reached. The reason that the market-risk document was issued in its present form is that New York Federal Reserve Bank President Corrigan chaired the Basle Committee, but under US law the Federal Reserve has no authority to set capital for Section 20 subsidiaries of banks or any other securities firms. The EEC's position on capital for equity risks is dangerously insufficient, according to

the SEC.[21] Will the United States lose market share to EEC exchanges in the future? The dangers of trading US equities in a secondary market such as London, which lacks the depth of the US market for US equities will prevent firms from defecting from the United States,[22] thus capital requirements will be higher for positions in the United States and consequently on almost all US equities than for equity positions on EEC markets and almost all EEC equities. However, this should not subsume the vast importance of the market-risk proposal that creates an international standard for capital requirement for debt instruments. Obviously, debt has always been more liquid than equity and more international in its marketability.

The specific application and implementation of the consultative paper will be pursuant to an SEC regulation which is in early stages of consideration by SEC staff. However, the restrictions on what constitutes eligible debt instruments will derive from various SEC no-action letters, which, for example, determine what constitutes eligible commercial paper, which, under the proposal, can be traded with 1/4 of a percent risk-weighting as opposed to the 8% that a bank would require to hold against a similar instrument. Thus, in current practice and under future implementation, securities firms and universal bank trading books enjoy a considerable advantage over banks holding identical assets.[23]

Under US rules, there is no consolidation requirement for broker dealers and their unregulated affiliates. Thus, capital adequacy treatment of foreign currency risks, interest rate swaps and financial futures and options that will apply to banks and regulated broker dealers will not apply to the unregulated affiliates of broker dealers.

NOTES

1. Consultative Proposal by the Basle Committee on Banking Supervision, "The Supervisory Recognition of Netting for Capital Adequacy Purposes," April 1993, Basle.

2. Consultative Proposal by the Basle Committee on Banking Supervision, "The Supervisory Treatment of Market Risks," April 1993, Basle.

3. Consultative Proposal by the Basle Committee on Banking Supervision, "Measurement of Banks' Exposure to Interest Rate Risk," April 1993, Basle.

4. See Chapter 3, *supra* note 25, and accompanying text.

5. "Supervisory Recognition of Netting," *supra* note 1, at 4.

6. See Chapter 1, *supra* note 226. The final version of the CAD is 93/6/EEC, O.J. Eur. Comm. No. L141, p. 1; the final version of the ISD is 93/22/EEC O.J. Eur. Comm. No. L141, p. 27.

7. See Chapter 1, *supra* note 57.

8. "Supervisory Recognition of Netting," *supra* note 1, at 4.

9. *Ibid.*, at 5.

10. *Ibid.*, at 6.

11. See, e.g., "Supervisory Treatment of Market Risks," *supra* note 2, at 36–37, discussing a bank's "structural position" in currency.

12. *Ibid.*, at 11. See also CAD *supra* note 6 at Annex V Own Funds, § 2(a), 3 and 6.

13. "Supervisory Treatment of Market Risks," *supra* note 2 (Section 2, Debt Securities), at 15.

14. *Ibid.*, at 25.

15. See Chapter 3, *supra* note 69, and accompanying text.

16. See *supra* notes 13 and 14.

17. See Chapter 2, *supra* notes 162–165, and accompanying text.

18. See Chapter 3, *supra* note 69, and accompanying text.

19. See Chapter 1, *supra* note 258, and accompanying text.

20. See Chapter 3, *supra* notes 52 and 53, and accompanying text; and "Supervisory Treatment of Market Risks," *supra* note 2, at 30.

21. This view has been propounded by the SEC Division on Market Regulation and by former chairman Richard Breeden at the IOSCO Conference, 1992.

22. Interview with staff, SEC Division of Market Regulations.

23. However, if no ready market exists for a debt instrument, it will be deducted from capital because it is illiquid and consequently bearing a 100% risk-weighting as opposed to the 8% that a similar instrument would attract under bank capital adequacy ratios.

Index

ABOUT THE AUTHOR

JOHN H. FRIEDLAND was a resident scholar at the Morin Center for Banking Law at Boston University Law School in 1992 and a guest scholar at the Brookings Institution in Washington, D.C., in 1993. He is associated with the law firm of Hoffinger Friedland Dobrish Bernfeld & Stern, P.C. in New York City, where he practices law in the area of real estate finance.